May '03

Freedom is still

America's

best investment!

Barack Obama

THE BEST IS YET TO COME

by
Barry Asmus

AmeriPress
Scottsdale, Arizona
1-800-225-3864
www.barryasmus.com

Library of Congress Catalog Card Number: 2001 129070

ISBN: (Cloth) 0-9709873-1-5

Cover design: Scott Taylor/Horizon Graphics

1st Edition

Published in the United States by
AmeriPress
Manufactured in the United States of America
10 9 8 7 6 5 4

CONTENTS

Dedication

To my grandsons

Andrew Jonathan and Raegan Robert Asmus

The Best is Yet to Come

It is mainly an economic journey —
    because I am an economist.

It is partly an American journey —
    because I am an American.

It is mostly a hopeful journey —
    because I am an optimist.

It is also a spiritual journey —
    because I am a Christian.

PART I

Powershifts, Shockwaves and the Triumph of Freedom

Late in the eighteenth century there was a revolution that had earth shaking consequences. For whatever reasons, a group of people realized that there will never be a really free and enlightened government until individuals were recognized as a higher and independent power from those of the state itself. It would be a government where individual freedom would be highly revered and derives its powers from the consent of the governed. By affirming the dignity and sanctity of the individual, the founders elected to frame a man-made state instead of a state-made man. The new American government, built on the foundation of limited government, is one of the great wonders of the world.

Unfortunately, after almost 150 years of success, the twentieth century represented an abrupt shift. Big government's control once again became popular in the United States. Governments in all other nations also grew larger. Reduced to a remnant, the ideas on freedom and limited government for most of the twentieth century were on life support. But late in the century the tide shifted again. The ideas of two Nobel Laureates in economics, the courage of an iron lady in Europe, the revolutionary shift of a military dictator in Latin America, the about-face of a communist ruler in China, and the startling presidential election of a movie actor from California, shifted the economic axis of the planet. Freedom got another toehold. It would eventually win the day.

Part I

As the twenty-first century dawns, the age of big government is drawing to a close. Every form of statism has been tried—from fascism to socialism to communism, from apartheid to the mixed economy to the welfare state—and failed. Under a system where the state is everything, the individual is but an incident. Under that system, the individual is a subject, rather than a citizen. Under that system, the individual has no rights, only state granted privileges. Under that system, the state is the reservoir of all power and is given the commanding heights of the economy.

In the new century, however, the commanding heights will be given to capitalism, markets and entrepreneurs. In the new century, both faith and freedom will experience a resurgence and the never ending struggle for economic success will run congruent with a human's desire for spiritual significance.

Of all of mankind's conquests, none have been more important than the conquest of tyranny's iron fist and the triumph of freedom. This section is about the visionaries who saw that freedom was the mainspring of both economic and spiritual progress and structured the ideas to accomplish both.

There are two ways to spread the light: light a candle or be a mirror. The candle is lit. Freedom's light will not go out. Part I is but a mirror to reflect it.

CHAPTER 1

The Triumph of Liberty

"They say that freedom is a constant struggle,"
goes the old song. It is. It is also more than that.
Freedom is *the* struggle. It is never achieved
except in the effort to reach it.

-Wallace Roberts

The scene: The American Bankers Association's annual meeting in Honolulu, November 10, 1981. In the audience are the who's who of American banking, 2,500 bank presidents dressed to the nines—in expensive suits and 50-dollar ties. They've come to hear Alan Greenspan, later to be chairman of the powerful Federal Reserve Board, previously a top economic advisor to President Gerald Ford and now an advisor to Ronald Reagan.

The ballroom is breathtaking. Every place setting has three forks, two wineglasses, perfectly folded napkins and beautifully sculpted pineapples. The master of ceremonies comes to the podium and the room goes silent.

"Ladies and gentlemen," he says, "we have some bad news and some good news. The bad news is that Alan Greenspan is in the hospital. We are sorry and we wish him a speedy recovery. The good news is that today, just in from Idaho, we have an associate professor of economics from Boise State University, Barry Asmus."

Up to the podium walks a young man in a lightblue leisure suit. His tie is the best that five dollars can buy at J.C. Penney's. He has been wearing his 10-dollar shirt for 20 hours straight.

Who is this guy? Me. That's right. I'm Barry Asmus.

Haltingly, I begin my speech. I'm scared to death.   I know that the bankers have paid a $75 luncheon fee to hear Greenspan. To say they are disappointed would be a major understatement. All the oxygen has been sucked out of the room.   After all, it's one thing to teach 18-year old kids just off the Idaho potato farms; it's quite another to command the attention of the upper crust of American banking, especially when their expectations are so high.

What could I tell them?

Actually, a lot. I had gone through a 20-year transformation from being a hard-core Keynesian socialist to being a free market, limited government conservative. Like many other misguided but well-intentioned citizens, I had believed that the Soviet Union had discovered the way to economic progress. And I campaigned hard in 1972 for Democratic presidential candidate George McGovern, who ran on the idea of taking $1,000 from everybody above the median level of income and giving it to everybody below the median level.   Since I was one of those "belowers," I thought McGovern's idea was great.   My mantra was: divide the wealth, spread it about, taxation is no sin.   When mine runs out, I plan to shout, let's divvy up a'gin, and a'gin, and a'gin.

By the late 70's however, I was reading Ludwig von Mises, Friedrich Hayek, Milton Friedman, and the editorial page of the *Wall Street Journal.*   Slowly, I was beginning to see how the world really works and not how professors wish it would work. World events, good books, and just growing up were all part of my metamorphosis. Belatedly, I realize that my dad, too, helped me see the light.

My dad loved to tell the story of the city slicker fella who found himself sitting next to a veterinarian at a dinner party. "Doctor" the man said, "I don't mean to trouble you for free advice . . . but you see I have this horse. Sometimes he walks normal and some times he limps. What should I do?" The veterinarian quietly answered, "Well, watch him closely, and the next time he walks normally . . . sell him!"

So, here I am, looking out over a sea of a thousand skeptics. It was my chance to sell America's most influential bankers on a new set of ideas promising prosperity and freedom. All of a sudden it dawned on me that words are important. For one word a man is often deemed to be wise, and for one word he is often deemed to be foolish. The difference between the right word and the almost right word, in this instance, is the difference between lightning and the lightning bug. While truth does not blush, one has to be careful with what one says.

I tell these pillars of capitalism that free markets and limited government have been the most liberating ideas in mankind's history. I tell them how freedom has allowed ordinary people to do extraordinary things—the oil wells in Texas, the Sears Tower in Chicago, Disneyland in southern California. I tell them that if you were to make a list of all the things that capitalism produces and provides, you would fill a library. Footprints on the sands of time are not made by sitting down. But now, I tell them, we have wandered a long way from freedom. Now, government takes almost half of our income and tells us what to do with the other half.

How, I ask, did this happen? I tell them of my farmer friends in eastern Colorado who believe in freedom and fought for it in World War II. They are willing to wave the flag of free enterprise with their right hand, but accept government farm subsidies with their left. With their right hands raised they say, "I'm for capitalism." And with their left hands held out they say, "but I need government price supports." They are not alone.

Many people say they are for free enterprise—but. Chrysler is all for free enterprise, but not if Chrysler goes bankrupt because Americans want to buy from Japan. Small business owners are all for capitalism, but many insist on federal subsidies and preferential loans from the government. Bankers also believe in capitalism, except when it comes to competition for small depositors. "I'm for capitalism, but . . ." "I'm for capitalism, but . . ." "Ladies and gentlemen," I say, "capitalism is drowning in a sea of buts."

They laugh. They're having a good time. I am relieved. I speak for 45 minutes and then this august audience gives me a standing ovation. Applause is always an appreciated interruption. In the next few years I will speak at bankers' conventions in 47 states. A week before this speech, I was an associate professor of economics at a small university. Now I will be speaking all across the country to Fortune 500 companies and to thousands of entrepreneurs. How did this happen?

Over a period of 15 years, I had given hundreds of free speeches and thousands of university lectures without ever once considering a career in public speaking. I'd never imagined that people would pay money to listen to a professor, especially a professor of economics. Even today, I don't think people pay to listen to me; rather, they pay to hear the message that I bring them.

I was always delighted to be invited to speak. And having taught the principle "TANSTAAFL" for over a decade (There Ain't No Such Thing As A Free Lunch), I was a bit surprised to discover that there were lots of free lunches. I'd give a speech—they'd buy my lunch. Trade, after all, is about voluntary exchange for mutual benefit. I always felt that I was getting the good deal. Words for food. Isn't an economist a man who gets invited to speak at banquets where he tells everybody there's no such thing as a free lunch? And then, in November 1981,

John Palmer, President of the National Speakers Bureau, called and asked me if I could possibly leave Boise immediately to give that infamous bankers speech in Honolulu.

I called my wife to let her know the details, and with nine dollars in my pocket, my light-blue leisure suit, no luggage, no toothbrush, no nothing, I was off. That was the start of a whole new career. And as we enter the twenty-first century, I'm still in it.

I am a professional speaker and a Senior Economist at the National Center for Policy Analysis, a public policy research institute that promotes private alternatives to government regulation and control. My passion is sharing my knowledge of economics and business with as many people as possible, to encourage them to use the best management practices and technology possible, and to explain the workings of a free-market, limited government system.

I try never to forget that the speech I am about to give succeeds in direct proportion to the way my audience responds. Will they enjoy it? Will they laugh? If I can't be funny, will I be interesting? Will they learn? Will they feel it? Is there something special about this presentation? Will they act upon it? Will it really make a difference? Reaching an audience is a process, one that starts with knowing the audience and then delivering with content, humor, and enthusiasm. Most of the time I have found that the importance of what you say can be enhanced by how you say it. A professor is a person who can take something simple and make it complicated. A communicator can take something complicated and make it simple. A yawn, to me, has always been a silent shout.

It was an honor to speak to 30 world bankers at the home of Harvard's president a few years ago. And I felt as though I'd returned to my agriculture roots when I spoke to 3,000 farmers in

Des Moines. I cannot even begin to explain the feeling of being raised in a town so small that the only thing that went out after 10 were the lights, and on a postage-stamp size farm in rural eastern Colorado, then finding myself speaking to 7,000 members of the Million Dollar Round Table at Radio City Music Hall in New York City.

I have appeared on the same stage as British Prime Minister Margaret Thatcher, management guru Tom Peters, and United Nations Ambassador Jeane Kirkpatrick. I have hobnobbed with Malcolm S. Forbes, Jr., Editor-in-Chief of *Forbes Magazine*; John Fund, a member of the editorial board of the *Wall Street Journal*; and Pete du Pont, former governor of Delaware. I have frequently appeared with Louis Rukeyser, and recently while lecturing in Africa had the privilege of meeting leaders of the South African government including Nelson Mandela. And now I am addressing the most demanding audience yet—that's you, the readers.

The ideas you will read in this book were distilled from my life experiences and the conversations with these thinkers, as well as from the important books I have read as an economist. I have seen and studied how the world works. I know how business works. I've talked to business people, workers, students, housewives, airline pilots, and consumers, and have asked them to tell me what works, what doesn't, and why. I know how government works—or doesn't. How do I know all of this? It's not because I'm smart. It's because I listen. You can often profit from being at a loss for words. I know my friends are smiling.

Choosing prosperity seems easy. It isn't. Two-thirds of the world's population is still poor. And the other third came close in the twentieth century to abandoning capitalism and freedom, mankind's only hope of creating prosperity. The world will always be in a never-ending motion of power shifts toward prosperity and shockwaves away from it. Freedom and limited government will always catalyze prosperity. Unlimited government will forever stifle it.

In 1986, I was part of the Statue of Liberty rededication ceremony. Since then, I've shared the following piece many times. It's my tribute to America and represents the essence of this book.

A Tribute to America

Ladies and Gentlemen, my name is the United States of America. I was born on July 4, 1776, conceived in freedom and liberty, and that freedom has caused millions of people to come to my shores and cast their economic plight with me. America is living proof that immigration is the sincerest form of flattery. The mission of America is one of benevolent assimilation. But that freedom has not been cheap.

Hundreds of thousands of my sons and daughters have lost their lives on the battlefields of Europe and Asia. Thousands of families have cried in anguish as they learned their fathers, husbands, sons and daughters were killed in the fight for freedom. In war, there are no unwounded soldiers. But thank God, those lives stood for something.

I am big. From the Atlantic to the Pacific, from the northern reaches of Alaska to the beautiful Hawaiian Islands, I have over three and one-half million square miles just pulsating with economic activity and opportunity. I have forests in Oregon, wheat fields in Kansas, oil in Texas and coal in West Virginia. I am the Empire State Building in New York, the Sears Tower in Chicago, and Disneyland in Southern California.

I have over two million farms whose productivity is unequaled anywhere in the world. I have given birth to thousands, nay millions, of producers and wealth creators. Historical entrepreneurs like Cyrus McCormick, Thomas Edison, and Henry Ford, as well as contemporaries like Jonas Salk, Stanford Ovshinsky, and Mary Kay Ash have literally changed the face of this country and this world for the better. I am Babe Ruth and the World Series, Vince Lombardi and professional football, Chris Evert and professional tennis. And, in my opinion, no one slams it better than Michael "Air" Jordan.

But more than a nation that just works and plays, I am a nation that prays. I have over 450,000 churches and synagogues where people worship the God who is there, because He is not silent.

Over 200 years ago, Thomas Jefferson penned a Declaration that still stands as a beacon for America: "We hold these truths to be self-evident, that all men are created equal, that they are endowed by their Creator with certain unalienable Rights, that among these are Life, Liberty, and the pursuit of Happiness."

A hundred years after Jefferson wrote that declaration, another President stood tall during the dark hours of the Civil War. Abraham Lincoln was asked the question, Can a nation of the people, by the people, and for the people survive? Hesitating for a moment, Lincoln replied: "I do not know how history will speak on America. But I do know that Americans were born to be free."

Brief Autobiography
Father Knows Best

I was born and raised on a farm. Some of you have had the same experience. You know there is something about milking cows both morning and night, sitting on a Ford or John Deere tractor cultivating sugar beets and corn 12 hours a day, and standing in cold irrigation water with hip-waders until your bones are about frozen that helps you decide what you don't want to do when you grow up.

"Dad, I don't want to be a farmer."

I realize now how difficult that was for my dad. Grandpa had come from Russia and was a farmer. Dad was a farmer. Why couldn't his oldest son be a farmer? Or at the very least, be involved in his tractor and implement business.

But my dad had the patience of Job. "What do you want to do, son?" he asked.

"Dad, I want to move into town and someday own and operate a Phillips 66 gas station. Pump gas. Change mufflers. Wash windshields," I replied. That sounded so much better than farming.

After I graduated from high school, my dad put his arms around me and said, "Son, Mom and I would be so proud if you went to college." "College," I said. "But Dad, we've never talked about it." When you live on a farm all you talk about is work. Morning, noon, and night, 365 days a year, there is work to be done. No one had time to talk about ideas. A farmer doesn't own cows. The cows own him. "I know college is a stretch, son." Dad replied. "But why don't you give it a try?"

So off to Colorado State University I went. The first week there I joined a fraternity. I'll never forget sitting on the roof of the ATΩ house, wearing my first pair of Bermuda shorts, surrounded by kegs of beer, and watching more pretty girls go by in an hour than I had seen in my entire life.

One day, Dad phoned. "Son, how do you like college?"

"Dad, I just love it," I answered. Now mind you, I had not even been to one class. I could not wait for success, so I went ahead without it.

In fact, I liked university life so well, I stayed there 10 years. Through persistence, I received my Bachelors degree, my Masters, and finally a Ph.D., all in economics. At graduation, my Dad said, "Son, if I would have known you were going to be in college 10 years—why, by now you and I could have owned Phillips 66!" He also told me a funny Dear Abby story that was most apropos. A man writes: Dear Abby, I have two brothers and two sisters. My one brother is an economist. My other brother is in prison for committing murder and my two sisters are in prison for burglary. My mother was committed to a mental institution when I was a young boy and my dad has never been able to support the family because of a gambling habit. Abby, I have fallen in love with this beautiful girl. We are going to get married. Abby, here is my question: Should I tell her about my economist brother?

So, with three degrees in economics, mainly Keynesian and liberal, I was ready to change the world. I was also able to repeat the mantra I heard over and over from my professors: "Take from the rich and give to the poor. Government should do this. And government should do that." And just like a good liberal, I wanted to give away everything I did not own. But while many professors are just people who talk in someone else's sleep, I was all ears and full of good advice.

I returned home to find that my dad had bought a new car. Feeling that his old car was good enough, and that he didn't understand how many poor people there were in this world, I told him that I thought conservatives were part of the problem. I strongly suggested that he sell his new car, take the money and give it to the poor. His reply? "Get your ass out of here. If I want your opinion I'll give it to you."

Of course, that was just a farmer's way of saying "Son, just because you have three degrees in economics does not mean that you know how to solve the world's problems. There is a big difference between a good sound idea and an idea that sounds good. Yours doesn't and isn't. Since when do the ends ever justify the means? Mom and I have been giving to our church and needy people our whole life. You know I would give the shirt off my back to help someone. Your grandpa was the same way. But just because someone is needy does not mean that I can steal someone else's money to help. There is literally no end to the good that do-gooders will do with someone else's money. So son, if you want to help the poor, that's great. But do it with your own money."

Dad didn't stop there. "I've been listening to you now for 10 years talking about socialism and Keynesian economics. I have heard you say that for some reason government spending is more powerful than private spending. You said that it makes good economic sense to tax more from the people and let the government spend it so that the economy will get back on track. You said that printing more money and running deficits improves our nation's health. Son, I'm no economist, but that is just plain crazy."

"Sometimes I think people can be educated beyond their intelligence; they know the way but can't drive the car. Where's the humility in all of this? Why would anyone believe that a few bright economists or government officials could ever improve the actions of millions of people working in the market? I cannot even plan my own life. How could anyone do it for an entire economy? Let a planner spend just a few years working on our farm—fighting the weather, the grasshoppers, drought, hail storms, broken down equipment, prices too low to meet costs, and the hundreds of other problems you face, and they too would acknowledge the extent of their ignorance. Let your socialist friends farm for just a year or two and let them see for themselves how tough, humbling, and difficult it is. People who think they can run the earth should begin with a small garden."

There is no one so irritating as someone with less intelligence but with more sense than we have. Few things are harder on a son than the annoyance of a good example. My dad was like that.

"Government is not God," he said. "It does not create miracles. Every job created by government is a job that was lost in the private sector. Whatever the government gives, it must first take away. If this keeps going, the incentive to be a tax taker will overwhelm the incentive to be a taxpayer. Now Son, I know that you voted for Lyndon Johnson in the last election and that's your right. But someday you are going to understand why I voted for Barry Goldwater. He ran a whole campaign on the premise of reducing government's size. He didn't want to streamline it. He didn't want to make it more efficient. His aim was not to pass laws but to repeal them; not to suggest new programs but to cancel old ones that violate the Constitution. Goldwater was not about finding taxpayers' money to help his Arizona constituents but to stand up for freedom and free enterprise. "Any government that is big enough to give you all you want," Goldwater said, "is big enough to take it all away. Ask not from government and you may save your ask! Ask from government and you will surely lose it."[1] On a lighter note, Barry Goldwater also said, "It's a great country, where anybody can grow up to be president—except me."

As the old saying goes, you can lead a mule to wisdom, but you can't make him pull the wax out of his ears and listen. Years later I would find myself back to my conservative roots, or as Irving Kristol was quoted, "a liberal who has been mugged by reality."

Just a decade earlier, I had taken my first economics class in college and was finally learning how the world works. It was the fall of 1960. The professor was a newly minted Ph.D. from the London School of Economics and a socialist to the bone. He sarcastically asked each member of the class: are you a capitalist or a doubting capitalist? A socialist or a doubting socialist? By far, the majority of students identified themselves as doubting socialists. He was very pleased. As an 18-year-old kid who did not know bull-diapers from baby food, I went along with the class. Going off to college as a Republican and a Christian, I soon learned that those beliefs were both politically incorrect and very ignorant. It took just a few college courses to recognize that while all animals are equal, some animals are more equal than others.

Two of my favorite fellow graduate students at Colorado State University were Lee Gray and Ed Hewett. Besides my dad, Lee was the only person I knew who voted for Barry Goldwater. Ed and the rest of us working for our Masters degree in Economics viewed Lee's vote as Neanderthal. How could anyone who was literate, who knew the events surrounding two world wars, who had studied the Great Depression, and who had watched the unbelievable success of the Soviet Union not see that government planning was the way to manage an economy? Barry Goldwater's platform of freedom, markets, and limited government sounded like it was from another planet. "Extremism in the defense of liberty is no vice and moderation in the pursuit of justice is no virtue," a Goldwater campaign phrase, was a scary and dangerous idea. Lee Gray and my good ol' dad were so easily fooled, I thought then.

All of us working on our Masters degree went on to get our Ph.D.s in economics. I know what you are thinking. Fifty thousand Ph.D.s awarded annually? Why, that's ridiculous! Where are they going to find that many cabs to drive? Well, Ed's

15

career was a most distinguished one. Receiving his Ph.D. from The University of Michigan and spending a good deal of his career in the foreign policy studies program at the Brookings Institution, his most important book was entitled *Reforming the Soviet Economy*, published in 1988. Ed became a Soviet specialist, spoke Russian fluently, and traveled to the Soviet Union many times to do research. Here are a few quotes from Hewett's book.[2]

"To underestimate the Soviet Union and to believe the Soviet economy is incapable of an adequate response to President Ronald Reagan's Strategic Defense Initiative is self-delusion." p. 33.

"If the Soviet Central Statistical Administration were to collect and publish unemployment statistics in a fashion similar to the U.S., the rate of unemployment would probably come under 2 percent for the mid-1980s. Western countries, and particularly Western workers, can only envy a society with such a consistently low level of unemployment." p. 42.

"The economic security provided in the USSR concerning the worth of income in real terms, is much higher in the Soviet Union than in Western countries. The relative security of job and real income combine to produce a high degree of personal economic security." p. 42.

And after discussing the quality of Soviet products, Hewitt concludes: "My admittedly subjective guess is that Soviet products probably cluster around the vertical axis, being of average quality by world standards." p. 83.

Untold numbers of liberal leaning Democrat academicians and media types wrote enthusiastically of the Soviet Union, Socialist governments and the efficiency of government planning and control. Laura Tyson, President Clinton's first head of the Council of Economic Advisors, did graduate and post-doctorate work on what she called the "miraculous Romanian economy." She was a student of Ceausescu's Romania, writing that it was in some respects more productive than the U.S. I wonder if she was a bit surprised when the Romanian people overthrew communism, and President Ceausescu and the First Lady were tried by a people's court and executed? Paul Samuelson, author of the most popular college economic textbook ever written, with dozens of editions, was saying as late as 1989 that the USSR would soon pass the U.S. in annual productivity.

It's been said that an economist's skills must include the ability to foretell what will happen tomorrow, next month, and next year—and to explain afterwards why it did not happen. The Soviet economy was even more difficult to forecast because the numbers were all fabricated. In defense of Ed, the Berlin Wall had not yet fallen and most of us were quite ignorant of what was really happening in the Soviet Union. America's intellectual elite were certainly fooled by the propaganda of Soviet success and five-year plans that, in Khrushchev's words, would soon "bury America." In Moscow, as it turns out, they ring the bells often, but not for dinner. To give them their due, however, I must say that Soviets for a very long time led the world in the volume and quality of lies produced.

Although a liberal, Ed ended his career by serving as President George Bush's main interpreter/advisor on the Soviet Union with Mikhail Gorbachev, who was trying to lead his country toward glasnost and perestroika. Ed's unfortunate death at an early age ended a productive career. The fall of the Berlin Wall a year later (1989) revealed what many professors could not see. The Soviet Union was a structure with no supports. Socialism cannot be made to work. The issue has always been the performance of capitalism against the hype of communism.

The human community, I gradually discovered, was involved

in a great twentieth century struggle between two fundamentally irreconcilable social systems. One is a system that emphasizes individual responsibility, private property, and voluntary social arrangements. It requires that government's role in economic and personal matters be strictly limited if freedom is to triumph. It is a system of competitive capitalism that can produce standards of living and opportunities for individuals that are unparalleled in human history. The alternative system relies on government planning, management, and regulation. It politicizes economic exchange, suppresses individual incentive, and is sustained by using coercion and force. Nationalization has always been one big attempt to legislate unsuccessful people into prosperity by legislating successful people out of it.

Of the two systems, socialism was the dominant economic system during most of the twentieth century. While a third of the world's population lived in totalitarian states and claimed an allegiance to communism, another third practiced quasi-socialism. Both required a large and coercive role for government in economic and social life.

Nations committed to competitive capitalism at the start of the twentieth century, on the other hand, accounted for less than one-third of the world's people. Its most important practitioner was the United States. But even there, prospects for liberty were on the decline for most of the century. The state's role was forever waxing. Government spending as a percentage of the total economy grew larger, taxes were increased, and regulations skyrocketed. Ambitious politicians and interventionist governments were encouraged by two main events in the 1930s and 1940s: the Great Depression and World War II. No two events could have done more to permanently affect the economic landscape and shape the way people viewed the role of government, their views of capitalism, and the embrace of governmentalism. Capitalism was almost reduced to a remnant. By 1945, only two countries were hanging on: the United States and Great Britain.

The Great Depression
Magnitude 8 on the Richter Scale of Social Shockwaves

The Roaring Twenties came to a standstill on October 24, 1929, when the bottom dropped out of the stock market. It was the beginning of the longest and deepest economic decline in our country's history.

The crash caused enormous hardship for tens of millions of people. Banks collapsed, farms failed, and business had no business. Even Siamese twins couldn't make both ends meet. When the economy sinks, desperate people look to government. Franklin D. Roosevelt responded by expanding government on a vast scale. His New Deal in the 1930s translated into an American version of the welfare state, where new government safety nets such as crop subsidies, social security, unemployment insurance, and federal family insurance were created as a response to a breakdown of the worldwide economic order. Institutions like the Securities and Exchange Commission and the Federal Deposit Insurance Corporation were created to protect people from the consequences of their own poor judgments, or from ignorance. Federal Wage and Hour laws were passed to prevent businesses from exploiting workers. Regulations specifying what businesses could and could not do in every sector of the economy were created or greatly expanded.[3]

The terrible irony is that the government did not sit on its hands: instead it made things worse. A lot worse. Congress in 1930 took a recession and turned it into a Great Depression.

Economists now agree that it was not the stock market that caused the Depression, but rather the wildly erratic shifts in the nation's money supply. When the stock market rose to unsustainable speculative excess, the Federal Reserve raised interest rates and tightened credit, bringing the frenzy to a sudden end. But this was no soft landing. When the world economy began its downward spiral, the U. S. government did exactly the wrong thing. It tightened credit, raised interest rates some more, and most devastatingly, shrank the supply of money. This stopped consumer spending and new investment in its tracks. Scarce credit and less money in circulation meant less borrowing, less spending, lower prices, and skyrocketing bankruptcies. When business and farmers couldn't repay their debts, banks failed, and the slump fed on itself by driving everyone to deeper and deeper levels of pessimism and despair. You know times are bad when Must Get Rid Of becomes a brand name.

International trade collapsed, and governments responded with a beggar-thy-neighbor approach. The United States joined in with the seriously misguided Smoot-Hawley Tariff, which only insured that trade would not revive. World trade, already shrinking in 1929, fell by two-thirds by 1933. These policies threatened the ability of the United States to remain on the gold standard, so government tried to protect the price of gold by keeping interest rates too high and money too tight. The resulting one-third contraction in the money supply perpetuated the devastating impact on credit, spending and prices. What should have been an ordinary, painful slump turned into a worldwide catastrophe of the first magnitude. Make no mistake about it—the Depression scarred an entire generation. Distressed citizens, not realizing that their governments had exacerbated the situation beyond all recognition, turned to government, demanding a quick fix. And today we are still living with laws, agencies, policies, and regulations that were created to solve problems that no longer exist in the technology-driven, Internet-quick world in which we live.

Although the Great Depression was mainly the fault of government, the media and intellectual elites laid the blame on capitalism. In 1936, John Maynard Keynes, a British economist, prolific author, and a vastly influential person in the twentieth century, wrote a book entitled *The General Theory of Employment, Interest and Money*. Keynes' book became the Bible for most economists for almost half a century. In it, he argued that the classical economics of Adam Smith was based on the mistaken assumption that the balance between supply and demand would ensure full employment. Watching the unemployment rate of the U.S. and Great Britain exceed 20 percent, Keynes concluded that private investment would not be adequate to create full employment. His policy prescription of government spending and investment through deficit spending represented a serious break with conventional economic thinking. Borrow money, sell bonds, or print money if you have to, he argued, but allow government to spend the economy back to health. As Keynesian economics became the dominant philosophy, the era of laissez-faire capitalism ended. Government would now manage the economy through monetary and fiscal policy, giving it considerable control. Using the carrot of subsidies and tax breaks and the stick of punitive taxes and regulations, the government would stimulate the economy and encourage businesses. Highly educated Brahmins from the "right" schools surely knew what was best for the economy. I certainly thought I did.

The new symbiosis between economists and politicians was mutually beneficial. As economists called for more public spending and tight controls on business, politicians were more justified in wresting control from private markets. Expert economists had to be employed to provide advice on the correct economic policies to follow. Power shifted from business and markets to politicians and economists. Everyone is in favor of a planned economy if they get to be the planners. The economics profession responded by developing a new set of tools called national income accounting, gross national product statistics, and mathematical models to use as tools to manage and guide the economy. Theoretically showing that the government spending multiplier was a more effective tool than the private investment multiplier in creating jobs, the policy of tax and spend was thought to be the key to jump-starting economic growth. More government spending, of course, meant more planning, control, and more state intervention in the free market economy.

For the next 50 years, the intellectual and media elite believed that government knowledge was superior to market knowledge. The state was wise, the market was not. Although the Great Depression was the most colossal and tragic failure of government and public policy in American history, what could the average citizen say? What did they know about running an economy? How could they argue with people who have Ph.D.s and buy ink by the barrel?

There was only one small problem. The Keynesian post-war idea that taxing and spending could be used in a precise way to control the pace of economic growth and employment did not work. The problem with this fine-tuning was enunciated by Austrian economist F.A. Hayek: lack of knowledge. Information about what is happening in an economy is always approximate and out-of-date. Governments and their legion of economists usually get the timing wrong, accelerating when the economy needed slowing down and vice versa. Moreover, the timing and size of government actions is driven first by political necessities, and only secondly by economic considerations. Almost always, justified in wresting control from private markets, expert government makes things worse. It reminds me of the fortune teller gazing into his crystal ball. "I see a long recession coming. Perhaps I see a short recession coming. I see high unemployment in the future, or is it full employment in the future? I see that I have a dirty crystal ball."

World War II
The Second Catastrophic Shockwave of the Twentieth Century

Of all the evils to public liberty, war is perhaps the most to be dreaded. War is the parent of armies; from these proceed debts and taxes. And armies, and debts, and taxes, are the known instruments for bringing the many under the dominion of the few. In war, too, the discretionary power of the executive is extended; its influence in dealing out offices, honors, and emoluments is multiplied; and all the means of seducing the minds are added to those of subduing the force of the people. No nation can preserve its freedom in the midst of continual warfare.

-James Madison

In 1945, when the United States had just fully mobilized its wealth and troops to defeat both the Nazis in Europe and then the Japanese in the Pacific, Americans' faith in government had never been higher. Browbeaten by 12 years of Roosevelt's New

Deal, by four awful, regimented years of a military-minded economy, by the socialist emanations of postwar Europe, it would seem that the war was proof that hierarchical management and control was the way to get things done. The Great Depression and the Wall Street crash had destroyed people's faith in the rationality of markets. During WWII, governments had seized control of basic industries, and America had out-produced its combined enemies by a tremendous margin. This was a further demonstration that the state could run things more efficiently and effectively than the private sector could. One wartime best seller, *Managerial Revolution* by James Burnham (1941), proclaimed that "the capitalist organization of society has entered its final years." But fewer mainstream thinkers stopped to consider that the war gave Americans a powerful incentive to produce, one that transcended whatever economic system was in place, and that such an incentive would not exist in peacetime.[4]

The war experience, which involved everybody pulling together for the national good, created widespread hope that government could create peace and prosperity. Capitalists had been depicted as myopic oafs since the trust-busting days of the early 1900s and the best chance for prosperity was intelligent planning and spending guided by benevolent politicians and wise professors. Places like the London School of Economics and Harvard University supplied the experts to put the political ideas into practice.

Meanwhile, returning veterans just wanted to get on with their tragically interrupted lives. They wanted schooling, a family, a nice home, a car, and a good job. The nation, which owed them a debt beyond calculation, showed its gratitude by showering them with all sorts of new programs and benefits: the GI Bill, low-cost VA and FHA mortgage loans, veterans' hospitals, and veterans' pensions. It was only a fraction of what we owed them, and besides, the government was "paying" for it. And, unlike most government programs, these programs worked pretty well for awhile. But these showcase successes hid certain deep problems that would inevitably surface. Eventually, the interest payments on the national debt would consume a growing and burdensome portion of tax receipts. Another problem was that these programs, and the bureaucracies that administered them, continued to grow long after the people they were designed to benefit no longer needed them and long after the free market had developed better alternatives. More insidiously, they reinforced the public's growing belief that the government was the first and best place to receive benefits.

Governments Ascend

When government was small and inconsequential, it possessed little concentrated power to endanger the life of an ordinary man. But interestingly, it also didn't have the power to do much good. But in a world of big government, with so many poor and so many social problems, the time was ripe for a bigger and stronger government to do good. No one doubted what could happen if government power were put in the right hands.

Meanwhile, Soviet economic propaganda sold people the idea that government ownership and government planning were better than capitalism and free markets. The Soviet government regularly reported outrageous rates of economic growth to prove its success. Reports of full employment and no inflation were all signals that a tightly planned and government-run economy worked better than a free market one. In addition, the Soviets reported that they had all but eliminated crime. The good news: the jails were emptied. The bad news: the asylums bulged to overflowing. What is the definition of a Soviet string quartet, someone once asked me? A Soviet string quartet is what is left of the Moscow Symphony after they have toured the United States.

In 1961, when Nikita Khruschev claimed that communism would bury capitalism, he was saying that a command economy would work better than a power-dispersing, market directed one. Government control was given the green light to manage the commanding heights of national economies. Politicians on every continent enthusiastically embraced the Soviet model.

In Africa, as countries gained their independence from their colonial oppressors in the 1950s and 1960s, state planning and management was always the preferred option. Many African leaders went to Moscow for advice and then adopted five-year plans and assigned government engineers to guide the economy.

In Latin America, elected leaders and dictators alike preferred a socialist approach. The military often ruled. Government management, high tariffs, a closed economy, and minimal personal freedoms were the prevailing prescription. Since the concern for national security reinforced and justified state control, the government took control of many sectors deemed strategic and in the public interest. Management of companies was given over to relatives and cronies, who then proceeded to enrich themselves.

With communism's grip on much of Asia, the Soviet model instituted in India, dictatorships controlling most of Africa and Latin America, the French playing off both sides of Soviet communism and Keynesianism practiced in America, Canada, and in Western Europe, it is fair to say that most of the world had ceded economic control and direction to government. But would it work?

One of the favorite tourist spots in London is St. Paul's Cathedral, considered one of the most beautiful buildings in the world. Its designer and architect, the famous Sir Christopher Wren, also designed another building just west of central London. Though also quite beautiful, the City Fathers criticized it for having too few pillars. So, Wren was asked to add some, and he obliged. The extra pillars of the Windsor Town Hall are still there today. They support no weight and in fact do not even reach the ceiling. As fake pillars, they serve only one purpose: to make the whole building look better. Ornamental embellishments would be how an architect would describe them.

Socialism and big government are like that: all show and no go. Always attacking the richest 1 percent. Always pitting the rich against the poor, the working class against the ownership class in a zero sum game. Promises of fairness, equality, justice, redistribution, and economic freedom are their clichés. But promises do not produce wealth. Neither does a redistribution of income. Eventually people want results, not rhetoric; positive outcomes, not promises; systems that work in reality, not just in theory. Man does not live by words alone, despite the fact that he sometimes has to eat them. And eat them the socialists did. Socialism does not work, cannot work and will never work. I take that back. There are two places where Socialism does work. One is a beehive and the other is an anthill.

The Berlin Wall Finally Falls

After World War II, German Chancellor Ludwig Erhard took a devastated Germany and began to encourage free enterprise in those areas under allied occupational control. He wisely rejected price controls, avoided nationalization and government intervention, and kept instituting free-market policies that began to produce a German economic miracle. The differences in living standards between East and West Berlin over the next four decades finally became too great to hide. In 1989, Hungary, a member of the Soviet bloc, announced that it would no longer control its borders and restrict the movement of East Germans to the West. Tens of thousands of Germans fled through Czechoslovakia across the Hungarian border to Austria and West Germany. When people are allowed to vote with their feet, they vote for freedom every time. Freedom is a virus for which there is no antidote. It is attractive because it produces prosperity and represents the victory of persuasion over force.

So, the totalitarian socialist system of Communism fell into the trash bin of world history on November 9, 1989. The Berlin Wall was toppled by Germans who would no longer knuckle under to poverty and dictatorship. Predictably, the collapse of the Soviet empire soon followed, and the Marxist-Leninist dictatorship of the proletariat, after 70 years of planning and millions of lives lost, was finally over. At last the world got to see how little substance was behind the facade of lies that had deceived so many for so long. Unlike the Windsor Town Hall, with its fake pillars that still stand today, Soviet communism collapsed. If freedom is the key to economic prosperity, then the poverty-producing systems of North Korea, North Vietnam, Cuba, and China are surely on their last legs. People today want prosperity, not promises. The Party is over.

By the 1970s and 1980s, it also became apparent that American liberals, too, had over-promised and under-delivered. Doubt about the ability of government to manage the economy was on the rise. People were worrying about inflation, an energy crisis, unemployment, and excessive government taxes and control. Far from picking up the slack created by inadequate private investment, Keynesian demand management was crowding out private investors. Far from smoothing out the economic cycle, it stoked up recurrent inflation-driven crises. Government continued to grow and malaise was setting in. The election of Ronald Reagan as President in November of 1980 was a first step toward reversing the trend. By the mid-1990s, even President Bill Clinton saw the writing on the wall. "The era of big government is over," he said. While hardly sincere, it was accurate.

Big government is running out of gas. Signs of its demise are everywhere. Government's ability to make war has been limited by the proliferation of nuclear weapons and public resistance to the draft. As the welfare state declines, the technological world and the Internet are allowing individuals around the world to have closer dealings with each other than they do with their own governments. Private fire departments, private prisons, private communities and private security are exploding in number. Citizens used to think that only the state could deliver security, prosperity, peace, and justice. Now they know better. You cannot create prosperity by governmental edict.

Each year the political leaders of the world are being stripped of their political control over the economy. The ability of governments to collect taxes, the ultimate foundation of state power, is reduced with every advance of the global economy. As information empowers citizens, top-down social engineering by government is increasingly rejected as an anachronism. Each day people send trillions of dollars along the electronic highway. The money goes to where it is wanted and stays where it is well treated. Low taxes are no longer a competitive edge; they are the competitive edge. The decentralization of information usually leads to a decentralization of power. The twilight of sovereignty is flickering its last.

The Best Is Yet To Come

As the twentieth century moved into its last two decades, citizens of the world knew that something was wrong. Government planning was not working. Many nations were getting poorer and people's lives were grinding down instead of ramping up. Government was not solving problems, but subsidizing, rearranging, and accentuating them. In many countries of Latin America, Eastern Europe, and Africa, state-led development was an ongoing disaster. Politicians did well, but everybody else suffered. In democratic but socialist India, poverty was more prevalent than ever. And when the economic picture of China and the Soviet Union finally cleared, it revealed economies in desperate condition.

Newly elected governments throughout the world had given way to authoritarians, totalitarians, and military rule. The likes of Ferdinand Marcos in the Philippines, Idi Amin in Uganda, and Mobuto Seko in Zaire (now Congo) all expropriated and stole enough money from their countries to become billionaires. Shortages were divided among the peasants. When, at the close of the twentieth century one-half of the world's population still had never used a telephone and three billion people were making less than $2 a day, it was obvious that poverty was still the dominant human condition. Interestingly, but not surprisingly, the suffering masses were clustered mainly in those countries that had rejected capitalism. By giving government the economic reins, whether by force or by ballot, most people remained dirt poor.

It was time to step back and examine once more what the founding fathers had in mind when they spoke of freedom, of being endowed by our Creator with certain unalienable rights, of what they meant when they said, "limited government and rule of law."

CHAPTER 2

Religion, Limited Government and the American Republic

> The history of liberty is the history of the limitation of governmental power, not the increase of it. When we resist concentration of power we are resisting the powers of death, because concentration of power is what always precedes the destruction of human liberties.
>
> - Woodrow Wilson

The USS Dwight D. Eisenhower is America's largest aircraft carrier. Weighing 95,000 tons, standing 22 stories high from keel to mast, containing 4½ acres of flight deck, and with the 6,000 sailors operating the ship requiring 18,000 meals a day, it is both a city, an airport, and technological fighting machine on the water. The Eisenhower has two anchors. Each anchor weighs 60,000 pounds. Total anchor weight including chain: 735,000 pounds each. The enormous weight of the anchors hold the ship in place and keep it from drifting.

America, too, has an anchor: rule of law and limited government. The idea of freedom, free enterprise, property rights, and capitalism are all tied to that anchor.

Questions: What one step can preserve liberty over all others? How do people maximize freedom and minimize personal interference? When can the commanding heights of an economy be given to freedom, capitalism, markets, and the entrepreneur? Under what conditions will people be permitted to keep most of what they earn? How do nations achieve the most individual prosperity? Our founders answered those questions with the simple to say, but difficult to implement idea, "limited government and rule of law."

> Despotism may govern without faith, but liberty cannot.
>
> - Alexis deTocqueville

Instituting a system of limited government could arguably be considered the most important power shift and singular achievement for freedom and prosperity ever instituted by mankind. Where did the idea come from? When and how did it happen?

It is difficult to discuss the topic of individual rights and limited government, no it is impossible to discuss the topic of individual rights and limited government without discussing religion. Every culture to a strong degree is a reflection of its beliefs about "ultimate reality."[1] Religious beliefs are the primary determinants of our fundamental attitudes about the world in which we live: Who created it? Who is man? Where do we fit in? What does it mean to be a human being? What is the purpose of our lives? Should we be governed? How should we be governed? Questions like these profoundly influence the way our social and economic institutions develop.

For freedom to exist, there has to be a nexus of primary assumptions about man and his intrinsic worth. Is there a respect for each human being? Do individuals count? If so, why? Can an individual be affirmed and dignified if there are no clear standards of right and wrong? Are the compulsions of one person against another limited in any way? On what basis? If there are no standards of moral conduct, can individuals be protected from the state? Can they be protected from a band of thugs? Do individuals have rights? Do they have property rights? In short, should people live under a rule of law, limited government and freedom, or should they live under a rule of men, unlimited government, and force?

History is clear. Freedom is the exception, not the rule. It is such a rare and precious thing that billions of people have had to endure tyranny living without it and often shedding their blood to attain it. Slavery was common and existed everywhere and in every century. Ancient Mesopotamia was filled with slaves. Egypt was literally built on the backs of forced labor. Chinese slavery goes back to the Shang dynasty in the second millennium. Early Asian history indicates that slavery was practiced and was the norm. Athens in the fifth and fourth centuries B.C. practiced slavery with a vengeance.

But slaves were not just unique to the ancient world. Medieval Europe's farmers were mainly serfs enslaved to the soil. Pope Nicholas IV in the mid-fifteenth century approved Portugal's efforts to enslave heathens and Pope Alexander VI in 1493 sanctioned Spanish slavery in the Americas. The saddest and most painful chapters of American history were its acceptance and legalization of the African slave-trade. And, unfortunately, slavery continues today: in Bangladesh, Brazil, Mozambique, Ghana, India, Sri Lanka, Thailand, Saudia Arabia, and Pakistan as documented in Milton Meltzer's book, *Slavery a World History.*

Even worse has been the enormous number of people who have died at the hand of their own government. The twentieth century was the most gruesome of all. Adolph Hitler murdered 21 million Jews, Balts, Czechs, gypsies, and homosexuals. Communist China murdered an estimated 35 million of its own, and another 27 million starved to death in one of their 1000 famines of the last 2000 years. The Soviet Union established its slave labor system, the gulag, which murdered at least 20 million of its own people. Political Science professor R. J. Rummel estimates that during the first 88 years of the twentieth century, almost 170 million men, women and children have been killed using dozens of brutal methods. It was like a modern Black Plague, but this was a plague of power, not germs. When limited government and rule of law does not restrain power, power is not restrained.

Paganism

In the pagan world, nature and its components were seen as aspects of divinity—mysterious, ultimate, and eternal. Pantheism, for example, believed there was a god of the sun, the moon, the sea, the forest, the wind and many others, including gods that were also men. The world for the pagans was a powerful and capricious place composed of deities and forces that ruined crops, killed people, and reigned havoc. Their belief in superhuman beings and awesome natural events lead to a belief in magic, astrology, witchcraft, child sacrifice and even cannibalism. Pagan cultures would often unite religious and secular functions in the state, thereby precluding the idea of limits on government power. Each person was subject to the vagaries of nature and to the compulsions of their leaders.

When everything in the world is godlike and magic, it is quite natural that the political systems stemming from those underlying assumptions would include elaborate public ceremonials, animal and human sacrifices, and the exaltation of priestly offices. A leader's main job was to communicate with and appease the deities. Kings, queens and village heads were often leaders of the religious cult and the state was the vital link between humanity and the gods. When man is thought to be a god, the political consequences are predictable: authoritarian leadership and an unrestrained state. If you spoke or acted against the rulers, the intercessories to the gods, you invited divine displeasure. To prevent this, your punishment had to be swift and final. No appeals were possible. Government compulsion, because it was fused with deity, gave the state total lien on the affections and energies of the people. Ideas like personal freedom and limited government were impossible to even imagine.[2]

Greco-Roman

Ancient Greece, including the Athenian democracy, often held their rulers in sacred and quasi-magical positions. Even in the Roman Empire, the monarch himself was thought to be divine. In these societies, according to the author of the highly recognized book, *The Ancient City*, Fusel de Coulanges: "Man felt himself at every moment dependent upon his gods and consequently upon the priest king, who was placed between them and himself—a consul is a mediator between man and divinity— he is, as it were, the tutelary genius of the city."[3]

In the Greco-Roman world, humanism was first postulated by a fifth century Greek philosopher named Protagoras who proclaimed that "man is the measure of all things." So where is truth? What is good for man and what is not? And for our purposes here, what is the status of government?

Plato maintained that the good life was discoverable. Goodness exists independent of man, but can be discovered and taught. Morality was not a matter of opinion. Man can discover "right" and "wrong" through the power of his intellect. Then he must train himself to live by those precepts.[4]

Aristotle, too, believed that the good life can be discovered through observation and that life had one main characteristic: happiness. Happiness, he argued was a dynamic quality of life that was advanced by finding a balance. His famous "doctrine of the golden mean" postulated that the correct amount of anything—eating, friendships, or intellectual pursuits, lies somewhere between too much and too little. Aristotle was a relativist.

So, although Plato and Aristotle taught virtue and discipline and called on people to live a healthy and balanced life, neither one believed that a creator God revealed the necessary morals nor was there a transcendent God above the state or human emperor.

Unfortunately, neither Plato or Aristotle sought to question the prevailing deification of the state. Plato wrote "By persuasion or constraint, the law will unite the citizens in harmony, making them share whatever benefits each class can contribute to the common good; and its purpose in forming men of that spirit was not that each should be left to go his own way, but that they should be instruments in binding the community into one." Plato wrote of "divine men" and "golden" men, men ordained to rule above "the herd." They are a living law; like a god among men.[5]

Among other things, Plato recommended rule by philosopher kings, the sharing of women and children among them, eugenic breeding, marriages controlled by the state, infanticide, abortion, and strict censorship. Molding citizens to the design of the ideal republic was Plato's utopian idea. Hundreds of years later the American Founding Father Thomas Jefferson would write: "Bringing Plato to the test of reason, take from him his sophisms, futility's, and incomprehensibility's, and what remains? His foggy mind is forever presenting the semblance's of objects which, half seen through a mist, can be defined neither in form nor dimension."

Now consider these excerpts from Aristotle's *Politics*, in turn, and ask if these set of ideas might have provided the underlying assumptions that would ever give birth to a nation based upon limited government and the rule of law.

> . . . that some should rule and others be ruled is not only necessary, but expedient; from the hour of their birth some are marked out for subjection, others for rule—it is clear—that some men are by nature free, and others slaves, and that for these latter, slavery is both expedient and right—no man can practice virtue who is living the life of a mechanic or laborer—the good of the state and not the individual is the proper subject of political thought—neither must we suppose that any of the citizens belongs to himself, for they all belong to the state.[6]

In ancient Rome, Pompeii, Julius Caesar, Anthony and others, all operated above the law. The law did not apply to them. In due course the Senate's responsibility for enforcing rule of law was obliterated, imperial power was deified, and Rome collapsed. The Dark Ages began. When the rule of law goes, it all goes.

No matter how much we admire Plato and Aristotle on other matters, we learned nothing about limiting government from them. "When a whole family," Aristotle writes, "or some individual happens to be pre-eminent in virtues as to surpass all others—then the only alternative is that he should have the supreme power, and that mankind should obey him, not in turn, but always." Are you surprised that two of our most famous philosophers would conclude that philosophers would make the best rulers?

So while both Plato and Aristotle imagined a government that could improve morals, it was an attorney/philosopher, Marcus Tullius Cicero, who articulated the idea that private property is an important piece of the puzzle of freedom and prosperity. Writing in 44 B.C. he said:

> The chief purpose in the establishment of states and constitutional orders was that individual property rights might be secured. It is the peculiar foundation of state and city to guarantee every man the free and undisturbed control of his own property.

What a breakthrough! Although not making the case for limited government, this principle would become a bedrock of liberty for the future modern world. But neither the ancients, nor Cicero, paganism, the Romans, or the Greeks possessed a theology that would limit government. Neither do most world religions. Even a mostly secular and non-religious country like Japan deifies the Emperor and thus, in that one idea, makes less likely the possibility of limited government.

Freedom cannot exist unless every individual counts for something. If individuals have unique value then rules to restrict compulsions of one person or a group against another must be agreed upon. If the underlying assumption, however, is that there is no god, or that man is god, or that nature is god, or when politics is founded on the denial of god, then there is no right and wrong. Individuals, per se, have no dignity. And when no limits are placed on the rulers or the rule of force, there is no hope for limited government or freedom.

Judeo/Christian

They that deny a God destroy man's nobility; for certainly man is of kin to the beasts by his body; and, if he be not kin to God by his spirit, he is a base and ignoble creature.

- Bacon

About five thousand years ago a view began to emerge that was truly revolutionary. Jehovah God spoke, "there shall be no other gods before me." God, in this religion, was first, man was second, and government of small consequence. What God did in that one statement was to subjugate all rulers to a higher authority. The first ten words of the first book of the Bible, in fact, would refute much of the error of ages past and ideas yet to come. And although not the subject of this book, I've included a paragraph to capture its flavor. Genesis 1:1 says:

"In the beginning God" – that denies Atheism with its doctrine of no God.

"In the beginning God"—that denies Polytheism with its doctrine of many gods.

"In the beginning God created"—that denies Fatalism with its doctrine of chance.

"In the beginning God created"— that denies Evolution with its doctrine of infinite becoming.

"In the beginning God created heaven and earth"—that denies Pantheism which makes God and the universe identical.

"In the beginning God created heaven and earth"—that denies Materialism which asserts the eternity of matter.

In this first testimony of Jehovah, God gave not only a declaration of Divine truth, but also a repudiation of human error. Liberty's origins can be traced to the ancient Hebrew doctrine of a high law that applies to everyone, even rulers. God's interest is not so much talking about the truth as it is revealing it.

God said, "Let us make man in our own image, according to our likeness—male and female He created them." The history of the creation of man and of the relation of our species to each other by birth, just cited in Genesis, is the best refutation that can be given to the divine right of kings and the strongest argument that can be used in favor of the original and natural equality of all mankind. In the opening chapters of this Old Testament book, we learn that human beings were made in the image of God to reflect his character. His creative activity is then reflected through human creativity—by cultivating the world, drawing out its potential, and giving it shape and form. A person's accomplishments are expressions of God's divine image. A person created by God has meaning, worth, purpose, dignity and rights. These rights come from a higher law, a law that came to be called the natural rights of man, the idea that every individual has the unalienable right to life, liberty and property, and is not subject to any ruler who denies those rights.

The Bible and The Natural Rights of Man

The Bible is a book of faith, and a book of doctrine and a book of morals, and a book of religion, of special revelation from God. But it is also a book which teaches man his own individual responsibility, his own dignity, and his equality with his fellow man.

- Daniel Webster

In subsequent centuries, the Biblical view stood in stark

contrast to the religions of the world. In most of those, government was the church and state rolled into one. There were no limits on state power and no competition to buffer it. Even the profoundest works of Greek philosophy placed few limits on the power of government. Personal freedom did not stand a chance. And because it did not, early civilizations were characterized by ruthless kings, government plunder, slavery and mass murder.

Even John Locke, in his book *Tyranny*, recognized that the natural law tradition went back to the ancient Jews. Rulers cannot legitimately do anything they want, because moral laws apply to everyone. Government is morally obliged to serve the people by protecting life, liberty and property. When government violates individual rights people may legitimately rebel. The Bible clearly reveals that every person, no matter how humble or poor, knows that God knew his name before he was born and that everybody is equal in God's sight. Furthermore, every precept of the New Testament gospel inculcates humility, servant leadership, and brotherly kindness, which are directly opposed to the pride of monarchies, kingly leaders, and the pageantry of exalted leadership.

The Biblical view states that God is supreme. Government is not. Man is not. God is neither nature, nor the sun, moon or stars. The state is not divine. The whole of man's existence is not absorbed by the state, but it too comes under the power of God. The king or emperor is neither god incarnate nor is he to be worshipped. Rather, both governments and citizens are under God and under His law.

Many Biblical accounts tell of people willing to obey the emperor in secular matters but not willing to bow down and worship him. Many of the early Christian martyrs were killed for this very reason. Nothing in the created order is entitled to be worshipped. "Thou shall have no other gods before me," is one of the Ten Commandments. The matter of the sovereignty of God and the refusal to worship any creature or any aspect of creation is the heart of many Biblical stories, including that of three men fighting idolatry: Shadrach, Meschach, and Abednego. These young Jewish men, who for the sake of conscience, would not obey the laws of the Babylonian Monarch Nebuchednezzar. "Here we stand", they said. "Kill us if you like. We will not bow to the king. Not now. Not ever."[7]

Listen to the Jewish prophet Samuel of some 3000 years ago give the Biblical reasons for limited government. The Israelites noticed that all their surrounding neighbors had a king and they wanted one too. The prophet Samuel confers with the Lord and tells them what would happen if they did so. I Samuel chapter 8, verses 10 – 20 states: So Samuel told all the words of the Lord to the people who asked him for a king. And he said:

> This will be the behavior of the king who will reign over you: He will take your sons and appoint them for his own chariots and to be his horsemen, and some will run before his chariots. He will appoint captains over his thousands and captains over his fifties and others to plow his ground and reap his harvest, and some to make his weapons of war and equipment for his chariots. He will take your daughters to be perfumers, cooks, and bakers. And he will take the best of your fields, your vineyards, and your olive groves, and give them to his servants. He will take a tenth of your grain and your vintage, and give it to his officers and servants. And he will take your male servants, your female servants, your finest young men, and your donkeys, and put them to his work. He will take a tenth of your sheep. And you will be his servants. And you

will cry out in that day because of your king whom
you have chosen for yourselves, and the Lord will
not hear you in that day.   Nevertheless the people
refused to obey the voice of Samuel; and they said,
No, but we will have a king over us, that we also
may be like all the nations, and that our king may
judge us and go out before us and fight our battles.[8]

Notice the Bible's view of what happens to human freedoms
when kings have all power.   People become slaves, it says.
Citizens belong to the state.   The state is a force which imposes
taxes, takes the best of your projects and personal initiatives, and
the most capable members of your family.   The Bible expresses a
continual attitude of mistrust of kings, the power of the state, and
fear of those who hold coercive force.   While the pagan view of
a king often led to uncontrolled power and to the subjugation of
the individual, the Biblical view sought limits on that power.
Without that, there would be no freedom.

The idea of a transcendent law reflecting the worth of man
and his property has deep historical roots, as even a cursory
survey makes clear.   In ancient Jewish culture, the law (Torah)
was revered as divine revelation. The Romans likewise appealed
to an eternal source of law, as reflected in Cicero's statement that
"law is not the product of human thought, nor is it any enactment
of peoples, but something eternal which rules the whole
universe."[9] By A.D. 380, Christianity was the official religion of
the Roman Empire, and from then on, Western law was largely
shaped by the Christian conception of law, based on the doctrine
of creation. Theologians like Augustine and Aquinas contended
that human law must reflect the moral order created by God—
knowable by believers and non-believers alike, since it is the
"law written on the heart."   The idea of a higher law was

expanded on by the Greeks and Stoic philosophers. Then during the English revolution a number of philosophers developed it, as we will see shortly, into a modern doctrine that liberty is about the sovereignty of the individual, that each man is responsible to himself and to his God, and that everyone has the unalienable right to life, liberty, and property.

Consequences of Limited Government

Under the Judeo/Christian tradition, when the kings and states of this earth are scaled back, the vacated space could then be filled by family, the church, and rule of law. Not only would there be a law above the king, but also a spiritual force far more important and always above him. Not only would the king be constrained, but the church could now address the issues of the spirit without intervention and superseded authority. Political rulers would then have the more limited, secular task of keeping order, protecting citizens, adjudicating property rights, and providing for defense of its citizens.

The Biblical model did just that. It scaled down the power of the state, while raising the status of the individual. It was a way of looking at people unheard of in world history. The Biblical view begins with affirming the inherent worth of every human being, created in the image of God, possessed of an immortal soul, and embarked on a journey in quest of their salvation. Each individual has a personal link to the creator and is independent of any earthly power. Each person has equal worth in the eyes of God. Judaic and Christian doctrine formed the very basis for the idea of limited government.

In Hebraic religion, as Will Herberg notes, "man's personality is taken as the inexpugnable reality of his being.

It is because man is a person that he can hear God's word and respond to it." Christian doctrine says the same thing. The Biblical world-view is a different mindset altogether than other world-views.

Property Rights

Thou shall not steal. Thou shall not covet.

-Two of the Ten Commandments

The Bible also discusses the underlying principles of economics, ranging from private property, to rules of commerce, to economic justice. It speaks clearly to the first requirement of economic liberty: that is, the protection of private ownership of goods and property. Private property is the natural bulwark of liberty because it ensures that economic power is not entirely in the hands of the state. Material things in and of themselves are not property; they become property only when humans creatively find ways to use them productively. Seen in this light, the defense of the right to property is not a defense of material things per se, but rather of the dignity of human creativity and inventiveness. Throughout scripture we find the right to private property recognized and protected. As a moral principle, this recognition and defense is implicit in the Ten Commandments: in the Eighth Commandment, which forbids stealing, and in the Tenth Commandment, which forbids coveting. In the Mosaic law, Exodus chapter 22, it is clear that those who stole another's property were required to make restitution.

Europe: The First Example of Limited Government

When the great struggle for human liberty began in Europe, the one interest that controlled the life and the mind of the continent was religion.   What men wanted most of all was the freedom to worship God in their own way.   Thousands of believers went to their death at the stake dying for that belief.

Europe was chiefly the product of Christianity.   The whole area of Europe was once described, in fact as, "Christendom." The church was the main institution in an area divided by language, custom, ethnic background and political ambitions. Religion was the one unifying entity. Christianity defined man, values, business, and provided the language of clerical and Latin officialdom. Christopher Dawson, a famous historian, said that, "the tribes and people and nations of the West acquired a common consciousness and sense of cultural and spiritual unity. It was the Christian religion that gave Europe a common outlook and distinctive view concerning the rule of the state."[11] It was here the limited government system took hold and thus produced a prosperity the world had never known. The foundations of modern capitalism were laid and European man was released from the vast bureaucratic system of administrative law and government control.

However, these developments did not always proceed in a straight-forward and peaceful fashion.   Christianity, like any other religion, can be twisted to false, secular ends. When the Catholic Church reached its zenith of political power, it had armies and engaged in wars, sold "dispensations" from sin for money (called "simony"), defined disagreements with its doctrines as a crime, and burned dissenters at the stake as heretics. Such practices led to the Reformation, and eventually to reforms within the Catholic Church, whose practices today look very different from those of a thousand years ago.

St. Thomas Aquinas (1224-1274) argued that the first focus of political power lies in the consent of the people. Since humans are born to be free, civilizations should not be constituted by force and by government power, but rather by conversation and the whole nation sharing in governing itself. There is absolutely no security for a particular individual if he must depend on the will of another man.

The Western political tradition that began in Europe assumed that in order to be valid, human laws must be grounded in the natural law by which God orders his creation. Human laws must work with eternal laws. This assumption was expressed in the Magna Carta of 1215, a groundbreaking charter guaranteeing certain rights and privileges to the nobles against the king. It was also the foundation of English common law. [12] However, it was only one step along the way.

The medieval genealogy of English freedoms, including the growth of Parliament, taxation by consent, safeguards for property, and legal privilege became leading features of the common law tradition. It is one thing to say the power of kings should be limited and quite another to do it. The English did it. The king was bound by the law, he must govern by consent. It was precisely this medieval concept of limited power that the settlers brought with them to America. And, in Britain as well as eventually on the new continent, the feudal notions of limited government were transmuted into modern theory by the Reformation and then the Founders. Text after text would indicate that Europe, by the mid sixteenth century, was learning that "all civil authority is derived from the will of the community as a whole. A king is merely a delegate and an agent." The main historical events of rule of law happened as follows.

The true rule of law emerged in the eleventh and twelfth century in two different places in Europe.[13] The Roman

Church fought vigorously to uphold its rights against both crowned princes and the feudal barons. Pope Gregory swore that his own courts would operate as a refuge for the physically weak and oppressed – not just for the clergy, but for women, children, the poor and the sick as well. His was an effort against the rule of force where the armored knight dispensed what law there was.

Unfortunately, Gregory was finally driven from Rome a failure. "I have loved justice and hated inequity and I die in exile," he said. But his successors carried on the struggle until churches and monasteries, nunneries and all consecrated ground was finally free from the arbitrary sword. These were the seeds of a rule of law to come.

At the same time the English crown, building on a different legal tradition, but still very Christian, moved by secular means toward the same rule of law. In 1154 the Angevin Dynasty, the richest and most powerful in the West, took over the English Crown in the person of Henry II. Restoring order after a period of feudal anarchy, Henry was determined to enforce the rule of law against the all powerful barons and their private armies. He used the flexible instrument of the old English common law with its general principles of justice and equity. Henry drew up comprehensive statutes and instructed his judges to administer the system, and because he was the tax collector, he could finance the enforcement of the law.

History records that a quarrel with Archbishop Thomas Becket of Canterbury led to Becket's murder in his own cathedral, but then Henry repented, and eventually a compromise was reached, which a generation later resulted in the Magna Carta. In this charter, the Church and state came together to force the crown itself, in the person of King John, to publicly submit for the first time to the rule of law. This 1215 document, stating and protecting the legal rights of many groups in society, is rightly classified as the first of the great English statutes of the realm and surely had earth shaking ramifications.

From these events emerged the permanent rule of law in the Anglo Saxon tradition from which even the monarch of the land was subject to the law of the land. While King Charles I disagreed, arguing that a king and his subjects are two plainly different things, the Parliament in 1640 proved him wrong. It took a civil war and Charles' execution to eventually make the point.

Gradually emerging over the decades, then, was a kingship under a rule of law, rule by Parliament, and the beginnings of a quasi-written constitution. By the early eighteenth century the Hanoverian Dynasty was actually ruled by a vote of Parliament, thus representing the first big step toward a genuine rule of law.

All of this, of course, gradually aligned with the doctrines of the church, which taught that earthly power should be subject to a higher law. The clerical spokesman Gratian proclaimed: "The law of princes ought not to prevail over national law— princes are bound by and should live according to (the) laws." In 1609, Scottish cleric Samuel Rutherford wrote a book titled *Lex Rex* ("the law is king"), asserting that the law stands above the king and that he is subject to it like all other citizens. The book was banned in Scotland and publicly burned in England, and Rutherford was arrested. [14]

The idea of limited government and limits on state compulsion is absolutely integral to the free society and the rise of capitalism. The American founders would later establish a new republic where citizens would be ruled not by men but by law.

This is not to say, however, that all of Europe understood freedom and limited government. The desire to regulate was strong and competing ideologies argued for a large role for the state. The belief that government could promote prosperity through massive intervention lead to wide-spread regulation of the economy. For instance, in France, just prior to the French Revolution, laws were passed so detailed that they specified the number of stitches allowed per inch on certain garments. Laws became so massive and inclusive that life itself became impracticable and impossible. Government power was subject to few constraints, despite the influence of the Christian religion and the Magna Carta.

The founders of America, however, saw things differently. In this new republic, citizens would choose to establish government in a better way.

America Next

> America is the only country ever founded on the printed word.
>
> - Marshal McLuhan

When historians write of the American Revolution, they often depict George Washington as its sword, Patrick Henry as its tongue, James Madison as its constitutionalist, and Thomas Jefferson as its pen. All people, Jefferson argued, have a right to liberty. He articulated a doctrine for strictly limiting the powers of government. His was a sophisticated, radical, and eloquent set of ideas that would set afire the imaginations of freedom loving people everywhere.

> "Oh! Ye that love mankind! Ye that dare oppose not only the tyranny but the tyrant, stand forth. We have it in our power to begin the world over again. Now is the time for union. The sun never shined on a cause of greater worth. The birthday of a New World is at hand."

These were the cries of the patriots, the founders, the framers, and the writers of America's Constitution and revolutionary government. These were also the cries of men of deep faith.

Michael Novak, noted historian, theologian and policy analyst at The American Enterprise Institute writes:

> If ever on a hot and muggy day in July, when you were young, you dove into the clear cool water of a mountain lake, you know the shock that greets you when you dive from the intellectual world of modern secular scholarship into a leisurely reading of the papers of the Founders. The latter were so plainly religious, compared to the intellectuals of today, and not merely religious, but pious—moved by sentiments of whose warmth and tenderness there can be no doubt. For the Founders, reason and revelation are not in fundamental opposition. Rather, regarding the character and centrality of liberty, they converge. In their view, the ideas and practice of Judaism and Christianity are the best foundation for republican government.

While modern scholars believe reason and revelation are radically opposed, please see Appendix A for the founders view.

As the early pioneers from England settled the east coast, they brought with them ideas of how to build communities, acquire land, settle property rights disputes, and construct a workable government. It was their "English law" that gave people the structure to buy and sell land, settle disputes over broken fences and settled property rights differences. It was their Biblical emphasis that gave them instruction on how to worship, marry, raise kids, treat their neighbors, and design a different and constrained government.

As many as twenty thousand Puritans poured out of England by 1642. Many of them came to settle in America for religious reasons. Their passion for their faith and the legacy of their belief prompted one American observer, G. K. Chesterton, to call the United States "a nation with the soul of a church."

The Puritans also brought with them the idea of limited government. John Cotton, chief Bible doctrine interpreter and theologian of early Massachusetts said:

> Let all the world learn to give mortal men no greater power than they are content they shall use, for use it they will—it is most wholesome for magistrates and affairs in church and commonwealth never to affect more liberty and authority than will do them good, and the people good; for whatever transcendent power is given will certainly overrun those that receive it. It is necessary, therefore, that all power that is on earth be limited, church power or other— It is counted a matter of danger to the state to limit prerogatives; but it is a further danger, not to have them limited.[15]

It was also unique to the West that competition among religions would prevent any religion from maintaining a monopoly and therefore all individuals could experience religious liberty. Freedom depends on the division of power. Competition does just that.

The Puritans based their church and civic institutions, on the concept of the rule of law, pointing toward the practices of limited government that Americans today take for granted. Indeed, the early history of our country shows how strongly that limited government was based on the teaching of religion. Biblical Christianity provided the blueprint. However, the Puritans remind us that we can never be too complacent about limiting government. The Puritans came to America to find religious freedom, only to turn around and want Puritanism to be a monopoly church. But, fortunately, this then produced Rhode Island, founded by Roger Williams, who was banished from Massachusetts for his political and religious beliefs, and then Pennsylvania, and so on.

Still, the fundamental proposition of the American revolution was that man is a child of God, created in His image, and that he carries within him a spark that links him with the universe and differentiates him from all other creatures. Each individual's spark gives to the principles of freedom a god-like validity. The essence of the American idea was not that every person would be on the same material level as everyone else, but that everyone would have liberty to be what God made him. Freedom is a weak cord if the focus is on rights rather than responsibility.

The American Revolutionists identified themselves with the Whigs of England who wrestled control of the Parliament from King John in the Magna Carta in 1215. They took care to adopt their constitution through a process of debate and deliberation. And for them, religion, the Christian Bible and the Protestant Churches were the sources of both revelation and revolution. While the revolution was ignited, in fact, by the Puritan preachers of New England, everything from the very beginning was done with prayer and Biblical insight.

It took the Biblical view of deity, nature, man and state to make the free society even a mental possibility. Prior to this attempt, history records an epoch where political power embraced the whole of life. Government was church and state rolled into one. There were no limits. But under Christianity, all of this was changed. The state was no longer divine nor the whole of existence, but was only a small part of life. The king was neither the law incarnate nor a divinity to be worshipped. The ruler "is under God and under the law."[16]

Limited government and freedom, then, begins with an idea. Man matters. Man matters because he was created in the image of God and has great worth. And because he has great worth, man has a natural right to liberty. Thomas Jefferson's "We are endowed by our creator with certain unalienable rights . . . ." means:

> Not endowed by government.
> Not endowed by politicians.
> Not endowed by armies.
> Not endowed by wealth.
> Not endowed by intellect. But rather,
> Endowed by our Creator.
> Endowed by God.

This single idea that people have individual rights did more to change the world than any other. Throughout history most men have been born in chains. Under this idea, they are born to be free. But to be born free is not to be born perfect.

Virtually everyone in our early politics, it appears, was a believer in Original Sin. The founders realized that everyone is prone to sin. Therefore, it is a fatal mistake to entrust too much power to any individual or group, including churches. They understood well that there cannot be power for good without having power for evil also. The idea of the sin nature of man—the inherited disorder of man's nature in which each of us is born—immediately puts the brakes on the utopian hopes of man's moral potency. Even a good government will disintegrate in time if not fortified by virtue, which itself is reinforced by religion. As a result, the founders established three branches of government—the judicial, legislative, and executive—based on the biblical teaching found in the book of Isaiah, chapter 33, verse 22, that God is our judge, lawgiver, and king. The founders also established a federal system in which state governments were to keep a check on the national government. This is why the Constitution originally reserved to the states the right to appoint senators, and even the election of the president was made the task of electors from the states (the electoral college). Samuel Adams stated that "ambition and lust for power are the predominate passions in the breasts of most men."[17]

In a grand, eschatological sense, the freedom for which the heart of man most deeply longs is the freedom from the bondage of sin and death. Yes, the founders like Samuel Adams tried to create a system that would deliver political, economic, and personal freedoms, but a large amount of their writing addressed not the freedom to do what we want but the liberty to choose what we ought. Even God himself, they argued, allowed man to choose sin, so great was His commitment to personal freedom and dignity. God never forces free will. But the Bible, they said, revealed what true liberty means. "If the Son will make you free, you shall be free indeed."

John Jay (1745-1829) was the first Chief Justice of the United States Supreme Court, having been appointed by President George Washington. He was a founding father, a member of the First and Second Continental Congresses and served as the president of the Continental Congress. Instrumental in causing the Constitution to be ratified, he wrote the *Federalist Papers* along with James Madison and Alexander Hamilton. On October 1, 1816 Jay made this comment: "The Bible informs us that our gracious Creator has provided for us a Redeemer, in whom all the nations of the earth shall be blessed; that this Redeemer has made atonement "for the sins of the world," and by reconciling the Divine justice with Divine mercy has opened a way for our redemption and salvation."[18] John Jay, like most all the framers, was a great skeptic of human nature. He understood man's sin nature and knew that any government must be constrained.

The anti-federalists were even more insistent about the evils of human nature. They wrote: "Every man has a propensity to power. It is the nature of man to be tyrannical."[19] Anti-federalists such as Richard Henry Lee, George Mason, and Patrick Henry never stopped worrying that "The ropes and chains of consolidation were about to convert this country into a powerful and mighty empire in which a standing army would execute the execrable commands of tyranny."

Thomas Jefferson said that "Free government is founded in jealousy and not in confidence—in questions of power, then, let no more be heard of confidence in man, but bind him down from mischief with the chains of the Constitution."[20]

Mistrust of human nature was universal among the founders, and it was this mistrust that formed the basis for limited government. Their hostility to unchecked power led to the checks and balances of two Houses of Congress, the Supreme Court, the Executive Branch, the Bill of Rights, and of course, the Constitution. The principle for the founders, was that every power should be a check to another power. Daniel Webster, the writer of the dictionary and framer of our government said:

> Never cease to give to religion, to its institutions, and to its ministers your strenuous support . . . those who destroy the influence and authority of the Christian religion, sap the foundations of public order, of liberty, and of republican government.

Constitutional Government

It is necessary from the very nature of things
that power should be a check to power.

-Charles deMontesquieu

Even though the beginnings of limited government were developed in Christian England, constitutional government took shape in America. In British government, while unchecked authority had been wrested from the crown, Parliament could still do as it wished. Law was whatever the Parliament decided. American Puritans did not accept that idea. All political power, they argued, was subject to a higher law, and this included legislatures as well as monarchs.

From all this came the thirteen American colonies on a new continent who elected their own representatives. When the infant American republic drew up its constitution, the framers understood they were upholding and reinforcing a system of government of laws, not men, and their written constitution was proof. The founders were very clear on what they believed to be the legitimate functions of government. Article 1, Section 8 of the Constitution said, in part: "The Congress shall have the power to lay and collect taxes, duties, imports, and excises, to pay the debts and provide for the common defense—to borrow money on the credit of the United States—to regulate commerce with foreign nations—to coin money—to establish post offices and post roads—to raise and support armies." The founders granted taxes and spending powers to support just a few activities. The Constitution, the Bill of Rights, and the offsetting powers of legislative, judicial, and executive branches of government clearly describe what the framers had in mind: limited government.

The Best Is Yet To Come

The Constitution separated the powers of the legislative, judicial, and executive branches, so that any two balanced the other. The authors understood that for a political system based on the rule of law to succeed, three conditions were necessary. First, the basic documents should be written in plain language, where everybody could understand and school children could even memorize. Both the Declaration of Independence and the Constitution met this condition. Second, it would be lawful to change the Constitution from time to time, but under conditions where its primary writer James Madison could say, "Let's make it possible but not easy." Third, the documents should be so written so that they could be interpreted in a conservative but enlightened manner.

The upshot was that Chief Justice John Marshall, appointed by President John Adams in 1801, effectively created the legal framework within which free markets in goods and services could flourish. Limited government and the rule of law thus produced the most successful economic system the world has ever seen. But no matter how prosperous, all participants of the system would still remain subject to the courts and to the rule of law.

Marquis deLaFayette summarized, "In the American colonies, the main problem of liberty has been solved, demonstrated and practiced in such a manner as not to leave much to be said by European institutions." And to my French friend, I say, oui.

The genius of the American political system was its respect for the dignity and rights of the individual. To counter the automatic tendency of government to grow, a constitution was created that strictly limited the powers of the national government while simultaneously recognizing that the greater powers given to state government would be held in check because of competition among them. Finally, in the Tenth Amendment to the Constitution, the founders clarified (again) that the rights of the individual were permanent, and that the powers of government must always be limited to preserve those rights: "The powers not delegated to the United States by the Constitution, nor prohibited by it to the States, are reserved to the States, respectively, or to the people."

There it is in a nutshell. All the powers of the U.S. government derive from the Constitution, which the people created, and any power not expressly granted by the Constitution is reserved (ultimately) to the people. Since the people can modify the Constitution via the amendment process, they can give the government new powers, such as the power to tax income (ok, even our founders had a bad idea once in a while), or take away powers, such as slavery, or the denial of fundamental rights due to race, creed, or sex. Their plan was simple, but brilliant.

In the few years following the American Revolution, each state would adopt governmental policies predicated on a Biblical world-view of limited government. In an amazing brief period of time, New England had created most of the features of a representative, limited government: constitutionalism, power wielded under the consent of the majority, annual elections, a legislature, and a Bill of Rights. As Tocqueville noted much later, "these ideas became the template for the American institutions that were to be developed later."

No, the Puritans were not democrats or proponents of toleration, or the libertarian types that would characterize the founders. They were devout believers in God who based their church and civil authority on their reading of scripture. But it is fact that they planted on American soil the very idea of limited government, the very idea of rule of law. The essence of things to follow was based squarely on Biblical precept.[21] "Limiting government will not work," said John Adams, "without religion." "Avarice, ambition, revenge, or gallantry would break the strongest cords of our Constitution as a whale goes through a net. Our Constitution is made only for a moral and religious people. It is wholly inadequate to the government of any other."

The Declaration of Independence said, "We are endowed by our creator with certain unalienable rights." Rights do not come from politicians or presidents. They come from our Creator. "We've limited government," said one of the founders, "to protect freedom from democracy and the individual from the majority." They understood that the majority is often wrong. The founders built a system that would protect against direct democracy – against any system where "the voice of the people is the voice of God."

Christianity/Limited Government/Freedom/Capitalism

From this brief discussion, we can conclude that religion and freedom go hand in hand and that America's institution of free government is based on religious precepts. Mistrust of human nature, as expressed by both the Bible and our founders, led to freedom by putting limits on political power. The Biblical world-view encouraged economic freedom because of what it did in the realm of politics and limited government. The principal thrust of Western religion, in political terms, was to impose effective boundaries on the power of the state. The result was to given rise to market economies. Judeo/Christian teaching is clear: man is created in God's image; manual labor possesses dignity and is important; man's responsibility is to steward the resources given to him; private property is important and protected; and government is limited. Free markets, after all, are what happens when government has not interfered with the transactions of private parties. The heart of the Judeo/Christian message was the idea that the individual worshipper could come into the presence of God without the mediation or intervention of any special class of men, or any group of people, or without subjection to any nation. According to this faith, the Lord is the creator and sustainer of life, and is close to every person, especially to the poorest of the poor.[22]

Think of what this belief does to tyranny. When man, no matter how humble, sees himself as a creature of God and potentially God's child, he certainly would not submit himself to the claim that government is ultimate reality. Every person has rights which government has no right to impair. Government is thus set up voluntarily by men to secure each of them in their "rights." James Madison, a Founding Father, and writer of most of the Constitution, said in his thirty-ninth Federalist Paper that the Founder's goal was "to rest all our political experiments on the capacity of mankind for self government."[23]

For the first time in history the individual person was not to be a creature of government, but instead had inherent rights endowed by God. Man could exert his energies in the way he sought and believes best without reference to government. When people obtain a strong measure of freedom by limiting government, private enterprise can and does emerge.

A culture is not something that just happens. Machiavelli once said that, "There is nothing more difficult to plan, more doubtful of success, nor more dangerous to manage, than the creation of a new system. For the initiator has the enmity of all who would profit by the preservation of the old institutions and merely lukewarm defenders in those who would gain by the new ones." It develops over time through the play of the old versus the new. Its spiritual foundation is constructed slowly and painfully, not unlike the building of a breakwater, where after throwing bag after bag of sand and cement into the water, the construction finally emerges and the breakwater is finally seen and in place. Building on the experience of Europe, America emerged with a new outlook, a new spirit, and a new set of values which released the human spirit like never before. The dead weight of the tyrannies of political government were thrown off and man's productive energies would now be geared to business, science, and economic growth as well as religion, education, medicine, and the liberal arts.

The material prosperity we have come to know in America is not an accident, but is rather the direct outgrowth of the spiritual, political, and social upheaval that Christianity produced centuries ago. The elements of the moral law as set forth in the Ten Commandments were the rules of conduct necessary for peaceful relations and voluntary exchange. It didn't take long for people to realize that mutual gains are more likely from cooperation motivated by the hope of reward than under the threat of violence. The only purpose for which power can be rightfully exercised over any member of a civilized community against his will, is to prevent harm to others. Otherwise, he is free to work and create. When freedom and limited government come together, they produce capitalism and prosperity. The peril of prosperity, however, is the peril of forgetting how it was achieved.

Tocqueville would write in 1835, after a long visit to America, "There is no country in the world where the Christian religion retains a greater influence over the souls of men than in America . . . I do not know whether all Americans have a sincere faith in their religion, for who can search the human heart? —

but I am certain that they hold it indispensable to the maintenance of republican institutions." [24]

We Americans say that the Constitution made our country. Well, the Constitution is a great document and we never would have been a great nation without it. But it took more than that. It was our forefathers and foremothers who made the Constitution work. The government they constructed did get great things for them, but it was not the government that put the great things into them. What put great things into them was their home life, their devotion to education, their love of liberty, their character, and most important, their religion and sense of personal responsibility to Almighty God. Every country and culture is to a strong degree a reflection of its religious beliefs. America was no exception.

The Best Is Yet To Come

CHAPTER 3

Ideas Have Consequences

Freedom Stalwarts: F. A. Hayek and Milton Friedman

> An invasion of armies can be resisted, but not an
> idea whose time has come.
>
> -Victor Hugo

It is the great ideas that inform the mind, fire the imagination, move the heart, and shape a culture. History is little more than the recording of the rise and fall of the great ideas—the world views—that form our values and move us to act. Some of these great ideas appeared in three very important books written in the twentieth century during the rise of governmentalism and the dark days of anti-capitalism. These books were largely responsible for the revived interest in the ideas of liberty and the socially beneficial implications of private property, the market system and limited government.

F. A. Hayek and the Austrian School

> Socialism as advocated by intellectuals and
> government is purely theoretical; practical socialism
> is totalitarian everywhere.
>
> -F. A. Hayek

The first prong of the attack on socialism and the politicized society originated in Vienna, then migrated to London, and finally to American soil. When the Austrian School of Economics finally came to the United States during World War II, its two brightest and most articulate expounders were Ludwig von Mises and Friedrich A. Hayek, the latter of whom would win a Nobel Prize in economics.

A man who wants to lead the orchestra must turn his back on the crowd. If any twentieth century economist was a Renaissance man, it was Friedrich Hayek. He made fundamental contributions in economics, political theory, and psychology. Many of his contributions are so remarkable that people still read them, more than 50 years after Hayek wrote them. The major problem for any economy, Hayek argued, is determining how people should coordinate their actions. He recognized that, while the price system and free markets could do a remarkable job of coordinating people's actions, they did so without any clear intent. Hayek maintained the free market is a spontaneous and unplanned order, not designed by anyone and nothing short of a miracle. It gives people the maximum latitude to use information that only they have and provides the data to act on that would not exist otherwise.

Friedrich A. von Hayek (1899-1992) was born in Vienna, the son of a distinguished botanist. Early on, he was an Adlai Stevenson-type intellectual and a government liberal. When he returned from service in World War I, his studies led him to a slow, intellectual conversion from government solutions to market ones. His study of the Austro-Hungarian Empire left him with a dour view of politicians. And the influence of his teacher and mentor Ludwig von Mises, author of *Human Action* and also a leading figure in the Austrian school, was profound. Mises had demonstrated conclusively the impossibility of rational planning under socialism. The market system, he said, is a self-adjusting order and far more capable than a horde of experts in "planning" an economy. Hayek, in his Nobel Memorial lecture, accurately summarized Mises' free market, pro-capitalist views:

> The recognition of the inseparable limits to his knowledge ought indeed to teach the student of society a lesson in humility which should guard him against becoming an accomplice in men's fatal striving to control society—a striving which makes him not only a tyrant over his fellows, but which may well make him the destroyer of a civilization which no brain has designed but which has grown from the free efforts of millions of individuals.

Hayek argued that it was unimaginable that any single person or group of people could have the necessary knowledge to institute an efficient centralized plan. In a modern society, information is always and everywhere widely dispersed among millions and millions of separate individuals. They have achieved a reasonably high order in their economic lives, despite modern complexities, only because their affairs have been guided, not by central direction, but by their own adaptations to the operations of the market and competition. It is the only way to ensure the adjustments and smooth functioning of a very diverse and complex economy.

Following a decade of Roosevelt's New Deal in the U.S., the massive growth in government's role in economic life in Europe, and the relentless march of communism throughout the world, Hayek's book *The Road to Serfdom* was just the antidote. Published in 1944, the book offered a grave warning to those who would follow the Soviet central planning model. The central tenet of the postwar economic consensus was that markets were much more prone to failure than governments were. In this book and others, Hayek argued the opposite. Yes, markets can fail, but they remain much more efficient than bureaucrats, who usually could not even understand what was going on around them, let alone predict the future. Government was driving out productive enterprises through planning, taxes and regulation. Hayek reminded his readers that a large increase in government's role in economic affairs would inevitably result in the use of force, the loss of freedom, and ultimately "the road to serfdom." Over and over he tried to demonstrate that markets, blind to status and not readily controlled by the elite, would produce more prosperity and achieve egalitarian ideals that government could promise but never deliver.

While it is true that a Saint is merely a dead sinner revised and edited, F. A. Hayek's work on freedom will one day be revered. As Daniel Yergin observed in his book, *The Commanding Heights* (1998), Hayek, the 1974 Nobel Laureate:

> Documented the beginning of a great shift in the intellectual center of gravity of the economics profession toward a restoration of confidence in markets, indeed a renewed belief in the superiority of markets over other ways of organizing economic activity.

John Cassidy wrote in the February 7, 2000, *New Yorker*:

> If there are two things most people can agree on these days, they are that free market capitalism is the only practical way to organize a modern society and that the key to economic growth is knowledge. So prevalent are these beliefs that their origins are

rarely examined, which is somewhat surprising, since both statements can be traced back in large part to one man, Friedrich August von Hayek.

Milton Friedman and the Chicago School
America's Bright Light

I know of no example in time or place of a society that has been marked by a large measure of political freedom, and that has not also used something comparable to a free market.

-Milton Friedman

Milton Friedman is the twentieth century's most prominent economist advocate of free markets. He was born in 1912 to Jewish immigrants in New York City. After receiving a B.A. from Rutgers University at the age of 20, Friedman went on to earn his M.A. from the University of Chicago in 1933 and his Ph.D. from Columbia University in 1946. In 1951, Friedman won the John Bates Clark Medal honoring economists under age 40 for outstanding achievement. In 1976, he won the Nobel Prize in economics for "his achievements in the field of consumption analysis, monetary history and theory, and for his demonstration of the complexity of stabilization policy."

In his book *Capitalism and Freedom* (1960), Friedman liberated the study of market economics from its ivory tower by making it understandable to the common man. He argued for, among other things, a volunteer army, freely floating exchange rates, abolition of licensing of doctors, a negative income tax, and education vouchers. His ideas spread worldwide with his book, *Free to Choose* (co-authored with his wife, Rose Friedman), the best-selling non-fiction book of 1980, and written to accompany a TV series on the Public Broadcasting System. Milton Friedman soon became a household name. No economist since Keynes has reshaped the way people think about and use economics as Friedman has.

The books by Hayek and Friedman encompassed a period during which a shift of power was beginning in the world of economic ideas and policy. The University of Chicago in the United States and the Austrian School of Economics in Vienna both became incubators of freedom. Both were bastions of scholarly activity on the benefits of private arrangements and the competitive market process. The powerful ideas of freedom were passed to a new generation of scholars, and then again to their students who, in the 1960s and 1970s, would lead the counter-revolution in favor of competitive capitalism. The century's long swing toward government solutions had begun to shift.

The fundamental message at Chicago ran counter to the conventional government interventionist dogma of the time. Often, when everyone is against you, it means that you are absolutely wrong or absolutely right. Eventually, the Chicago school was proven absolutely right. Truth always passes through four stages before it is recognized. At first, it is ridiculed. Then, it is opposed. Third, it is regarded as self-evident. And finally, some politician takes credit for inventing it. Milton Friedman, Frank Knight, Henry Simons, James Buchanan, Warren Nutter, Roland McKean and dozens of other famous Chicago scholars demonstrated conclusively that there is somebody wiser than any of us, and that is everybody. Freedom really is the mainspring of economic prosperity.

In 1999, Robert Mundell was the latest Chicago scholar to become a Nobel Laureate in economics. The central figure of supply-side economics and the intellectual grandfather of Ronald

Reagan's economic revolution, Mundell's policies set in motion the trends we are still enjoying today. The Mundell policy mix of tight money to cure monetary inflation and tax cuts to stimulate growth in the real sector was a direct challenge to the liberal Keynesian orthodoxy that had dominated the economics profession for forty years. In the last 23 years, in fact, Chicago's faculty have been honored with the Nobel Prize 11 more times, three times in physics and eight times in economics. In the mountains of truth, you never climb in vain.

Milton Friedman won the prize for his study of monetary policy, its mismanagement and the catastrophic effects it had on the economy of the 1930s. Nobody taught the world more about the causes of inflation than Friedman. And in every path-breaking idea he pioneered—controlling inflation, a consumption tax, vouchers in education, competition in the health care system, among others—his countenance was pleasant, his smile infectious, and his mind always manufacturing original and important ideas. Nothing lowers the level of conversation more than raising the voice. Friedman knew that in quarreling, the truth is often lost. Few people can win an argument and respect at the same time. Friedman did.

Theodore Schultz's prize was for his work on the relationship between education and economic development. George Stigler was cited for his research on government regulation. Gary Becker believed that people make rational decisions and are affected by personal incentives. His research applied free-market economics to the many diverse aspects of human behavior. Robert Fogel applied economics and statistics to the analysis of history. These University of Chicago Nobel Laureates each cast light on the advantages of a free market, voluntary exchange, and limited government. They were willing to challenge conventional economic thinking and explore the uncharted territory of a world based on freedom and free markets. The ideas of the Chicago School were never mainstream. For half a century, they have shocked the intellectual, political, and media elites, who even today lean the other way.

Nevertheless, humanity was about to embrace a better way. The ideas of a limited government and the free market economy, though enunciated by many, were stated most clearly during capitalism's most desperate hour by Hayek and Friedman. And while millions of Americans would credit Friedman for their understanding of capitalism and freedom, Friedman himself said, "I have again and again asked fellow believers in a free society how they managed to escape the contagion of their collectivist intellectual environment. No name has been mentioned more often as the source of enlightenment and understanding than Friedrich Hayek. I, like others, owe him a great debt. His lucid and always principled exposition have helped to broaden my understanding of the meaning and the requisites of a free society." That said, Friedman himself was America's greatest champion of liberty. He carried the torch in the media, in academia, and his influence extended around the world.

Who would have believed 50 years ago that freedom and capitalism would be so widely embraced today? Who would have believed that the opening of the twenty-first century would find America so dominant? In 1970, United States per capita income was only 10 percent higher than that of other major industrialized nations. Now at $32,000 per capita GDP, the gap is 22 percent. Though single country domination has happened before, Portugal in the fifteenth century, Spain in the sixteenth, and Britain in the nineteenth, the world has ever seen a country's influence as dominant as America's is today. Motorola cell phones, McDonald's and Federal Express trucks, Michael Jordan sweatshirts, Starbucks coffee houses, waiters speaking English in restaurants everywhere, the teenagers around the globe singing tunes from MTV and watching Hollywood movies—these all make today's world look like Planet America. Think about what Asia's Rollerblade generation, age 10 to 24, prefer compared to their parents: their parents drank tea, they drink Coke; their parents wore sandals, they wear Nike's; their parents ate rice, they eat Chicken McNuggets; their parents purchased things with cash, they purchase things with credit cards.

P.J. O'Rourke summarizes it well. "Omnipresent amid all the frenzy of Shanghai is that famous portrait, that modern icon. The faintly smiling, bland yet somehow threatening visage appears in brilliant red hues on placards and posters and is painted huge on the sides of buildings. There are those who say his military reputation was inflated, yet he conquered the mainland in short order. Yes, it's Colonel Sanders."

Hayek and Friedman on Free Markets

When government is limited and property rights are protected, freedom flourishes, capitalism works and prosperity predominates.

-Barry Asmus

Capitalism and Freedom

There can be no freedom of the individual without the private enterprise system. Capitalism and freedom are, in the end, inseparable. Those who would destroy freedom have only first to destroy the hope of gain, the profit of enterprise and risk-taking, the hope of accumulating capital, the hope to save something for one's old age and for one's children. For a community of men without property, and without the hope of getting it by honest effort, is a community of slaves and a despotic state.

The challenge of human beings has always been to find ways to coordinate their actions with others to achieve mutually beneficial gains. Government planning, coercion and despotism is one alternative. Freedom is the other. It's dynamic. It's untidy. It's innovative. And it's complex. Preservation of freedom is a fresh challenge and a fresh conquest for each generation. It is based on the religious concept of the dignity of man. When man is free, he becomes a wealth creator.

Why is it that America, with 5 percent of the world's population can produce 70 percent of the world's Nobel Laureates and 90 of the 100 most important inventions of the twentieth century, and currently produces 35 percent of the world's annual wealth? Why is it that if you live in the United States, Canada, the Western rim of Europe or Australia, you represent only 15 percent of the world's population but produce over 60 percent of the world's output and control about 95 percent of the value of its equity markets?

The answer is that most of these people live in a system that protects property rights, compete in a system called capitalism, enjoy free trade and voluntary exchange, and live under a tax, monetary and rule-of-law system that permits the accumulation of wealth. The answer in one word: freedom. People have freedom to choose. Hayek and Friedman both wrote that freedom is the mainspring of prosperity, that private property and rule-of-law were necessary prerequisites to freedom, and that the commanding heights of an economy should be given to capitalism, the markets, and entrepreneurs. Freedom, they argued, is the most powerful prosperity producer ever devised by mankind, a virus for which there is no antidote. They spent a lifetime telling people how and why it works.

Property Rights

> The system of private property is the most important guaranty of freedom, not only for those who own property, but for those who do not. It is only because the control of the means of production is divided among many people acting independently that nobody has complete power over us, that we as individuals can decide what to do with ourselves.
>
> -Friedrich A. Hayek

The free-market system we call capitalism is a set of ideas based upon private property rights. Individuals may own, buy, and sell property as long as they don't do it fraudulently or harm others. Private property is the natural bulwark of liberty because it ensures that economic power is not entirely in the hands of the state. The glue that holds the market together is a judicial framework and a system of laws to maintain a sound currency, the protection of property rights, the enforcement of contracts, and a rule of law. Those tasks are usually taken over by government.

Government, instead of trying to do too many tasks and doing them poorly, should try do only a few things that it can do well. That's what we call *limited government*. Government's main job is to protect and adjudicate property rights, making sure that everyone follows the rules and plays fair. The business of prosperity cannot be carried out in a society in which property rights are weak or even nonexistent, where graft and corruption the rule, and where contracts are broken and debt cannot be collected. We have only to look at the current situation in Russia to see what happens when capitalism is introduced without rule of law, property rights, and the judicial infrastructure to maintain order in commerce. Ruthless communist businessmen, such as the "Russian Mafia," pillage the country. Former communist leaders organize the privatization efforts, sell the stock in the new companies and quickly transfer the collected money to personal Swiss bank accounts. When property rights are not defined, deeded, titled and protected, capitalism will not work. Nobody has a chance for prosperity, least of all the poor. But when an individual has the exclusive right to his property, the complex issue of property rights is resolved.

When social critics complain that "property rights" take precedence over "human rights," Hayek and Friedman respond that inequality and scarcity exist in all societies. The purported conflict between property rights and human rights is a mirage— indeed, property rights *are* human rights, and they represent the best means humans have for producing prosperity. If one upholds freedom, then individual rights are preeminent. But individual rights are meaningless unless you uphold each person's right to their own life, their own liberty, and their own pursuit of happiness. Without property rights, no other rights are possible. If you don't have a right to the product of your effort, you have no means to sustain your life. There is no freedom. The only dependable foundation of personal liberty is the personal economic security of private property.

Property is a broad term that includes labor service, ideas, literature, and natural resources, as well as physical assets such as homes, buildings, machines, and land. Private ownership of property is about the right to exclusive use and the legal protection against those who would want to take it. It means that an owner has the right to sell or transfer his property if another person wants it. Private ownership not only allows individuals to decide how they will use their property, but it also makes them accountable for their actions. People who use their property in a manner that invades or infringes upon the property rights of another will be subject to the same legal forces that were set up to protect their own property. For example, private property rights prohibit me from throwing a rock through your window, because if I did, I would be violating your property rights. Your right to your home restricts anyone else from using or abusing it without your permission. Similarly, my ownership of my property restricts anyone else from using it without my permission.

There are many reasons why private ownership works. First, private ownership encourages wise stewardship. If owners fail to maintain their property or if they allow it to be abused or damaged, they will bear the negative consequences. When you own an automobile, for example, you have a strong incentive to change the oil and have the car serviced regularly. Why? Because if you are careless with your car's maintenance, its value to both you and potential future owners declines. With private ownership, wise stewardship is rewarded. Without it, there are few positive incentives. When, for example, was the last time that you washed a rental car?

Private ownership also encourages increased productivity. With private ownership, individuals have a strong incentive to improve their skills, work harder, and work smarter. Similarly, they have a strong incentive to enhance capital assets such as houses, office buildings, and farms. Positive incentives are always improved when personal efforts are rewarded.

Another attractive feature of private property is that it

eliminates the use of violence as a competitive weapon. People you do not buy from are not permitted to burn down your house. Nor are competitors permitted to slash your automobile tires or threaten you with bodily injury. Private ownership keeps power dispersed and expands the area of activity that is based on voluntary consent. The only dependable foundation of personal liberty is the personal economic security of private property.

The story of four people named Everybody, Somebody, Anybody, and Nobody is illustrative. There was an important job to be done and Everybody was asked to do it. Anybody could have done it, but Nobody did it. Somebody got angry about that, because it was Everybody's job. Everybody thought Anybody could do it, but Nobody realized that Everybody wouldn't do it. Consequently, it wound up that Nobody told Anybody, so Everybody blamed Somebody.

The point? Everybody's business is Nobody's business. Public ownership socialism doesn't work because the incentives to take personal responsibility do not exist. Private property capitalism, on the other hand, limits economic power; produces positive economic incentives; makes people accountable for their actions; promotes harmony; encourages stewardship; and in the final analysis is the only dependable foundation of personal liberty ever tried.

The Price System and Economic Coordination

The price system of a market economy is made up of many different kinds of prices—wage rates, interest rates, rents, stock market quotas, retail prices, wholesale prices, charges for professional services, and others. All of those prices are continually fluctuating in response to underlying conditions of supply and demand, and in so doing, they direct every phase of economic activity.

Prices are the language of the market economy, a summation of a great amount of knowledge and information, not necessarily known to most market participants. As the price of bauxite rises, for example, the producer of aluminum may not know why. Nonetheless, the aluminum producer knows that the real cost of an important raw material has risen and, thus, production plans must be altered. If the going wage rate for skilled labor rises relative to the wage rate for unskilled labor, an employer's hiring practices will probably change, even if he knows nothing at all about why this change in relative wages has occurred. Nothing conveys information faster than prices. Blind to race, sex, and religious preference, the price system is an incredibly efficient way to determine price, supply and demand.

Prices transmit information. The higher they are, the more suppliers will supply and the less buyers will buy. Markets transmit prices to help everyone decide what to do. Prices also provide the incentives necessary to produce in the least costly way and use resources for the most highly valued purposes. The coming together of supply and demand to determine price is probably the most complicated interaction in the universe. Millions of producers, sellers, and buyers are all simultaneously making it happen. The price mechanism is probably the only possible device yet conceived that can weld the personally and individually determined preferences, desires, and ambitions of people into a peaceful working social order.

A delightful story called "I, Pencil: My Family Tree" as told by my late friend and the longtime President of the Foundation for Economic Education, Leonard E. Read, dramatizes vividly how voluntary exchange enables millions of people to cooperate with one another. Read tells his story through the voice of an ordinary yellow pencil. "Not a single person knows how to make me," the pencil says. Could that be true? Compared to a house, a car, or a computer, a pencil seems so easy. Then he proceeds to tell about all the things that go into the making of a pencil. First, the wood comes from a tree, a cedar of straight grain that grows in Northern California and Oregon. To cut down the tree and transport the logs to the railroad siding requires saws and trucks and rope and countless other gear. Thousands of people and hundreds of skills go into the making of just the "wood" part. The mining of ore, the making of steel and its refinement into chain saws, axes, motors are just the start. The growing of hemp and bringing it through all its productive stages to finally become heavy and strong rope; the logging camps with their beds and mess halls—untold thousands of persons had a hand in the making of my many components.

Think about all the skills it takes to bring the logs to the mill, all the millwork involved in converting the logs to slats, and the trucks to move it from place to place. Up to now we're still talking only about the outside wood of the pencil. The "lead" center is not really lead at all. It starts as graphite mined in Sri Lanka. After many complicated processes it ends up as the lead in the center of the pencil. The bit of metal—the ferrule—near the top of the pencil is brass.

Think of all the persons: who mine zinc and copper and those who have the skills to make shiny sheet brass from these products of nature. What we call the eraser is known in the trade as "the plug." We think it's rubber, but Read tells us the rubber is only for binding purposes. The erasing is actually done by "Factice," a rubber-like product made by reacting rapeseed oil from Indonesia with sulfur chloride. After all of this and much, much more, says the pencil, "Can anyone challenge my earlier assertion that no single person on the face of the earth knows how to make me?"

The thousands of persons involved in producing the pencil performed their tasks not because they wanted a pencil or even knew what a pencil was for. They simply saw their work as a way to get the goods and services they wanted. Every time we go to the store and buy a pencil, we are exchanging a little bit of our money for the small service that each of many thousands contributed toward producing the pencil. How did they all know what to do?

Competition, Prices, and Economic Coordination

The single summary statistic—the competitive market price of all the processes just discussed—provides suppliers of goods or services with everything they need to know to make a supply decision and bring their decision into harmony with the preferences of others. Competition is a constant force. It makes things happen, constantly tries to lower costs and price, and continually tries to improve people's lives. Competition happens so automatically and so naturally that most of us don't even give it a second thought. Some people might not like each other, but nevertheless cooperate with each other peacefully. Think about it. The goods people value are produced in approximately the right quantities that people want. Very few people in America stand in long lines or are told "sold out until next week." Yes, it sometimes happens, but very seldom. And when it does, it's not bread, milk or other necessities that we can't get; it's "Tickle Me Elmo" and "PlayStation 2." The invisible hand of the marketplace produces order, coordination, harmony, and diversity. Isn't it amazing that a process that works so wonderfully and quietly is so little understood and so seldom appreciated?

Consumers love competition. When Reebok slips, Nike is right there with a better shoe. When the quality of Ford and GM cars goes down, America's demand for Toyota, Nissan, and Honda goes up. We all seek competitive bids for a project we have planned. Competition is a very positive force for consumers.

Hayek and Friedman said that competition would not lead to chaos, but to a spontaneous and productive social order, a fundamental concept of basic economics. Competition, for example, replaced the horse and wagon with railroads, automobiles, and airplanes; the washboard and clothes line with the washer and dryer; whisky with Novocain and other modern drugs; the ship and pony with a modern, digital telecommunications system.

Interestingly, competition is not the creation or even the by-product of a capitalistic system. Competition exists everywhere in nature and in all economic systems. The difference between social systems is not in the presence or the absence of competition, but in the type of competition different systems unleash. The rivalry, for example, to become a central planner in the Soviet Union was just as great as the rivalry to become an executive in an American Fortune 500 firm. The difference is that, to be successful as a planner, you had to get good at bureaucratic politics. To be successful as an American CEO, you had to excel in productive efficiency.

The driving force of competitive capitalism are the entrepreneurs, who wrest progress from the clutches of scarcity and place it at the disposal of all mankind. When an entrepreneur's ship doesn't come in, he swims out to it. Entrepreneurs attempt to read the market's signals, anticipate previously undeveloped consumer demands, and take risks, usually with their own money. If successful, they earn a profit.

The media can be counted on to bring attention to the winners, while the majority of entrepreneurs, who incorrectly anticipate consumer preferences, are little nor long remembered.

Competition is as much a system of cooperation in the market economy as anything else. Within a firm or family, or between a customer and a supplier, everyone must cooperate to achieve their ends. It's the kind of competition that counts. When competition takes the form of violence and plunder, wealth is destroyed. But when it takes the form of productive cooperation, it is win/win.

The story of the man getting his car stuck in a country ditch helps make the point. He knocked on the farmer's door to ask whether the farmer might use his tractor to pull his car out of the mud. The farmer replied that he was retired and had sold his John Deere, but that he had a blind horse named Dusty in the barn who could pull the car out. After putting a harness on blind Dusty and leading him out to the car, he hooked the harness to a chain and then to the car. The farmer then asked the owner to step back and watch. "Pull Clyde pull," the farmer barked. Nothing happened. "Pull Bonnie pull," the farmer cried out. Again, nothing happened. Finally, "Pull Dusty pull," and Dusty pulled the car right out of the ditch. The car owner politely asked, "Why all that pull Clyde and pull Bonnie stuff?" The farmer replied, "Well listen mister, I didn't want Dusty to think that he was pulling all by himself."

Competition and cooperation are like that. Pulling together and acting in tandem, they are a very strong team. Coopetition is literally the lifeblood of a market economy. It places pressure on producers to operate efficiently, caters to the preferences of consumers, and forces out the inefficient. Firms that fail to provide consumers with quality goods at competitive prices will experience losses and eventually be driven out of business.

Successful competitors always have to outperform rival firms. No matter their methods—quality of product, style, service, convenience of location, advertising, or price—they must consistently offer consumers as much or more value than they can get elsewhere.

Choice and Win/Win

Some critics have charged that economic analysis only explains the actions of self-centered, greedy owners. This view is false. It also explains the actions of self-centered, greedy laborers and consumers. People, whether owners, workers, or consumers, act for a variety of reasons, some selfish and some humanitarian. The basic postulate of economics applies to both the altruist and egotist. The choices of both will be influenced by changes in personal costs and benefits.

Consider a person's action in the following situations: 1) a baby is drowning in a shallow swimming pool; and 2) the same baby is in the middle of the Niagara River, just moments away from going over the falls. Most people would rescue the baby in the small pool. But what about the baby ready to go over Niagara Falls? In that case, the rational person would likely conclude the personal costs would be too high and the probability of success too low. The same baby, but with different costs, produces a different response. Although most choices involve decisions that are less extreme, people are constantly prioritizing and making choices that involve both benefits and sacrifices. Not surprisingly, we all choose differently. And, not surprisingly, monetary costs are not always the main consideration. It has been said that one never dives into the water to save a drowning man more eagerly than when there are others present who dare not take the risk. Heroes have many faces. Because people see things differently, they choose differently. A free society is the only society where it is safe to be different. Nevertheless, in both literature and love, we are astonished at what is chosen by others.

What's remarkable about an economy based on private property and voluntary exchange is that market prices will bring the actions of self-interested (even selfish) individuals into harmony with the general prosperity of the community. While the entrepreneur might have intended only his personal gain, the secondary effect was to promote an end (economic prosperity) that was not even part of his intention. "It is not from the benevolence of the butcher, the brewer, or the baker that we expect our dinner, but from their regard to their own interest," said Adam Smith, the world's first famous economist.

Money

> Although money as money is nothing, it also isn't everything. But it sure keeps you in touch with your kids.
>
> -Milton Berle

First and foremost, money is a means of exchange. It is more efficient than barter. It reduces the costs of all our exchanges because it provides a common denominator into which all goods and services can be converted. Money allows us to engage in complex exchanges over lengthy time periods and gives us a way to store purchasing power for future use. As a unit of accounting, money enhances our ability to keep track of revenues and costs that are incurred at different times and in different time periods. To say the least, an economy would not work very well without money. Money has for its basis the axiom that every person must work to gain it. It's not about force or fraud but about voluntary creative effort to enable the exchange of goods. Money has little meaning and is of no value unless there is production and exchange behind it.

The productive contribution of money, however, is directly related to the stability of its value. In this regard, money is to an economy what language is to communication. Without words that have clearly defined meanings to both the speaker and listener, communication is impossible. So it is with money. Many would argue that money does not talk nowadays, it just goes without saying. Seriously, if money does not have a stable and predictable value, it will be more costly for borrowers and lenders to conduct exchanges; saving and investing will involve additional risks; and time-dimension transactions (for example, paying for a house or automobile over time) will be fraught with additional danger. When the value of money is unstable, exchange is retarded and the gains from specialization, large-scale production, and social cooperation are reduced.

Inflation

Prices must be going up. This morning I saw a gum-ball machine that takes bills. Inflation is being broke with money in your pocket.

-Steve Allen

"There is no surer means of overturning the existing basis of society than to debauch the currency," said John Maynard

Keynes. "Inflation distorts price signals, undermines a market economy, is the one form of taxation that can be imposed without legislation, is really taxation without representation," says Milton Friedman. They both agree on the absolute necessity of monetary stability.

The language of an economic system is prices, wages, interest rates, profits, and losses. They comprise the signaling system telling people what to do. When inflation occurs, the signals are confusing. Inflation is like a country where nobody speaks the truth. It is an enemy because it gives us the illusion that we have more money than we really do have. With inflation, future buying power is reduced, interest rates are forced up, lenders become more unwilling to lend money over longer periods of time, fixed mortgages disappear, and credit becomes less available. A little inflation is like a little pregnancy—it keeps on growing.

Inflation is the loss of the purchasing power of a currency, usually expressed as a general rise in the prices of goods or services. Although no gauge of inflation is truly reliable, the most widely watched measure in the U.S. is the consumer price index.

It is always tempting to view the sectors of the economy in which prices rise the most as the causes of inflation. But blaming a storekeeper for high prices, says Milton Friedman, is like blaming the thermometer for the fever it records. Boycotting the storekeeper is like breaking the thermometer to cure the fever. Prices always rise and fall. They are a natural feature of the way a market economy adapts to changes of supply and demand. Inflation is not simply the sum total of a collection of independent price changes, but rather the degree to which all those prices move. When we watch the tide come in at the beach we know it is not caused by the waves but rather by the gravitational pull of the moon. Individual waves are the independent price changes of each product. Inflation is the gravitational pull. Or, as a student once said to me, "Inflation wouldn't be so bad if prices didn't keep rising."

There is no mystery about the cause of monetary instability. Like other commodities, the value of money is determined by supply and demand. When the supply of money is constant or increases at a slow, steady rate, the purchasing power of money will be relatively stable. In contrast, when the supply of money expands rapidly and unpredictably relative to the supply of goods and services, prices are inflated and the purchasing power of money declines. This often happens when governments print money (or borrows from a central bank) in order to pay their bills. You wake up one day to find out as Yogi Berra said, "a dime isn't worth a nickel any more."

Milton Friedman, titular head of the Monetary School at the University of Chicago said this about the causes of inflation:

> There is perhaps no empirical regularity in economic science that is based on so much evidence for so wide a range of circumstances as the connection between substantial changes in the stock of money and the level of prices. To the best of my knowledge, there is no instance in which a substantial change in the stock of money per unit of output has occurred without a substantial change in the level of prices in the same direction. Instances in which prices and the stock of money have moved together are recorded for many centuries of history, for countries in every part of the globe, and for a wide diversity of monetary arrangements.

As we enter the twenty-first century, two powerful factors have combined to seriously wound the inflation bear: the global economy and the productivity resulting from the technological revolution. As global markets become more competitive and trade barriers continue to fall, price pressures, absent government monetizing deficits and cranking the money supply, will be downward. Intense global competition puts a big lid on prices. The other lid on prices is productivity. Large increases in productivity make it more difficult for the supply of money to outstrip the supply of goods and services. When that happens, inflation remains minimal, interest rates trend downward, the price signaling system works, and both Main Street and Wall Street are prosperous.

Taxes

> I hate taxes. Every time my ship comes in, the government unloads it. Taxing people to spur the economy is even less useful than applying a tourniquet to a guillotined man.
>
> -Unknown

"Taxes are paid in the sweat of every man who labors. If those taxes are excessive, they are reflected in idle factories, in tax-sold farms, and in hordes of hungry people tramping streets and seeking jobs in vain," said Franklin Delano Roosevelt. "People will produce more only when they are permitted to keep more of what they earn," said Milton Friedman. John Marshall, a former Chief Justice of the United States once remarked, "The power to tax involves the power to destroy."

There are few things in life that change behavior more than tax policy. Incentives matter. When things cost more, people buy less—and vice versa. When you reward a particular activity, you get more of it. When you penalize it, you get less. Incentives matter. Taxes matter.

The global economy makes labor and capital very mobile. Labor can move to wherever it wants. Taxes are the prime mover. Swedish tennis star Mats Wilander and German tennis star Boris Becker, for example, have left high-tax Sweden and Germany and now live in Monaco. Exempt from income and capital gains tax, a low tax country not only attracts sports stars but anyone in the higher tax brackets. In France, where the top personal income tax rate is 54 percent, the value added tax adds another 20.6 percent, and piling injury on insult, the government restricts people from working more than 35 hours a week. Is it any wonder that 40,000 French engineers and technicians have moved to the Silicon Valley of California? Is it surprising that 1.7 million French, or 7 percent of the work force, are employed outside the country? Guess the reason for one-quarter of the graduates from French universities now leaving the country after graduation? Personally, what I gained most by being in France was learning to be even more satisfied with the United States.

Labor today is highly mobile. It's no surprise that the mega-states of Texas and Florida, with no state income tax, grew their economies and their population faster than other parts of the country. The Cato Institute's Steve Moore calculates that 1,000 people move every day from the 42 states with a state income tax to the nine states without one. Many people are willing to move when they see a better deal. Lower taxes are a better deal. High taxes in any one country make it even more so. Capital is also mobile. It will go to the country that wants it most and will stay where it is well treated.

There are many reasons why high marginal tax rates reduce prosperity. First, they discourage work effort. As tax rates rise, the opportunities for employment fall. Higher taxes reduce the possibility to trade with other human beings. When marginal tax rates soar to over 50 percent, individuals get to keep less than half of what they earn. People who do not get to keep much of what they earn tend not to earn very much. Some will even drop out of the labor force. Others will simply work fewer hours. Still others will decide to take more lengthy vacations, forgo overtime opportunities, retire earlier, be more particular about accepting jobs when unemployed, and forgo entrepreneurial opportunities. Some will join the underground economy, lie on their tax returns, or file no return at all. In some cases, high tax rates even drive a nation's most productive citizens to countries where taxes are lower as we just discussed. When government taxes work, production, savings, and investment and subsidizes leisure and consumption, should we be surprised when we get less of the first and more of the second?

Free Trade

Free trade consists simply in letting people buy and sell as they want to buy and sell. Protective tariffs are as much applications of force as are blockading squadrons, and their objective is the same—to prevent trade. The difference between the two is that blockading squadrons are a means whereby nations seek to prevent their enemies from trading; protective tariffs are a means whereby nations attempt to prevent their own people from trading.

- Henry George, 1886

Less trade means less prosperity and more trade means more. This was the economic mantra of the Austrian and Chicago

School scholars of the twentieth century. Commerce and trade is the great civilizer. We exchange ideas when we exchange fabrics and goods. The crossroads of trade are the meeting place of ideas. Rivals and customs are re-thought, diversities become advantages, superstitions cancel each other, and reason begins.

Voluntary exchange and trade is a form of social cooperation that permits both parties to get more of what they want. Mutual gain is the foundation of trade: parties agree to an exchange because they anticipate that it will improve their well-being. The motivation for market exchange is summed up in the statement, "If you do something good for me, I will do something good for you." Exports are the price we pay to get imports. Man is always seeking to make bargains. Have you ever seen a dog exchanging bones with another dog?

Specialization and trade are just common sense. They permit a skilled carpenter to specialize in the production of frame housing while trading his earnings to purchase food, clothing, automobiles, and the thousands of other goods that the carpenter is not so skilled at producing. Total output is enlarged and everyone gains when they are allowed to do what they do best. If a person can do something better than anyone else, let us, in the name of prosperity for all, let them keep doing that job.

Free trade allows the U.S. to specialize in software, financial products and services, advanced technology and high value-added manufacturing, biotechnology, health care, and Internet applications (among other things). Other countries can specialize in textiles, clothing, consumer electronics, petroleum products, what they do best. As less developed nations gain key production and technical skills, they can move up the value-added chain to higher value products, as Japan, Korea, and Taiwan (to name a few) have done. In turn, newly developing nations, such as Mexico, Thailand and Indonesia can move into the lower-tech rungs of the ladder and begin the transformation of their societies. Everyone gains. Prosperity spreads.

International specialization and trade also allow domestic producers and consumers to gain from reductions in per unit costs that often accompany large-scale production. It also benefits domestic consumers by permitting them to purchase from large-scale producers abroad. The aircraft industry provides a vivid illustration of this point. Given the huge designing and engineering costs, the domestic market of almost all countries would be substantially less than the quantity required for the efficient production of jet planes. With international trade, however, consumers around the world are able to purchase planes economically from a large-scale producer, such as Boeing or Airbus. International trade also promotes competition in domestic markets and allows consumers to purchase a wide variety of goods at economical prices. And while we are told to worry about the exports of other nations to the U.S., we forget to understand that the U.S. sells more goods to the rest of the world than any other country. Over 10 percent of U.S. jobs can be tied directly to exports and more than 25 percent of America's economic activity is related to international trade.

In 1992, Ross Perot ran for President. He warned that if the North American Free Trade Association (NAFTA) treaty between the United States, Canada, and Mexico was approved, there would be a "great sucking sound" of jobs being lost from the U.S. to Mexico. The real "great sucking sound" was Ross's claim itself. In the years since NAFTA has gone into effect, the economies of the U.S., Canada, and Mexico have all gone on to record prosperity. In the United States, we experienced the longest economic boom in our history, the stock market rose to record highs, approximately 15 million new jobs were added to non-family payrolls between 1990 and 2000, and unemployment fell to a thirty year low. So much for job loss.

In the decade of the nineties, U.S. exports to Canada approximately doubled, while Canadian exports to the U.S. rose about 130%. This mutually beneficial increase in trade exceeded the rate of growth of both economies. But the greatest beneficiary of NAFTA, as expected, was Mexican-American trade. U.S. exports to Mexico more than tripled in the decade, from $28 to $103 billion dollars. At the same time, Mexican exports to the U.S. quadrupled, growing from $30 to $126 billion. Companies from all over the world are rushing to set up manufacturing plants in Mexico. For example, the world auto industry has invested $13.6 billion in Mexican operations just since 1994. U.S. Mexico trade in vehicles and parts rose from $14.6 to $37.6 billion over those same six years.

Newly elected Mexican President Vincente Fox talks of building on the success of NAFTA and lowering trade barriers even further. His vision is that in a decade or two economic opportunities in Mexico will be so good and so widespread that the illegal immigration from Mexico to the U.S. will simply begin to atrophy away, victim of the growing prosperity and prospects of the Mexico economy. And that, finally, is the strongest argument for free trade. It's not just numbers, not just carrying out the proven success of free markets. It is most importantly about spreading prosperity to hundreds of millions of ordinary men, women and children around the globe, who in the absence of free markets and free trade, would face a life of grinding poverty and without hope.

Migrants from southern Mexico working in large television assembly plants in Tijuana, native Mexicans working in new apparel plants located throughout the Yucatan, bright engineers holding good jobs in high tech factories in Monterey and Guadalajara, these are the jobs that would not have been possible without free trade. There is no surer way to keep a developing country a bad neighbor than to keep it poor.

CHAPTER 4

U-Turn on the Road to Serfdom

Augusto Pinochet and Chile

Chile was the first developing country in the world to consciously put Hayek's and Friedman's arguments into practice. All of Latin America was engaged in some form of socialism when General Augusto Pinochet staged a coup against communist Salvador Allende, who had tried to nationalize all of Chile's business. When Pinochet militarily took over Chile in 1973, the country was an economic basket case. High unemployment, abject poverty, and rampant inflation were all symptoms of a very sick system. Although Pinochet knew little about economics, he turned to 10 economists at Catholic University in Santiago, all trained at the University of Chicago.

One of their first questions of the General was: "Have you read John Locke or F. A. Hayek or Milton Friedman?" They then gave Pinochet a mini-history lesson on freedom: freedom is the main spring of economic prosperity and private property is a primary pre-requisite for freedom. Pinochet apparently grasped the new set of ideas on privatization, deregulation, and lower taxes and began to order earth-shaking privatization programs.

The facts are clear: by every measurement, Chileans are far better off economically than they were 25 years ago. Twenty-five years ago Chile was on the brink of communism, facing shortages, black markets, extreme poverty and weekly inflation rates of 13%. The introduction of free-market policies changed all that.

At first, the Hayek/Friedman guys made some damaging mistakes by selling off state companies too cheaply. It was a totally new experiment that met with huge political resistance. Nevertheless, Pinochet's government instituted several fundamental reforms: privatization of government businesses and copper mines; deregulation of government-run utilities and the financial sector; removal of wage and price controls; and a move toward free trade. State-owned companies, numbering 500 in 1973, were reduced to just 25 by 1980. The irony of using the dictatorial hand of government to "force free enterprise" was not lost on Pinochet's detractors, or on his supporters. His political and social policies were less than desirable, but no one can gainsay the results his economic reforms produced.

Although there were many difficulties along the way, Chile by the late 1980s was the outstanding Latin American example of free-market reform. While its Latin American neighbors face double digit inflation, Chile's inflation rate is well under 10%. While most of its neighbors have stagnated economically, Chile's real growth has averaged 6.0% for 20 years, creating more than a million jobs, twice that of the U.S. on a per capita basis. And while many of Chile's neighbors practice economic protectionism, Chile's tariff rates, which in 1983 averaged 95%, are now down to a uniform 10% on all imports. Because of Chile's open borders and many items entering duty free, its average tariff rate is 7.5 percent. Additionally, Chile has diversified its export markets aggressively to Asia, Europe and the rest of Latin America. For two decades, exports have been growing at a real rate of 12% per year. Since government jobs are constructed from the body parts of superior jobs killed in the private sector, the goal of the privatizers has been to reduce government and emphasize market solutions. Government expenditures were slashed from 29% to 17% of the gross domestic product from 1985 to 1995, and per capita GDP went from the second lowest in Latin America to the highest.

Although the impressive macroeconomic statistics capture the facts, they do not capture the feel of what is going on in this buzzing economy. How do you measure excitement? How do you convey "fire in the eyes?" Whether taking a bus ride or talking to a waiter or visiting with workers in an Antofagasta factory, as I did a few years ago, there is electricity in the air. The vision guiding Chile's social reforms has been to enable the poor to earn higher income. The government did this through privatization reforms in education and housing and through economic growth. Chile's government has improved education by moving to a voucher system. The average years of schooling has increased from 4.5 to 9, and only 5% of poor children lack a basic education, down from 43% in 1970. The government has also eliminated direct personal welfare payments. Subsidies, if thought to be necessary, are targeted to the poorest, provided by entities closest to the beneficiaries, and given to those in need rather than to the providers. In 1970, almost 30% of the population were in extreme poverty. Of all South American countries, only Paraguay had lower social indicators on health, education and infant mortality. By 1990, the percent of Chileans in extreme poverty had fallen to 11%. Moreover, infant mortality, which in 1970 was 79 per 1,000 live births, has fallen to 11 per 1,000 in 1995. Life expectancy has increased to 72 years from 64 as the new century dawns.

On November 6, 1981, the same day that Ronald Reagan won presidency of the United States, Pinochet also privatized Chile's social security system. Led by the American trained economist Ph.D. José Pinera, he organized an unbelievably successful privatization of Chile's government-run pension system. Retirement accounts were set up that could not be raided by national politicians or political parties. Every individual had control over their pension funds. Each could choose among many prudent investment possibilities and at any time could see how much was in their accounts. Every worker in Chile now has a "blue book" to track their pension fund growth. By requiring all workers to save for their own retirement, the Chilean program destroyed the structural flaw of a pay-as-you-go social security system that has no relationship between contributions and benefits, rights and responsibilities. Interestingly, ninety percent of workers chose the private option and were given bonds in recognition of their past contributions to the government system. With everyone required to save at least 10% of his salary for retirement, each person can choose from any of 22 privately managed pension funds. Twenty percent of their pension can be invested in the U.S. stock market. These accounts have produced annual real returns of 12% over the past 20 years. Many ordinary Chileans now retire with hundreds of thousands of dollars in their privately managed pension accounts. Chilean families and businesses have prospered as their economy grew by more than 6 percent a year from the late 1980s onward.

Every continent needs a model to show the way. Chile was that light in Latin America for the last two decades of the twentieth century, and today, Argentina, Mexico, Brazil, and others are privatizing and moving towards free markets and free trade. Who would that leader be in Western Europe?

Margaret Thatcher and Great Britain

By the end of the nineteenth century, Great Britain was the premiere world power. Even at the mid-point of the twentieth century, Britain had one of the highest standards of living in all of Europe. But by the mid-1980s, the full consequences of socialism left it with one of the lowest standards of living in Europe.

A small, obscure think tank in Great Britain, the Institute of Economic Affairs (IEA), a tiny lighthouse of free-market, limited-government ideas during the 1960s was organized to do something about it. While Great Britain was awash in socialism with a Keynesian flavor, the IEA was building its platform on the ideas of Hayek and Friedman. Protesting the unfettered welfare state, the union power of labor, Keynesian demand management, the impossibility of economic calculation under socialism, and the economic disaster of nationalizing industries, the IEA set the stage for decades of policy discussion and change. Wealth creation through the market economy was their bedrock idea. IEA championed personal responsibility, lauded wealth producers, and transformed the word "entrepreneur" from a pejorative word into a term of respect.

Nevertheless, the British government, unaware of the IEA and opposed to the free market, kept moving the country even further into socialism. Higher taxes, more government, and a growing welfare state continually worsened the nation's economic condition. Strikes were rampant. Standards of living went down. Newspaper headlines regularly proclaimed, "The Trains Aren't Running Today." When British Rail was having difficulty running its trains on time, executives solved the problem by redefining "on time." Now trains ran on time if they arrive within an hour of schedule. Government garbage collectors stopped collecting. Union gravediggers stopped digging. Government truckers, steelworkers, and coal miners went on strike. Something was not working—certainly not labor. British trade unionism had become a formula for national misery. As welfare rolls expanded, other industrial countries raced past Britain, whose ability to compete in international markets was suspect. Their once-proud currency, the pound, continuously lost value compared to the dollar. The United Kingdom was in deep trouble, possessing the miraculous power of turning wine into water.

Then Margaret Thatcher entered the picture. Born Margaret Roberts in 1925, she was an extremely bright, lower-middle-class girl who was raised with the ideals of hard work, achievement, and personal responsibility. After receiving a degree in chemistry from Oxford University, she accepted a position with a plastics company. Around that time, she read F.A. Hayek's book, *The Road to Serfdom.* In 1951, she married Dennis Thatcher and studied law to become an attorney. In 1952, Thatcher won a seat in the House of Parliament as one of only 17 female MPs out of 625.

In the early 1960s, Thatcher became familiar with the IEA's proposals of privatization, deregulation, and letting the private sector work. Better mentors for Thatcher than Keith Joseph, a British politician, and Ralph Harris, founder of the IEA, would have been hard to find. She became a serious student of the Austrian School and often held up Hayek's book *The Constitution of Liberty* and said, "This is what I believe." Her trademark was to listen, to observe, to weigh the arguments, but then to stand up and take action. She said: "The cock can crow and crow and crow, but then the hen has to lay the egg. No one would remember the Good Samaritan if he had only good intentions. He had money as well."

In 1979, Margaret Thatcher was elected Prime Minister of Great Britain. On that day, the Earth shifted a bit on its 23° axis. Thatcher became the "mother hen" not only of conservatism, but also of direct action against impossible odds: she was about to turn a socialist, statist, unionized economy in an entirely different direction. "Government was doing too much," she said. "Markets should be depended on to produce prosperity. An enterprise culture must be embraced and labor unions must be reined in."

Had the Pope declared he was a Protestant, he would have been better received in Rome than Thatcher's declarations were in London. People fought, battled, and ridiculed her. Yet Thatcher seemed only to gain strength from the hysteria among her opposition. At one point, 364 economists took pains to write the *London Times* to urge Thatcher to reverse direction and return to the policies of government management and nationalization. But Margaret believed that, for Britain to regain its former greatness, it had to open its economy to global competition, engage the free market, and reduce government. Despite all opposition, she abolished controls on the flow of international capital and began to de-regulate business. Once, while announcing her new policies to a friendly crowd, the chant of opposition grew louder: "Turn Margaret, turn. Turn Margaret, turn." But the Iron Lady from the Midlands, with a singular capacity to be bull headedly firm if necessary, emphatically replied, "Turn if you might. Turn if you might. But this lady's not for turning." Thatcher was very democratic. She'd talk down to anyone—even members of her own party. The opposition party, of course, thought that she had the delicacy and charm of barbed wire. Few women have so comforted the distressed and distressed the comfortable as has Margaret Thatcher. Even her well-timed silence was a commanding expression. Silence is one of the hardest arguments to refute.

Drawing the framework of her ideas from the writings of Hayek, Friedman, and others in the classical liberal school of thought, Thatcher denationalized Great Britain. She privatized one-third of the government work force, three million public housing units, and many nationalized companies such as British Coal, British Steel, and British Telecommunications. She cut the top income tax rate from 83 percent to 40 percent and removed the burden of income tax altogether for low-paid workers. It worked.

She presided over a doubling of British productivity, and Britain's unemployment rate went from the worst of European economies to the best. Britain's rate of growth in the 1980s, in fact, was double that of West Germany. The country was now headed in a different direction. The numbers tell the story. By 1992, almost two-thirds of Britain's state-owned industries had been moved into the private sector. Fifty major businesses employing 900,000 employees were privatized. Privately, many citizens were becoming stockholders, purchasing triple the shares of stock of just a decade earlier. As strikers stopped striking and labor started working, a collective sigh of relief could be heard. Thatcher was said to have remarked, "We've got more people striking than other countries have working." In 1979, almost 1,300 working days were lost to strikes for every 1,000 people working. (As the story goes, a shop steward told his union members that management had agreed to all their demands: "Wages are doubled, holidays are increased to 10 weeks per annum, and we only have to work on Fridays." A man from the back of the room shouted, "You don't mean every bloody Friday?"). But, by 1990, the number of strikes was down to 108. Workers were paid better wages. The growth rate of the British economy, which before 1979 could only be seen under a microscope, increased to respectable, then strong, levels. While inflation fell, employment rose, and the pound stabilized, the political and economic culture of Britain was being permanently altered. Eventually, all of Europe would move in the same direction. Ideas do have consequences.

"It always starts with ideas," said Thatcher. "You must believe. It all starts with beliefs." It also takes a brave politician to institute those ideas. Britain's first female Prime Minister, Thatcher served longer than any other person in the twentieth century—eleven and a half years—and won an unprecedented three consecutive terms. Despite ferocious opposition, she had a dynamic vision of liberty and the strength and perseverance to see it through. Some leaders choose to live by consensus, convenience, and comfort. Thatcher chose to live by conviction, commitment, and courage. "You may have to fight a battle more than once to win it," she said.

Just two years after Thatcher's election, a movie actor and former governor of California would become President of the United States. Ronald Reagan, like Thatcher, would re-light the lamp of freedom.

Ronald Reagan and the United States

America is what it is today because, of all the countries of the world, we have prospered under the Siamese twins of limited government and economic freedom. 'We the people' tell the government what to do; it does not tell us. 'We the people' are the driver; government is the car. 'We the people' decide where it should go, and by what route, and how fast. America is about 'We the people.'

- Ronald Reagan

If you'd gone to sleep in 1980 and not awakened until 1990, you would certainly have noticed an enormous difference in the United States. A modern day Rip van Winkle would have nodded off in a nation that was undergoing a political-economic crisis on the home front and reeling before the challenge of Soviet communism abroad.

By the end of the 1980s, however, everything had been transformed. The U.S. economy was completing the longest peacetime expansion in American history, raising the average income of everyone. And overseas, the change was even more dramatic: the communist menace was undergoing its terminal spasms of collapse.

These generalizations, in fact, understate the enormous changes that swept over America and the world in that decade. If we recall the grim facts of our national situation when Jimmy Carter was in the White House, and compare them with corresponding facts 10 years later, the transformation is even more apparent. In domestic affairs under Carter, we endured crippling shortages of petroleum, double-digit inflation and interest rates, a large and growing burden of federal taxes, and high and rising levels of unemployment. Americans began to doubt themselves. Maybe America's time was past, and now it would be Asia's turn. How could we compete with the Japanese, who seemed to have the patents on low cost and high quality? And the domestic economy was suffering from stagflation—an almost unheard of combination of inflation and low economic growth. Some economists even said that the engines of growth have shut down and are not likely to return for years to come.

In foreign affairs, the situation was even worse. Fifty-two Americans were being held hostage at our embassy in Tehran, and our military couldn't even keep its helicopters working long enough to fly a rescue mission. On a larger screen, while the forces of communism seemed unstoppable, it proved to be the worst curse of the twentieth century on the planet. Aside from destroying economic system after economic system, it destroyed people. The total death toll from communism has been estimated to be over 150 million people. The Soviet Union stole America's nuclear secrets, deployed thousands of nuclear missiles aimed at the U.S., and was making inroads of influence in Asia, Africa, and the United States. America's citizens, allies, and security interests seemed everywhere in danger.

Strategically, there was widespread consensus that the defenses of the United States were inadequate to protect our people and our interests. Military experts pointed to a "window of vulnerability," that would allow the Soviets to inflict colossal damage on the United States, thus crippling our capacity to respond—our only deterrent against attack. Given this American vulnerability, members of the Western alliance openly doubted the value of our strategic guarantees to Europe.

As this brief summary suggests, the prospects facing the United States in 1980 could scarcely have been worse. Nor did the authorities in the nation's capital have any strategy to improve our situation. Instead, congressmen went out on the steps of the Capitol, smashing Toshiba television sets with sledgehammers. They needed the exercise, I suppose, and it made good television. But it wasn't much of a plan for improving things.

Intellectuals had long given up on America and American capitalism. Professor John Kenneth Galbraith, a Harvard economics professor said in the *New Yorker* magazine (1984): "The Russian system succeeds because in contrast with the Western industrial economies, it makes full use of its manpower." Economics Professor Lester Thurow in 1989 hailed the "remarkable performance of the Soviet Union."

Politicians, professors, and bureaucrats were in a fog. Americans were told, in essence, that we would simply have to learn to accept our lagging conditions. The future was not rosy. Growth was no longer sustainable because we were running out of resources. The children of the '70s would be the first generation of Americans to have a lower standard of living than their parents had. Americans were told to use less gasoline; turn down thermostats; stop using the air conditioner; and submit to the ever-rising burden of taxation and the slowdown of the economy. We were supposed to sit by idly while Marxist forces took over one country after another and hope that, through agreements with the Soviets, we could persuade them not to exploit our growing weakness. And if we acquiesced to the Organization for Petroleum Exporting Countries, maybe they'd consent to keep sending us petroleum at prices that would only double every few years.

Of course, so-called experts were ready and willing to manage this New World of shortages and declining standards of living. Only experts could make vanishing resources last longer. Only experts could insure that these scarce resources were allocated equitably, that we would all share equally the pain of not enough. In America, during the height of the energy crisis, "experts" at the Federal Energy Administration (FEA) told farmers they'd have to plant their crops a month later, and harvest them a month later, to do their part in conserving scarce fuel. The fact that there would be no crops to harvest if farmers followed that order was of no concern to the FEA because their job was energy, not food. And if we had chosen to follow such foolish prescriptions, the bureaucrats would have been proven right: the children of the '70s would have had a lower standard of living than their parents.

President Ronald Reagan saw all these matters differently. He was a leader—leaders lift and bring about change. They have vision. They knock down walls. What opinion leaders called radical, Reagan called right. What they called dangerous, Reagan saw as policies desperately needed. And leaders often have a great sense of humor. During the Iran Contra affair the President declared "I have to admit we considered making one final shipment to Iran, but no one could figure out how to get Sam Donaldson [of ABC News] in a crate." When Sam Donaldson yelled over the noise of a helicopter on the South Lawn, "What about Walter Mondale's charges? What about Mondale's charges?" Reagan shot back, "He ought to pay them."

Reagan repudiated the notion that the problems we suffered had somehow fallen on us from the sky, and that we could do nothing about them. The troubles we faced, he said, resulted from mistaken government policies, not from any decree of fate or some "malaise" among the American people. Governments, he argued, tend not to solve problems, only to rearrange them. The country and its basic values, he believed, were as sound as ever. If our nation adopted proper policies, he concluded, we could reverse the record of decline in both domestic and foreign affairs. Reagan was devoted to enabling the common man to reach his full potential. Like Thatcher, he had carefully read the classical liberal writers like Mises and Hayek. Milton Friedman, he said on many occasions, was his favorite economist.

To an extent that not even his staunchest admirers could have predicted, Reagan accomplished these objectives. Reaganomics, historians would agree, was the most serious attempt to change U.S. economic policy since Roosevelt's New Deal in the 1930s. Reagan's 1981 Program for Economic Recovery had four major policy objectives: 1) reduce the growth of government spending, 2) reduce the marginal tax rates on income for both labor and capital, 3) reduce regulation, and 4) reduce inflation by controlling the growth of the money supply.

Because of a huge national defense buildup in the 1980s, Reagan was not able to reduce the growth of total government spending as he planned. Nevertheless, compared to Jimmy Carter's four years, the annual increase of federal spending declined from 4.0 percent during the Carter Administration to 2.5 percent during the Reagan years. While absolute numbers went up because of a record peacetime increase in real defense spending, the annual relative increases of government spending went down.

Unemployment rates declined from 7.0 percent in 1980 to 5.4 percent in 1988. The inflation rate declined from 10.4 percent in 1980 to 4.2 percent in 1988. In short, the malaise described by President Carter and the stagflation that plagued the U.S. economy from 1973 through 1980 were transformed into the largest peacetime expansion in American history up to that time.

Unfortunately, there were no major reductions of any federal programs, such as Social Security and Medicare, and Reagan proposed no substantial reductions in most domestic programs. Nevertheless, he pushed through an economic program that spurred phenomenal economic growth. Supply side economics works. He advanced a national security policy that turned the Cold War tables on the Soviets—and was a major factor in the collapse of the communist regimes of Europe and the idea of Marxism itself. Giving a speech at the Berlin Wall on June 12, 1987, Reagan declared "General Secretary Gorbachev, if you seek peace, if you seek prosperity for the Soviet Union and Eastern Europe, if you seek liberalization: Come here to this gate! Mr. Gorbachev, open this gate! Mr. Gorbachev, tear down this wall."

Finally, in late 1988, Gorbachev cut his armed forces and told his communist puppet states that he would no longer prop them up economically. Late in 1989 the Berlin Wall came tumbling down. Not only communist countries but most of the world recognized that the Reagan ideas of markets, private property, rule of law, constitutional rights, human rights, and freedom were the institutions that produced prosperity and growth.

The combination of Reagan's domestic and foreign policies sparked a worldwide revival of the cause of freedom. "Freedom is the key that unlocks prosperity's door", he said in speech after speech. "It is a virus for which there is no antidote."

In sum, our Rip van Winkle of the 1980s would have

awakened to a world that had been radically changed in 10 short years. From a situation in which freedom was embattled, often losing, amidst uncertainty of its principles and prospects, our sleeper would not have believed he had returned to the same country—or even the same planet.

Ronald Reagan's presidency was about the relationship of the individual to the state; about freedom; about what works in government and what doesn't. Government, he said, is like a baby: an alimentary canal with a big appetite at one end and no sense of responsibility at the other. Government must be constrained. "You and I," he said, "have a rendezvous with destiny. We will preserve for our children this, the last best hope of man on earth [America], or we will sentence them to take the last step into a thousand years of darkness. If we lose freedom here, there is no place to escape to. This is our last stand on earth." Reagan only meant to change a nation. Instead, he changed the world. Freedom, he said, was not only profoundly productive, freedom also was profoundly good.

What else but our sturdy reliance on freedom could explain the enviable record this country has made? In less than 200 years it rose from nothingness to become the world's greatest power and brightest light for freedom. The greatness of the United States is due in large part to the fact that under the principle of individual liberty, human incentive has been given its widest scope. Great Britain in Europe, Chile in Latin America, now once again an America that offered a bright hope. Would there be light in Asia, and if so, where would it be?

Deng Xiaoping and China

Throughout history, relatively few individuals have had the privilege of living in freedom and with material well being. Even today, many people live under totalitarian regimes, political dictatorships, and inevitable poverty. Though Greece and Rome experienced some freedom for a time, for the most part, freedom has been the exception, not the rule. Poverty seemed the natural condition, wealth an aberration experienced by only a tiny few. Yet, a thousand years ago, it appeared that China would be different. Blessed with abundant natural resources and a strong work ethic, the country produced both wealth and culture. Impressively inventive, China's achievements included papermaking, moveable type, the compass, gunpowder, the production of fine silk and porcelain, and significant advances in medicine, mechanics, education, and astronomy. In contrast, although block printing was used in seventh-century Europe, Gutenberg's reinvention of moveable type in a more effective form didn't impact European progress until late into the fifteenth century. Papermaking and printing in China, however, go back at least 2000 years.

The Chinese possessed a singular advantage in that they could record and store knowledge efficiently. Information was made accessible and this proved beneficial to all disciplines and lines of progress. For example, by discovering the magnetic properties of the lodestone, the Chinese were the first to use the compass, which led to ocean navigation because of trade. Advancement and higher living standards were the direct result of such activity. China led the world in attempting to better the human condition. A "classical age" took hold in which its most memorable prose was written, domestic and international markets were opened, and a money economy appeared.

But though the Chinese made impressive advances in human culture, their economic progress broke down. Subservience to government took precedence over individual freedom. Viewed through the long-view, the story of China is one of an extraordinary decline over hundreds of years, precipitously so from 1820 until 1978. China, for centuries, has done its best to shut out foreign influence and ideas, always trying to keep foreigners at bay. Rather than importing technology, China banned foreign contracts; rather than letting farmers make enough money to buy consumer goods, the government squeezed farmers to try to help industry; rather than establishing the rule of law, including clear property rights, successive regimes destroyed rights and confiscated property; rather than working for peace, Chinese leaders succumbed to and fostered war. Bureaucrats devoted all their energies to maintaining and increasing the power and wealth of the Emperor. Artists reflected "Socialist Realism" by glorifying the Emperor and his works. Lower and mid-level functionaries learned that corruption was their only ticket to a better life. And, in the twentieth century at least, China's practice of socialism and government by communism stopped progress altogether. The infamous 'Great Leap Forward' was a great leap all right, but in the wrong direction. The mass mobilization of rural labor to build dams, irrigation and other infrastructure resulted in rural famine, in which perhaps 35 million Chinese died.

Fox Butterfield, first head of the *New York Times* bureau in Peking, writes in his book *China: Alive in the Bitter Sea*:

> Almost every Chinese I got to know during my 20 months in Peking, had a tale of political persecution— [F]rom their stories it seemed as if a whole generation of Chinese (over 600 million since 1949) had known nothing but arbitrary accusations, violent swings in the political line, unjustified arrests, torture, and imprisonment. Few Chinese I knew felt free from the fear of physical or psychological abuse and a pervasive sense of injustice.

111

Mao Tse-tung once mentioned that he had been accused of being ruthless. "I am not ruthless," he said. "And if I find the man who is calling me ruthless, I shall destroy him." His outward appearance matched his ugliness inside. He did not take baths or brush his green teeth, and defending his non-stop chain smoking, declared that it was, "a form of deep-breathing exercise." The dictatorship of the peasant, according to Chairman Mao, is nothing less than power based upon force and limited by nothing—by no law and absolutely no rule. His tactic was terror and immediate execution: it is better to kill a hundred innocent people than to let one guilty person escape.

In America, you can always find a party. But in China, the Party always finds you. Could it be that Chinese leaders failed to recognize that the wealth of a nation is its people? That to energize people you must secure their property rights? Did they not see that a government must encourage personal incentives and deliver the freedoms it promises? But how do you do all that when your government is communist and your system is socialist?

Mao Tse-tung was responsible for at least 35 million deaths in less than 30 years, which is equivalent to 6% of the population of 545 million he took over in 1949. Finally, in 1978, two years after Mao's death, Deng Xiaoping became Premier. The son of a prosperous landowner turned local government official, Deng was sent to Moscow for his college education, where he was trained as a socialist and became convinced as a communist. After Mao's 1949 victory and the establishment of the People's Republic of China, Deng labored with Mao as one of the senior leaders of the Communist Party. During this time, Deng watched as Mao forced farmers into collective communes and exerted an iron grip over every aspect of Chinese lives—the so-called

"Great Leap Forward." And as Deng watched, he learned an important lesson: socialism doesn't work. People starved during the Great Leap. Industrial production fell dramatically. Experienced managers and workers were shuttled off to "reeducation centers" until they could recite the sayings of Chairman Mao backwards and forwards. If workers are standing around chanting "Political power grows from the barrel of a gun," they are not making a lot of steel, clothing, or other things people need. Experience is a tough teacher, says history. First you get the test and then you get the lesson. Mao gave both.

Yes, Deng Xiaoping was a communist. And yes, Deng would take your head off at Tiananmen Square. He believed in freedom of speech, just not freedom *after* the speech. In spite of this, though, Deng had lost his faith in socialism. Not because he read Hayek or Mises or Friedman, but because he was a first-hand witness to its disastrous consequences. Watching the Cultural Revolution and the Great Leap Forward of the 1960s bring poverty and starvation to China, Deng was eyewitness to the failure of his country's flawed economic theories and was jailed for disagreeing with Mao's policy. With the death of Mao Tse-tung, he was finally released from prison and returned to power.

When the Third Plenum of the 11th Congress of the Chinese Communist Party assembled in December 1978, Deng made a break with the crimes of Mao. He said, "I can distribute poverty or I can distribute wealth." Seeing plenty of the former and little of the latter, Deng opted for wealth and began to privatize China. Two factors were catalysts for Deng's first new policy: a severe drought that made the land so hard it could not be broken and peasants living under socialism and starving. They simply refused to do the back-breaking work unless they were promised a return to the Old Ways, the pre communist ways. Privately held farms were those ways, and so Deng granted 30 year leases on land for millions of Chinese. The familiar Chinese proverb of "Give people a 100 year lease on a desert and they will turn it into a garden; but give people a one year lease on a garden and they will turn it into a desert," became Deng's creed.

The responsibility system was adopted, leases on land were approved, material incentives were put in place, and each family was made responsible for a piece of land and its product. Deng had launched free enterprise. He introduced market prices for farmers; established property rights for the first time since 1949; allowed towns and villages to build their own light industry; and opened China to trade and foreign investment. In other words, Deng instituted a wide range of economic freedoms.

But what about other freedoms, like freedom of speech? Not really. You could say anything that you wanted, but only once. But you could keep most of what you grew for food and sell the rest for profit. In 1978, less than 10% of farm output was sold in the open market. By 1990, the share had gone to 80%, and farm incomes grew significantly each year. China's GDP grew at nearly 10% average annual rates, its income per person rose six times as fast as the world average and nearly 20% of the population was raised out of subsistence-level living. Deng Xiaoping's privatization programs and market reforms in the 1980s and 1990s brought the biggest and most rapid reduction of poverty the world has ever seen.

Deng's idea was that of building socialism with Chinese characteristics. In 1984, he published a book with that title. But who was he kidding? Socialism with Chinese characteristics really meant free markets, personal incentives, leased land, and contract responsibilities.

Deng Xiaoping's life journey took him from Paris to Moscow to Beijing and then, of all places, to Chicago. His guiding lights ran the gamut from Marx and Stalin, to Mao, and finally to

Milton Friedman. He made up his own language. "Market economics need not be surnamed capitalism," Deng said. "Markets can be called socialism." By labeling the changes in his country as a shift from a "socialist planned economy" to a "socialist market economy," Deng demonstrated that he never let the facts get in the way of a good theory. Communists never lose their ability to tell lies, even to themselves. China's strong economic growth during the last two decades of the twentieth century was the first time in history that "socialism" had worked. Institute capitalism—call it socialism—and China began to produce miracles.

As the twenty-first century dawned, 125 million Chinese had been lifted out of poverty. Seventy percent of all the construction cranes in the world are now located in China. Many Chinese, with cell phones to their ears, are sharing entrepreneurial ideas with their friends. There are four million cell phones in China today, and by 2002-2003, there will be 150 million. Soon, Internet browsers will be built into phones, and our Chinese neighbors will even have the ability to visit Yahoo!, AOL, or Amazon.com. "Become a modern citizen," they say. "Let's build a modern China."

On a personal note, however, I think China is getting kind of greedy. First, they take Hong Kong. Now they want Britain to hand over The Spice Girls.

The Close of the Twentieth Century

The events described in the last two decades of the twentieth century has turned the tide. Chile, Britain, the U.S., China, and now much of the world are moving to privatization and free market capitalism. Thus began what the *Wall Street Journal* called the "Sale of the Century"—one of the largest global transfers of property in modern history: from Buenos Aires to Budapest; from Washington to Auckland; from steel mills to delicatessens, privatization and free markets have become the new mantra.

When Margaret Thatcher became Prime Minister in 1979 the word privatize was not in the dictionary and did not appear in Webster's New Collegiate Dictionary until 1985. Since then, privatization in new and emerging markets has surged. "Margaret Thatcher privatized three or four firms a year," said Prime Minister Vaclac Klaus, Chief Architect, of the Czech Republic's lightning privatization campaign. "We've been privatizing twice that figure per day."

President Fox in Mexico asks why the standard of living varies so greatly between the Texas border towns adjacent to Mexico? Why is the contrast between San Diego and Tijuana so markedly different? Is it because Mexicans are lazy? He knows, everyone knows that Mexicans are hard working and very entrepreneurial. Then, what is the problem?

Fox realizes that incentives matter. When taxes are high, people produce less. When government runs companies, productive efficiencies are destroyed. When tariffs are high, trade is impaired. When the Peso is devalued, working class incentives are wiped out. Fox plans to change all that. Most of Latin America will be moving in freedom's direction.

Even France is beginning to see the light. After winning the French presidency in May 1981 on an anti-globalist platform, Francois Mitterand proceeded to nationalize industry after industry. Unfortunately, his policies were totally out of sync with how the world works. He could no longer contend with the economic chaos his policies were creating. Rather than suffer further humiliations at the hands of international currency speculators, he pegged the franc to the deutsche mark, and

France's fate was now connected to the integration of Europe. No, the French would not embrace privatization quite yet, but Mitterand at least gave it an air-kiss as he switched gears. Even former socialists like Brazilian President Henriqué Cardoso have changed their tune. Mr. Cardoso still professes a suspicion for the market, but now accepts economic liberalization of markets and free trade as the necessary ingredients for overcoming poverty.

In 1989, the Argentines elected a strange, slightly messianic Peronist named Carlos Menem, who seemed to want to nationalize everything and print money. But once in power, he sold off state businesses, introduced a currency board to kill the 20,000 percent per year hyper-inflation destroying Argentina at the time, rapidly reduced tariffs, deregulated the burdens of business and then proceeded to carry off one of the world's largest privatization programs ever. Dozens of world leaders have done the very same thing. The postwar consensus of socialism has collapsed. Nationalization is hopefully over.

When the Berlin Wall fell, it was more than the collapse of a wall. It was the collapse of an idea. Capitalism and freedom would now replace government and socialism. Globalization would equate to capitalism, the market, and the entrepreneur. The commanding heights were now shifted to freedom and free markets. And the new digital technologies would further shift entire economies.

Information has always equaled power. But it used to be that only the kings, queens, presidents, and generals had all the power. Now everybody has it. CNN, the Internet, the World Wide Web, photo copiers, fax machines, television, radio, and wireless telephones are shifting the whole balance of power from government to the individual. With a decentralization of information comes a decentralization of power. Microelectronics are pulling decisions downward and outward from central authorities of all kinds. The shift is away from governments toward markets, from the political model to the market model. Every function of government is a candidate for privatization and every government activity can be returned to the market. When riding a dead horse, for heaven's sake, dismount!

CHAPTER 5

Freedom and the Developing Countries
Turning Have Nots into Haves

> Why are some places wealthy and other
> places poor? It occurred to me, at least,
> that this might have something to do with
> money.
>
> - P.J. O'Rourke

Mapping the Earth: Geographically and Economically

The space shuttle Endeavor recently completed an earth-mapping mission that provided information on the world's terrain. Ten hours after blast-off, its astronauts deployed a large radar antenna from the ship's cargo bay and put a second antenna out on the end of a long "fishing pole." As the Endeavor orbited 145 miles above our planet, yet another antenna beamed radar signals toward earth. The twin beams swept across the planet in a swath almost 150 miles wide, bounced back into space, and then were captured by both the cargo bay antenna and the antenna on the long fishing pole more than 200 feet from the craft. By combining the two sets of data, scientists were able to triangulate an image and thus compile 3-D snapshots of the world with unprecedented accuracy and clarity.

While the economic snapshot of 2001 planet earth is not as accurate, it does reveal a clear picture. The Heritage Foundation, the Wall Street Journal, the Fraser Institute, the National Center for Policy Analysis and others have completed their freedom/prosperity analysis of the earth's nearly 200 countries.[1] Each country was surveyed for differences in wealth and poverty

119

and then numerically evaluated for its level of economic freedom. The criteria used were: fiscal burden of government; over-all government intervention in the economy; monetary policy; foreign investment opportunities; banking and finance laws; overall wages and prices; property rights; government regulations; and the extent of the black market economy. The linkage between economic freedom and a nation's prosperity is overwhelming. As it is with an individual, so it is with a nation: one must produce to have, or one will become a have-not. Freedom produces.

Unfortunately, many of the poor countries continue to make poor choices. In 1970 the world's richest industrial economies, the U.S. and Great Britain, had per capita incomes roughly nine times that of poorest countries. In 2000, America's income per head was over 55 times greater that of Chad or Ethiopia. The gap is still widening everywhere. Why?

The 11 economic think tanks that have been part of the mentioned studies say that most of the explanation lies in the way poor countries are governed. Economic freedom means the ability to do what you want with the property you have legally acquired. Since wealth does not fall out of the sky, but depends on property rights and the incentives to create it, the questions are: have property rights and deeds been granted; are they protected; are people hemmed in by government regulations and trade barriers; are savings under attack from inflation? When people are free, prosperity ensues. When government protects property rights, sets clear market-oriented policies, avoids inflation, and, just as important, does not grab all the money for itself, good things happen. That good thing is capitalism.

If the twentieth century has taught us anything economically, it is this. Socialism does not work. It's not only inefficient, it's immoral. Collectivization is shorthand for envy, malice, and the lust for power of a few who rule and are afraid of freedom. It has been tried and found to be woefully lacking.

Capitalism, on the other hand, is the system of choice because it rewards and celebrates the best in human nature, and because it does, it works.

Globalization Friedman Style

Thomas Friedman's book *The Lexus and the Olive Tree* has a most clever explanation of the choices people in the world have today. "I believe in the five gas stations theory of the world," he says. He goes on to explain:[2]

> First, there is the gas station in Japan charging $5 a gallon. A handful of men in uniforms and white gloves, with lifetime employment contracts, pump your gas, check your oil, and do all your windows. Services completed, they give you a friendly smile as you drive away fleeced, but well served.
>
> Second, is the gas station in the U.S. Gas costs about $2 a gallon, but you pump it yourself, wash your own windows, check your own tires, and then you might purchase a snack, beverage or movie video before you exit.
>
> Third, is the Western European gas station. Gas there costs at least $5 a gallon. Since there is only one person on duty, he grudgingly pumps your gas and complains about having to change your oil. He reminds you that his union contract says that he does not wash windows. He'll pump your gas and change your oil, but that's all. His

union limits his work time to 32 hours a week, with 90 minutes off each day for lunch, during which time the gas station is closed. He also gets six weeks vacation every summer somewhere in France. Across the street, his two brothers and uncle are playing soccer. They have not worked in 10 years because their government unemployment insurance pays more than their last job.

Fourth, is the developing country gas station. A dozen people work there and they are all related. When you drive in, no one waits on you because they are all too busy talking to each other. Gas is usually less than 50 cents a gallon because it is subsidized by the government. Unfortunately, only one of the six gas pumps actually works, and the others are inoperable and waiting for there replacement parts to be flown in from Europe. The gas station is shabby and run-down because the owner lives in Zurich and takes all the profits out of the country. The owner has no idea that half his employees actually sleep in the repair shop at night and use the car wash equipment to shower. Interestingly, most of the customers at the developing country gas station either drive the latest model Mercedes or a motor scooter. The place looks like a beehive, however, because so many people stop in to use the air pump to fill their bicycle tires.

Lastly, there is the communist gas station. Gas there is only 50 cents a gallon, but guess what? There is none. The four guys working there have sold it all on the black market for $5 a gallon. Just one of the four guys who is employed at the communist gas station is on premise. The other three are working at second jobs in the underground economy and only come around once a week to collect their paychecks.

There you have it. You choose. America's works best. But not everyone, of course, likes America's version of global capitalism. Both the Western European and Japanese versions of capitalism insist on government assurances and guaranteed job security. While employing fewer people, Western Europe nevertheless pays higher wages and collects higher taxes to subsidize those people who don't or won't work. Japan chooses to pay less, but, until recently, has guaranteed lifetime jobs. Communists, of course, choose to exercise complete control over the people and over the market. But will those kinds of practices work in a competitive global capitalistic world? Can't just any gas station get the job done?

Prosperity is not about personal preferences. It's about what works, the choices a nation makes. If they choose to open their economy to foreigners, to deregulate their main industries, and embrace free trade, it's a good choice. If they stabilize their currency, lower taxes and tariffs, and allow the private sector to be the main engine of economic growth, they are on their way to prosperity. But when they make sure that property is deeded and protected, that the rule of law is practiced, and that limited government and balanced budgets are important goals, the country's path to prosperity is unstoppable.

Countries do not have to privatize, but if they do, their entrepreneurs will produce wealth. Countries do not have to stabilize their currencies and lower their taxes, but if they do, they create enormous incentives to increase production and efficiently allocate resources. Countries do not have to open up their countries with low tariffs, encourage free trade, and welcome foreign investments, but if they do, they will enjoy the win/win benefits of mutual gains from voluntary exchange and comparative advantage. Countries do not have to deregulate their industries, allow the free flow of labor and specialization, and protect property rights, but if they do, the magic of markets and competition inevitably work their prosperity-creating wonders.

India/South Korea

> A full bag is heavy to carry, but an empty one is
> even heavier.
>
> -Indian proverb

Fifty years ago, both India and South Korea were very poor. While India's per capita income was about $150 a year, South Korea's was estimated to be about $350. Both countries had about 70% of their population involved in agriculture. Life expectancy was 40 years in India and 50 years in South Korea. In most other economic comparisons, however, India had the edge. It had a greater savings rate (12% vs. 8%), more natural resources, and considerably more infrastructure of railroads, schools, and roads that the British colonialists had left behind. India would easily have been a historian's choice to achieve prosperity first.

The dawn of the twenty-first century tells a different story. South Korea's per capita income was $11,123 compared to India's $444. South Korea had grown at annual rates greater than 6 percent while India's growth rate over the same 30 year period had averaged less than 2 percent. While South Korea became an unbelievable success, India until very recently has been a development failure. Why?

South Korea lowered taxes to create incentives, lowered tariffs to ensure free trade, limited government by privatizing some of its companies, encouraged foreign investment to capitalize on comparative advantage, and most importantly protected property rights. India, on the other hand, had raised taxes, and tariffs, discouraged free trade, remained leery of foreign investment, and often failed to protect property rights. Criminal gangs in all four of India's southern states have been known to attack rivals and deny people equal access to justice. In addition, businesses still face long procedural delays in Indian courts, which involve very slow judiciary processes and, thus, reinforce the snail-like pace of economic growth.

Most unsuccessful developing countries copied India. They rejected market economies and capitalism and chose to have their economies guided by "expert planners." Developing country constitutions are still, by and large, socialistic. They contain pages of promises for health, security, and welfare to all. They call themselves "social market economies," and hence permit government to be the main command and control operative, essentially empowering the elected politicians to transfer wealth arbitrarily. Is it any wonder that private property rights are insecure and that entrenched interests can stave off competition?

"When the state has unlimited power," says Mary O'Grady who edits the America's column in the Friday *Wall Street Journal*, "democracy is destined to create a cycle of populist promises and bitter disappointments, regardless of the fairness of elections. Only global competition and free trade is likely to eventually force the political class to limit its own power and let the market flourish." In short, most poor countries either let government run their gas stations or regulate them.

These models are failing because people were not free to choose. India, much of Latin America, most of Africa, and, of course, the Soviet Union, China, and all their satellites were economic disasters. Countries that embraced free-market economics, such as Chile, Colombia, Malaysia, Ireland, and South Korea, however, experienced remarkable growth. Any country can choose prosperity if it wants to.

A Verbal Contract Isn't Worth the Paper It's Written On

As the twenty-first century opens, dozens of countries are giving the commanding heights of their economies over to capitalism, privatization and the market. Nevertheless, this still may be capitalism's greatest hour of crisis. The fire that appears to be extinguished often is just slumbering beneath the ashes.

Socialism is never dead. As they have come to recognize capitalism as the best and only choice, Third World and former communist nations have tried to privatize, reduce their government budgets, cut subsidies, allow foreign investment, and encourage freer trade. But many of their efforts have been largely in vain, and they are seriously considering socialism once again. Starving, rioting, and looting has intensified. There are renewed calls for government to do something. A recent *New York Times* editorial said, "For much of the world, the marketplace extolled by the West in the afterglow of victory in the Cold War has been supplanted by the cruelty of markets, wariness toward capitalism, and dangers of instability." When capitalism triumphs only in the West and seemingly cannot be made to work among the poor, serious international upheavals are inevitable. So, what is the problem? More importantly, what is the solution?

Property Rights, Again

While the value of savings among the poor is significant, the poor unfortunately hold these resources in defective forms. They live in houses where ownership rights are not recorded. Businesses have undefined liability and no statutes of incorporation, and people cannot be made to pay their debts.

126

Many businesses are located where neither bankers nor government can find them; nor do they have verifiable addresses. And, because there are no documented property rights, assets cannot readily be turned into capital or traded outside of immediate friends and family. Loans are nonexistent because there is no collateral. Few can benefit from the fact of rising asset values when nothing is legally titled. In other words, what makes capitalism work is the set of rules, procedures and laws wrapped in property rights.

Yes, the world's four billion poor do have some savings, they do have meager homes, and they do have assets. It has been estimated that they hold nearly $9 trillion of real estate. The problem, however, is title, not wealth. Lacking title to their house, their land and their animals, and bedeviled by local government from ever getting it, the poor remain squatters. Lacking title, they have no hope of buying another cow because there is no collateral. They can't grow and they can't expand. The road out of poverty is blocked. Thanks to ill-defined property rights, their assets are as dead as their ancestors. One can hardly mortgage what one does not officially own, or get an electric company to deliver power to a non-verifiable address.

Most governments of developing countries literally thwart a citizen's effort to get title or start a new business. If you want to start a business or provide a service, they require you to fill out forms, get permission from different bureaus, show that you are qualified, indicate that you have sufficient financing and meet various impossible regulatory tests. Even if you do pass muster, officials may still refuse your application unless you are willing to pay a bribe or make a significant contribution to their political coffers. In free countries the process might take only days or weeks. In countries that are not free, the process might take years and even decades.

The procedure to formalize urban property in the Philippines, for example, takes 168 steps and from 13 to 25 years to accomplish. The cost is tens of thousands of dollars. In Egypt, a person must go through 77 bureaucratic procedures and at least 31 public and private agencies to acquire and legally register a lot on state-owned desert land. The process takes anywhere from five to 14 years and costs thousands of dollars. The total time to gain lawful land in Haiti is 19 years. To open a perfectly legal business in Lima, Peru, might take nearly a year of filling out forms, standing in lines and hassling with bureaucrats. The cost would be roughly $1,200 or 31 times the monthly minimum wage in Peru. Most Third World countries, in fact, create such a maze of procedural costs of both time and money that most citizens choose to go underground and illegal. People do not want to break the law. It is the law that breaks them.[3]

In the West, by contrast, every piece of land, every building, and every piece of machinery is represented in a property document that is protected by rule of law, a visible sign of a powerful hidden process that connects all assets to the rest of the economy. Government does little to impede the titling of property rights. When governments around the world stop blocking property rights, capitalism changes from a cold, unworkable theory into a prosperous and workable system.

As Fernando deSoto says in his powerful book, *The Mystery of Capital,*[4] the poor have houses but not titles; crops but not deeds; businesses but not articles of incorporation. The unavailability of these essential representations explains why people who have adapted every other Western invention, from the paper clip to the nuclear reactor, have not been able to produce sufficient capital to make domestic capitalism work for them.

Imagine yourself living in a country, deSoto writes, where

nobody can identify who owns what, where addresses cannot be easily verified, where people cannot be made to pay their debts, where resources cannot conveniently be turned into money, where ownership cannot be divided into shares, where descriptions of assets are not standardized and cannot be easily compared, and where the rules that govern property vary from neighborhood to neighborhood or even from street to street. You have just put yourself into the life of a developing country or former communist nation. More precisely, you now see the life of 80 percent of a poor country's population.

Preemption

> Early American property rights laws were, in essence, a recognition that people like my grandparents were assets to the country and not trespassers.
>
> -Barry Asmus

To understand how to solve this seemingly intractable problem, imagine the nineteenth century United States being carved out of its own wilderness. The U.S. had inherited from Britain not only its complex land laws, but also a vast system of overlapping land grants. The same acre might belong to a person who had received it as part of a vast land grant from the British Crown, to another who claimed to have bought it from an Indian tribe, and to a third who had accepted it in place of salary from a state legislature. It may be that none of the three had ever actually seen the property. Meanwhile, the country was filling up with immigrants who settled boundaries, plowed fields, built homes, transferred land, and established credit long before governments conferred on them any right to do so. Those were indeed the days of the pioneers and the "Wild West."

One of the reasons the West was so wild was that these early settlers, like my grandpa, insisted that their labor, not formal paper titles or arbitrary boundary lines, gave land its value and, therefore, established ownership. Under English law, even if an individual farmed and improved the property, the land would not revert to the farmer, and he could not claim any of the value he had produced. In America, however, most local governments accepted the fact that farming a formerly barren piece of soil and making improvements on the land were enough to establish property rights. Squatters were allowed to purchase the land at a price set by a local jury. This innovative legal provision of allowing the settler to buy the land he improved became known as "preemption." This provision would be the key to unlock the extralegal property arrangements in American law and thus allow capitalism to work.

My grandparents were part of the later stages of this process. They came to Ellis Island from Russia at the turn of the century, migrated to Michigan for a year, and then were shipped by government immigration officials by train out West to Colorado to work in the sugar beet fields. Grandpa explored the Platte River Valley in Eastern Colorado, staked out a snake-infested, sandy piece of ground, and declared ownership. He built a little cabin, dug a ditch from the river, and farmed the land far from even the closest little town of Hillrose, population 90. When a government official finally came out to ask him who owned this land, Grandpa said, "I do!" When the official said, "You have no title," my Grandpa responded "Yes, I do. I farm it. That corn is my title. So is that rifle over there." The government man left because America had legal preemption.

The U.S., after all, was a Third World country for the first half of its history. Federal and state governments constantly contended with migrants, gold diggers and squatters. Many officials simply gave up. The "whole land system is broken," they argued. Even the famous Homestead Act of 1862, which gave 160 acres of land to those who would settle it, was simply government's way of recognizing that, for decades, Americans had been settling the land, improving the land, and hence, in their view, "legally" occupying it. It was just a difference in time line. Instead of laws coming first, and then the pioneers settling, the pioneers first settled and then the law was established. But, once the laws regarding deeds, title, and contract were in place, American pioneers were ready to make both hay and the system work for them. The American government saw that law must cooperate with what people were actually doing.

In retrospect, this was critical because legalization of property literally set the stage for generating capital, garnering collateral, making loans, and rapidly expanding markets. The search for the right legal order was the turbo charger that private property, entrepreneurship, trade, and competition needed to succeed.

Early American property rights laws were, in essence, a recognition that people like my grandparents were assets to the country and not trespassers. America's past is the Third World's present. America's land law and property rights history must now be duplicated in developing countries everywhere. The difficulty of legally buying the property they occupy must be changed. Even today, America's biggest source of new startup capital comes from entrepreneurs taking out second mortgages on their homes. Deeds to private property are everything.

Property Rights and the World's Poor

In March 2000, the Young Presidents Organization invited me to lecture in Capetown, South Africa. The essence of my lectures was that any African country could choose prosperity if it wants. Forty years ago Ghana was richer than Thailand and Nigeria was richer than Indonesia. Much of Africa was growing and on the mend. What happened? The new liberators, who threw out the oppressive Colonialists, became dictators. Many of them were communists, almost all of them were socialists and they collectively destroyed Africa.

Simply stated, much of Africa has to start over. They were, and can be again, entrepreneurial. But this time the base must be capitalism, not socialism. They must: allow the entrepreneurial private sector to be the main engine of growth; stabilize their currency; lower taxes; privatize; encourage foreign investment; limit government; lower tariffs; and encourage free trade. Unfortunately, the collapse of many of the countries to the north of South Africa encourages hopeless immigrants to migrate south, with almost three million people ending up in Capetown alone. The situation becomes less stable each day. Millions of squatters, living in 15x15 cardboard shacks with no toilets or electricity, must daily observe the enormous wealth built over the century by blacks, whites, Indians, Chinese, Jews, Greeks, Turks, and others. Typical of the world's wretched poor, they, too, have houses, but no titles; crops, but no deeds; and their underground economy jobs have no chance of being recognized and sanctioned by government. Much of Africa is a microcosm of the world's poor. African governments must go into the settlements, survey the land and homes, give them a verifiable address and grant government-backed deeds of ownership to those who squatted on government property. These policies, and preemption, would immediately empower them and give them the missing ingredient of capitalism's powers: deeds, titles and thus collateral and incentives.

A last quote from deSoto's book captures the essence of these world-changing ideas: [5]

> One of the greatest challenges to the human mind is to comprehend and to gain access to those things we know exist but cannot see. Time, for example, is real, but it can only be efficiently managed when it is represented by a clock or calendar. Throughout history, human beings have invested representational systems—writing, music notation, double-entry bookkeeping—to grasp with the mind what human hands could never touch. In the same way, the great practitioners of capitalism, from the creators of integrated title systems and corporate stock to Michael Milliken, were able to reveal and extract capital where others see only junk by devising new ways to represent the invisible potential that is locked up in the assets we accumulate.

How Property Rights and Rule of Law Enhance an Economy

When property rights are secure, legally granted, and protected, and when government commits to minimal influence over the economy, freedom has a chance. Prosperity-producing economics is about rule of law, not rule of man. Contracts are defined and enforced. Government rarely, if ever, expropriates property. The judiciary is free of corruption, and delays in judicial decisions are infrequent. When government guarantees private property, an efficient court system enforces contracts, and a justice system punishes those who unlawfully confiscate private property, the table is set for entrepreneurial activity just waiting to be unleashed.

While a country's economic performance depends on many things, no aspect is more important than the quality of its political, legal and economic institutions. Differences in property rights protection have proven empirically to be among the most important determinants of differences among countries in rates of economic growth and investment. It is so easy to forget that the right to acquire property and have it protected by title favors the interests of the poor and the wealthy. When government protects the product of one's labor, it eventually enables the large majority of the poor to become self-sufficient by their own efforts. Consequently, basic reforms that improve such protections provide one of the best routes for transforming a country economically.

Democracy, Rule of Law and Prosperity

Interestingly, while enhanced property rights and the rule of law (everybody, including all leaders, must live under the law) will likely encourage economic activity, the overall effects of expanded democracy, particularly in the sense of voting rights, are ambiguous. Democracy does not, by itself, have much of an effect on producing prosperity. Investors, both within and without the country, are more concerned with institutional matters such as the prevalence of law and order, the capacity of the legal system to enforce contracts, the efficiency of the bureaucracy, the likelihood of government expropriation, and the extent of official corruption. Many studies have shown that stable property rights and the rule of law are more important to a nation's prosperity than is democracy.

Improved rule of law tends to stimulate economic growth and that often sets in motion democracy and the expansion of electoral rights. When former U.S. Secretary of State Madeleine Albright was asked whether it is was sometimes necessary to sacrifice democracy in the short run to promote economic growth, she replied that there is no such trade off because democracy is a prerequisite for economic growth. Sounds good, but it's simply false.

People must remember that although democracy is nice, democracy is not the key. How the rulers are chosen is far less important than what the rules are. Rules of private and stable property rights and market competition must precede the democratic rules of government taking, arbitrary confiscation and government managed competition. Freedom, after all, is quite different than democracy. Democracy means we get to vote for someone who chooses for us what we might want in the public sector: bomber planes, warships, and public parks, for example. Freedom means that you get to vote with your money in the private sector. A public choice gives you little, if any, control or effect. With freedom, you get to determine your choices, and therefore, you do have control over outcome.

The Heritage Foundation, the National Center for Policy Analysis, the Fraser Institute and many other reputable research organizations have found that democracy is not the main driver of economic growth. In fact, the extent of democracy has little relation to subsequent economic performance. For many, democracy is just the surrogate faith of intellectuals deprived of religion.

For a country that starts with weak institutions, with little democracy and little rule of law, an increase in democracy is less important than an expansion of the rule of law as a stimulus for economic growth and investment. In addition, democracy does not seem to have a strong direct role in fostering the rule of law. Thus, one cannot argue that democracy is critical for growth. Whenever there is a limited amount of energy to accomplish institutional reforms, it is best spent in a poor country by attempting to implement rule of law, deeded property rights, and free markets. These are the institutional features that matter most for economic growth, and these features are not the same thing as democracy.

In the long run, however, the rule of law does tend to generate sustainable democracy. But economic development should happen first. Even if democracy is the principal objective, the best way to proceed is to encourage deeded property rights and the rule of law in the short run. U.S. advice to poor countries should focus on just that.

Founding Father James Madison had it right when he said, "We've designed this government to protect freedom from democracy and the individual from the majority." Freedom produces wealth; democracy does not. The collective wisdom of individual ignorance has always been a dicey proposition.

South Korea, Thailand, Indonesia, and Chile are all recent examples of countries that reversed direction and chose prosperity. Others will do the same. To reinforce the idea that countries can make choices to go from rags to riches, let's briefly examine one of the twentieth century's outstanding economic turn-arounds.

Singapore as a Model

Singapore, formerly pitifully poor, is an inspiring example of how a city-state can make choices to create prosperity. It literally went from being one of the world's poorest places to being one of the richest, having today a per capita GDP of nearly \$31,000, equal to that of the U.S. Singapore has exceptionally low tariff rates, averaging less than 1 percent, and approximately 99 percent of all its imports are duty free. It has no labeling requirements, no import quotas, and no non-tariff barriers to foreign trade. Singapore's taxes are relatively low; its top income tax rate is 28 percent, and the average taxpayer faces a marginal tax rate of 12 percent. Government expenditures as a percent of GDP are approximately 18 percent, very low compared to most other countries. Singapore also tightly controls its money supply and, therefore, experiences little inflation—averaging less than one-half percent annually for the last 10 years[6]. The investment laws in Singapore are clear and fair and pose few problems for business. Foreign and domestic investments are treated equally under the law. Almost all prices in Singapore are set by the market, free of any government intervention. Obtaining a business license is easy, with few government encumbrances, and business regulation is minimal. It has very little black market activity.

To ensure economic growth and prosperity, Singapore not only does things right economically, but also does what good governments must do: protect property rights. The court system is very efficient. There is no threat of expropriation. Since its constitution authorizes an independent judiciary, titles, deeds, articles of incorporation, and property right laws are all secure and protected by the Singaporean government.

Despite all these economic freedoms, Singapore, unfortunately, has severe restrictions on personal freedom: fines for spitting in the street; prevalent defamation laws; and, sometimes, curtailed freedom of speech. It has a death penalty for drug smugglers; hijackers are given a rapid trial with "due process of law" at the airport, and then jailed; and authorities seem to stop at nothing to preserve their clean, healthy, and beautiful city. Yes, it's a fine city—you get fined for this and get fined for that. Nevertheless, Singapore is one of the miraculous Asian tigers that is raising standards of living for its citizens faster than almost any other country on earth.

Developing countries do not have to follow exactly the American model of free markets and personal freedom or the free market economic model of Singapore, with its severely limited personal freedoms. But it is clear to anyone who looks, that contact with free market countries most often results in the elimination of epidemics and endemic diseases, the mitigation or disappearance of famines, and a significant improvement in the material standards of living for all. If history teaches anything, it is that nations that choose freedom and free markets seem to prosper. Unfortunately, many developing countries only behave wisely when they have exhausted all other alternatives. Everyone must learn the first rule of holes: when you're in one, stop digging.

PART II

Throttling Government

Utopias Promised

Those who promise us paradise on earth never produced anything but a hell.

-Karl Popper

History has shown that the grandiose expectations of the elites are almost always confounded by what actually does happen. They always propose a hard-nosed bargain of exchanging freedom for security and economic progress. Experts are then given authority to organize society by scientific methods and make decisions that private parties could not. The assumption is always that planners are smart, ordinary citizens are dumb. But like all complex societies run by political and economic elites, they fail. Expect to pay dearly for chasing what is cheap. The most daunting problems of rulers become an overbearing hardship for the people. Why? Because economies set up in this fashion do not have the incentives needed to encourage anything close to productive efficiency. When planners, rather than markets, tell people what and how to produce, watch out. Always trying to solve yesterday's problems using yesterday's data, they apparently don't realize you can never plan the future by the past. Tomorrow's problems are always different. Eventually, the system breaks down and then collapses. Whether the planners are dictatorial monsters or mild-mannered civil servants of a political democracy matters not.

Generation after generation in all centuries has tried to square its circle by imagining a world that might be. There is nothing that government cannot do if given the time and money. Is it pride that feeds a man's instincts to imagine a world run according to scientific principles? Perhaps. But though nature is identifiable by the simplicity and elegance of its laws, to which all natural phenomena must readily conform, people's lives are much different. They are a beehive of countless and surprising variables that cannot be even understood, much less managed according to scientific laws. When such principles are applied to economic man, the result is economic disaster. As the history of the twentieth century clearly shows, even when something so discreet and systemic as an economy is directed by economists and politicians according to scientific economic principles, it ends in dismal failure. The principal lesson of government planning has been to teach us how it should not be done.

Each generation must relearn the reasons for government failure and why government limitation is so important. What government calls "the downward trend of a sliding tendency" is frequently the economic malaise resulting from some well-meaning government policy that did not work.

CHAPTER 6

The Anatomy of Government Failure and Reasons for Privatization

Giving money and power to government is like giving whiskey and car keys to teenage boys.

- P.J. O'Rourke

Flaws One, Two and Three:
Doing Good with Money, Spending Money, and Getting Money

Big government did not happen because evil people had evil intentions. On the contrary, it happened because a lot of good people had good intentions. Opera houses, tennis courts, public buildings, food stamps, pension funds, welfare checks, and free health care are all well-intended social programs. But as Nobel Laureate Milton Friedman has said for fifty years, there are major flaws in the process.

First, people are doing good with other people's money. There is no end to the good that do-gooders will do with other people's money.

Second, you never spend someone else's money as carefully as you spend your own. Neither the government nor the politicians are spending their own money. They have no incentive to strive for economic efficiency: the money they save will not be their own, nor will any of the savings go to them.

141

And third, you cannot do good with another's money until you get it. So government must use the force of law to take your money away from you. Taking money requires coercion, which is the fundamental requirement of government doing anything. Taking other people's money by force and then using it to do good predictably leads to unforeseen consequences and disastrous results.

In the beginning it's easy. You have a lot of people paying taxes and a small number for whom you are trying to do good. Take a little from the many and give it to the relatively few. Politics works best when you localize benefits and diffuse costs. You have to tax everybody just a few dollars to subsidize the special interests you want to help. Those who pay the bill hardly notice. What's a few dollars, after all?

But then the game gets tougher. As the number of people on the receiving end grows, you have to tax more and more, until you end up taxing 50 percent of the people to help 50 percent of the people. Early on, you take one dollar away from each of fifty people and give the fifty dollars to a needy person. A dollar does not ruffle anyone's feathers. But in the latter stages of the welfare state, the number of taxpayers falls because they rationally choose to be receivers rather than payers. In turn, those taxed become more obstinate because the amounts needed from them are now much larger. Give it long enough and the process inevitably breaks down.

Flaw Four:
Wasting It

By any objective standard, government's performance as an efficient user of taxpayers' money over the last half century has been demonstrably atrocious. Great expectations for government programs have repeatedly given way to pathetic outcomes. Our government used our money to build vast housing projects to provide the poor with adequate housing, but today we get to watch that same government blow up those buildings it had such high hopes for. The head of the Federal Energy Administration flies around the country speaking to business and civic groups about the need to conserve energy. On one escapade alone he spent $25,000 of taxpayer money on 19,000 gallons of fuel to spread the word not to waste energy. The U.S. Consumer Products Commission bought 80,000 buttons for a campaign promoting safe toys. There was a small problem. All the buttons had to be recalled because they were too sharp and coated with lead paint. Ten years after the government installed automatic elevators in the Capitol Building, taxpayers were still paying the salaries of elevator operators—to operate what were now automatic elevators. In 1999, the U.S. Post Office printed a batch of stamps featuring the Grand Canyon. The message on the stamp: Grand Canyon, Colorado. Being born and raised in Colorado, I thought that was great, especially since the Grand Canyon is in Arizona. And the list goes on.

You name it and government will spend your money on it. Six million dollars to the National Seafood Council; $500,000 to study the effects of cigarette smoking on dogs; $13 million to repair a privately owned dam in South Carolina; $500,000 for an annual American Flora Exposition; $49 million for a rock and roll museum; $66,000 to determine the average length of a flight attendant's nose (2.8 inches); $942,000 for fishing gear entanglement research; $375,000 to renovate the House beauty parlor; $8 million for Senate elevators; $2 million to renovate the House restaurant; $98 million for Congressional franked mail, and on and on. Add it all up: two trillion dollars of government spending for 2001. The 1985 fiscal year federal budget was more than three times larger than the $268 billion federal budget in 1974. The year 2001 budget, almost two trillion dollars, and another threefold increase in 15 years, represents a huge absolute increase and is near historic highs as a percentage of the economy. It's a budget that makes you wonder if the ship of state has lifeboats.

Flaw Five:
Unintended Consequences

Adding further insult to the quantity of money spent is the quality of programs produced. Government seems incapable of bringing about the kind of social improvements its enthusiasts promise. Welfare, as we now know, cannot abolish poverty; nor can the National Endowment for the Arts create grace and beauty. Medicare cannot provide comprehensive health care; government industrial policy does not pick winners; and government civil rights laws do not spread tolerance. Instead, government welfare creates dependency; art grants reward vulgarity; Medicare bureaucratizes health care; civil rights laws foment litigiousness; and government subsidies encourage corporate flaccidity. While taxpayers are disappointed with the results, so are the intended beneficiaries. Accepting government money is like taking drugs—pleasant at first, habit-forming later, and damning at last. Programs that promise the wonderful things to be accomplished with taxpayers' money often end with consequences that are disappointing at best. Government is not the answer.

Flaw Six:
Free Flaws

There is a fundamental distinction between the political model and the market model. Market models, that is, competitive market processes, are characterized by a selective access to goods and services. If an individual wishes to have a pair of shoes or see a movie, he or she must provide something in exchange. In contrast, when government provides goods or services, equal access is usually guaranteed. The direct, out-of-pocket cost of using municipal tennis courts, public libraries, highways, neighborhood police patrols, or the city park, is zero. The good or service is provided "free" to all comers and the cost is covered by the taxpayer. Those who use the service seldom have to pay, and those who pay often do not use. No attempt is made to match benefits and costs. This game has to fail. Everyone wants to get, and nobody wants to pay. In the case of the marketplace, however, the benefits of a new CD or a new coat are tied directly to a purchase price. If the potential consumer does not pay, he or she is excluded from enjoying that good.

Providing something for "free" has another important implication, one that supports the argument for market solutions. Inevitably, free means cross-subsidization. Those who use the city parks or the municipal transit system are subsidized by those who pay their local taxes but use and financially support a private park or drive their automobile to work. The gross mismatching of consumer benefits and tax costs generates both an efficiency and an equity argument in favor of a system in which those who benefit from a service should be those who pay for it. The fundamental issue, after all, is freedom of choice. Individuals must be permitted to choose the services they want and determine the ways they wish to spend their money.

145

Another unfortunate limitation of providing things for "free" is the false economic information elected officials receive concerning the intensity of demand for municipal services. The function of price is to ration goods, services and resources. Most people would prefer to drive a Mercedes until they see its sticker price—the $60,000 price tag convinces them that a Ford or Honda will do. Price not only measures the cost of acquisition, but it also indicates the intensity of demand. Goods and services provided "free" encourage wasteful consumption. Grocers would hardly be astounded to see their shelves emptied quickly if food prices were zero. Yet, government officials are quick to ask for larger budgets, whether for bridges, highways, education, tennis courts or whatever, citing the intense demand or need for the good or service in question. Providing things "free" only encourages people to want more, whether or not they need it.

Unfortunately, the anatomy of government failure goes far deeper than just six flaws. Government spending and provision of services is also characterized by systemic problems that cannot be overcome. Here are just five of those problems.

Problem One: Rational Ignorance

Is rational ignorance preferable to just plain ignorance?

- Barry Asmus

It can be shown that voters lack any kind of meaningful incentives to monitor government effectively. As Anthony Downs' book, *An Economic Theory of Democracy*, points out, voters don't monitor government because they are largely ignorant of political issues and that ignorance is totally rational.

146

Why? Because even though a voter might be deeply concerned with the outcome of an election, an individual's particular vote would rarely, if ever, decide it. The direct incentive of casting a well-informed vote is almost nil. People must choose how to spend their valuable time. People usually deem work, family, church, sports, and a myriad of other activities more important than becoming informed on political issues. Casting one intelligent vote is very costly in terms of time. Remaining rationally ignorant on political issues and being actively busy with one's personal life makes eminent sense to most people.

The incentive to be ignorant in the private sector, however, is rare because personal choice is decisive and immediate, and you pay for only what you choose. If your choice is wise, you benefit. If your choice is unwise, you have to suffer the consequences. Voting lacks that kind of direct result. And since it does, voters are largely ignorant about the position of the people for whom they vote and uninformed about most of the issues. In fact, the vast majority of Americans cannot even name their congressional representative. As time is best spent elsewhere, the number of "intelligent" voters declines, and the number of people choosing not to vote at all usually exceeds 50 percent of the population.

Problem Two: Special Interests

> Politics is a strife of interests masquerading as a contest of principles.
>
> -Ambrose Bierce

Volumes of empirical research reveal that special interest

groups control the apparatus of government at the expense of the individual taxpayer. At one and the same time, government creates miracles for one group (entitlements, price supports, exclusive franchises, import restrictions, government benefits), while taxing everybody to pay for it and ensuring that citizens pay higher prices and have fewer choices (the anti-miracle). Concentrating enormous benefits on a special interest group, while distributing the costs thinly over all taxpaying citizens, government would have us believe in the tooth fairy. What the taxpayer gets is a root canal.

Inevitably, some special interests place great value on particular political outcomes and are prepared to provide vote-gaining resources to political candidates who sympathize with their objectives. The idea of democratic government comes to this: if enough people get together and act in concert, they can get something without paying for it. The average voter has little interest in stopping a particular program because the out-of-pocket cost is small, and the time required to oppose it could be significant. We all can find at least one government program that directly benefits us at the expense of someone else. The end result is that the political process responds more favorably to special interest groups than it does to the taxpayer. Government programs with immediate, concentrated benefits and widely dispersed costs, especially if those costs are borne later, are likely to be approved. People always favor something for free—now. On the other hand, politicians find it much more difficult to vote for programs with readily identifiable and concentrated costs and with benefits only realized later.

Sugar beet growers promise to deliver votes and make contributions to the politician's campaign war chest in exchange for quotas on sugar imports and price supports. The National Education Association supported mainly Democratic candidates in the 2000 Presidential election. Its primary goal was to obtain more U.S. Department of Education money to ward off the possibility of choice and competition that threaten their government school monopoly. The AFL/CIO unions support candidates who will vote for minimum wage laws, oppose free trade, and enforce the Davis-Bacon Act. The American Dairy industry makes large contributions to politicians who are expected to support the dairy price support programs. Tennessee State Representative John Bragg said on more than one occasion that the reason he was for price supports for milk, but against it for liquor, was that, "I've got 423 dairy farmers in my district and I've got to rise above principle." At least that's better than the city political candidate telling the farm community, "Yes, we must grow more wheat." A heckler yells out, "What about straw?" The candidate replies, "We'll get to your specialty in a few minutes."

The incentives then, for good management for the public interest are weak. In contrast, the special interest groups have every reason to work hard and convince the politician they need government money to do whatever they want to do. While the monetary benefits to the special interest group are large, the economic cost to each taxpayer is so insignificant that most people are unaware of the program or the cost. However, the people who organize special interest groups are the very people who become the program's principal beneficiaries. In return for grants, money and political favors, the quid pro quo are campaign funds and workers. The net result is that politicians behave in ways that are very costly to the nation as a whole. A billion dollars here and a billion dollars there does add up to real money.

Problem Three: Politicians

Politics is perhaps the only profession for which no preparation is thought necessary.

-Robert Louis Stevenson

P. J. O'Rourke writes:

I have only one firm belief about the American political system, and that is this: God is a Republican and Santa Claus is a Democrat.

God is an elderly, or at any rate, middle-aged male, a stern fellow, patriarchal rather than paternal and a great believer in rules and regulations. He holds men strictly accountable for their actions. He is politically connected, socially powerful and holds mortgage on literally everything in the world. God is difficult. God is unsentimental. It is very hard to get into God's heavenly country club.

Santa Claus is another matter. He's cute. He's non-threatening. He's always cheerful and loves animals. He may know who's been naughty and who's been nice, but he never does anything about it. He gives everyone everything they want without thought of a quid pro quo. He works hard for charities, and he's famously generous to the poor. Santa Claus is preferable to God in every way but one: there is no such thing as Santa Claus.

Regardless of ideological stripe, the politician's goal must be to win the election. Entrepreneurs all, they must obtain more votes than their opponents. Most will say or do almost anything to win. There are some politicians who, if their constituents were

150

cannibals, would promise them missionaries for dinner. To remain in office, they must constantly sell favors to people who are prepared to deliver votes at election time. A politician that robs Peter to pay Paul can, as a rule, count on the support of Paul. And if a politician paints Peter as misogynist, then he can also count on the support of Mary. You have to hand it to politicians, they're going to get your money anyway.

H. L. Mencken speaks to the issue:

> They [politicians] all promise every man, woman, and child in the country whatever he, she, or it wants. They'll all be roving the land looking for chances to make the rich poor, to remedy the irremediable, to succor the unsuccorable, to unscramble the unscrambleable, to dephlogisticate the undephlogisticable. In brief, they cease being sensible, candid, and truthful men and become simply candidates for office.

Their palms are soft, their grip lacks clout, yet they win votes with each handout. Seldom protecting the general taxpayer, they promise to build a bridge even when there is no river.

Problem Four: Bureaucracy

> Feeling good about government is like looking on the bright side of any catastrophe. When you quit looking on the bright side, the catastrophe is still there.
>
> -P. J. O'Rourke

The anatomy of government failure does not stop with the

151

misguided incentives of the elected politician, the rational ignorance of the voter, or the get-something-for-nothing special interest groups. While legislation authorizes government action, and always sounds so lofty, the day-to-day operations of government are carried out by bureaucrats. Just like the politician, the bureaucrat has incentives that are skewed against the taxpayer. Bureaucrats pursue their self-interest as readily as do private individuals. They are not transformed into altruistic beings when they gain political power. Rather, they invariably pursue more power, higher budgets, bigger bureaucracies and more tax money.

We should not be surprised by the cliché: old bureaucracies never die, they just grow larger and more oppressive. William A. Niskanen, in his book *Bureaucracy and Representative Government*, made the convincing case, supported by a number of other studies, that the provision of a good or service by a government agency would, on average, be roughly twice as expensive as the same provision accomplished by the private sector. Many economists refer to this phenomenon as the "rule of two."

Private bureaucracies are more cost-efficient than their public counterparts because they face the continuous threat of competition in the marketplace. Profits and losses (i.e., "the bottom line") communicate important information on whether or not consumers' wishes are being served. Bankruptcies get rid of the inefficient. Unlike a private organization, government bureaucracies usually have complex sets of objectives, most of which are difficult to measure. Bureaucrats do not have a profit goal to guide their behavior. And without profits and losses, there is simply no way to know how well government serves customers—useless work usually drives out useful work.

My worst experiences living in Arizona have to do with dealing with Arizona's government. Why do I stand in line for two hours to get a license plate and less than two minutes to get a hamburger? And why, when I finally reach the clerk to purchase my plates, is she sitting behind a screened wall with only a small opening through which to pass paperwork, checks, and plates? The tellers in my bank are not protected by screens. Why should government workers be protected?

Well, I asked her why, and this was her reply: "Sometimes citizens try to reach across the counter and grab my throat." Does it ever dawn on government that putting customer services staff in cages to protect them is an attempt to solve the wrong problem?

What is it about government that makes dealing with them so exasperating? Why do government bureaucracies organize themselves as a complex maze? Why does it take ten minutes or longer to route a phone call asking for a particular service to the right department?

The average state government has between 50 and 70 different agencies, and finding the right one can be a daunting task. When you do get the right department—hang on—it's just the start. Even a relatively simple, straight forward task, such as licensing a business, selling a house, or registering the birth of a child, requires at least two or more agencies, each demanding that you fill out a plethora of forms, get permits or licenses, pay numerous fees, and spend significant amounts of your precious time to complete the process.

Consider the obstacles you face when trying to hire a child care provider. Even in the easiest of states there are at least four or five agencies involved, each with its own set of forms. FICA, unemployment and workers' compensation insurance forms and fees are the least of your problems. The Department of Labor will insist that you provide adequate rest breaks for your child care worker. OSHA will—well, don't even go there. The process is endless. Even generals, cabinet members, senators, and many law-abiding citizens have chosen not to comply, not because of the cost, but because of the sheer difficulty of complying with all the rules. Dealing with government usually involves an intimidating knot of uncoordinated agencies, mind-numbing regulations and tension-filled scenarios.

Often the services state governments provide cannot be reconciled by single agencies but require a complex collaboration among employees across departments. We know they should communicate with each other. Why don't they? Because the underlying structure of government conspires against it. The way governments function forces employees to concentrate only on their internal organizational needs and not the broader needs of citizens and businesses. The job of each agency, department, and bureau is to administer and enforce the laws and regulations for which it is chartered. As a result, each focuses on administering its laws and regulations and not on the most efficient way to serve you.

Problem Five: Non-Peaceful Solutions

There is no act of treachery or meanness of which a political party is not capable; for in politics there is no honor.

-Benjamin Disraeli

Political solutions have another important defect. Have you ever stopped to wonder why politics is so dirty, why elections are so emotional, why so much dirt is thrown, and why so many personal attacks take place? Why is it that most elections, campaigns, and government solutions get so ugly? Is it because deciding things politically is inherently flawed? Voting is simply a way of determining which side is the stronger without putting it to the test of a fight. When four fellows sit down to dine, for example, each will choose from the menu what he wants. But, if the group has to vote on their selection of one wine for the table, they are confronted with a political problem: they must reach a collective agreement. The person who insists on getting his way might have to use persuasion, coercion, name-calling, and as a last resort, his fists. Allowing each person to choose the exact wine he wants eliminates the problem. Democratic decision making—forcing the minority to accept the majority's decision—brings with it a minefield of problems. "Voters are collared under democracy, not by talking sense but by talking nonsense," said H. L. Mencken.

Democracy, on the one hand, gives people a vote on public things: choosing politicians who then choose for us the extent and kind of national defense, welfare laws, highways, and other goods and services the government will provide. Freedom, on the other hand, gives people a vote on everything else. It is personal and specific. When you settle things by a majority vote, the psychological effect is to create the impression that the majority is right. The majority would always choose jazz over Chopin, Grisham over Tolstoy, and a heavy weight boxing match will always draw a bigger crowd, larger gate receipts and wider newspaper publicity than any new revelation of goodness or truth. Democracy is a clumsy instrument for making choices. Personal freedom and markets are elegant ones.

To decide issues such as creation/evolution, abortion/right to life, euthanasia and vegetarian/meat eating by a democratic vote is more than troublesome. Majority vote forces the minority to accept the will of others. "Majorities, compose them how you will, are a herd, and not a very nice one at that," said Mark Twain. As many decisions as possible, therefore, should be left to market solutions, where peace pervades. An impersonal market separates economic activities from political views and, thus, prevents discrimination based on factors that are irrelevant to people's contributions, such as their skin color or religious views.

Consider, for example, the controversy over teaching the origins of mankind. School boards everywhere have to decide whether to teach that human beings evolved or were created. Whatever they decide, the fight is on. People who disagree with the board's decision organize marches, write letters to the editor, lobby, hire lawyers, and often become quite exercised. Collective decisions such as these leave decision-makers in a no-win position. If the school board allows creationism to be taught, evolutionists will be angered. If they decide to teach evolution, creationists will be outraged.

Please consider for a moment what the evolutionists are asking the creationists to accept and what the creationists are asking the evolutionists to accept. Then ask if a democratic, majority-determined, one-size-fits all political solution will work. Since few of us believe in the collective wisdom of individual ignorance, we must minimize the number of decisions handled that way.

The Big Bang Theory of how the universe was formed has been the most durable, if fanciful, cosmological theory of the twentieth century. Sometime between ten billion and 20 billion years ago, adherents believe, an indescribably esoteric pinprick of transparent, empty space exploded to cosmological proportions in less than a second. Eventually, subatomic particles collided and coalesced across the heavens, forming the 40 billion or so known galaxies. Then, roughly 4.5 billion years ago, the remains of an exploded star condensed into our own solar system. Life has evolved ever since. Or briefly—in layman's language— from goo, to the zoo, and now you.

Once, a great scientist finished his polished lecture on the evolution of the cosmos, all the way from the Big Bang to man's eventual entropic heat death. Up from the audience popped a little old lady to ask the professor how he reconciled his depressing theory with the more uplifting and common-sensical idea that the earth, in fact, is posed gaily and perdurably on the back of a giant turtle. "But Ma'am," the great scientist inquired, "What is it that holds up the turtle?" The woman responded, "Another turtle, of course." "And what holds *it* up?" coolly pursued the scientist. "Oh, don't you see?" the little old lady replied patiently. "It's turtles all the way down." It was her way of saying the idea of the "Big Bang" is absolutely preposterous.

It's like eating a wonderful meal and then arguing whether the meal "just happened," questioning if there was a cook. Could a 747 jumbo jet be created from a tornado blowing through a junkyard? Does the existence of a Rolex watch necessarily mean there was a watchmaker?

People are going to believe what they're going to believe. But people should be allowed to choose what they want to believe. Different children need to be educated differently, and profoundly religious ideas (creationism) and anti-religious (evolution) should not be declared true for everyone. It would be foolish for atheist parents to have to subject their children to either the Genesis creation account or the Judeo-Christian Ten Commandments. They should have the freedom to choose schools that will reflect their views and send their children to people who will best serve their kids. But even atheist parents must be careful. Nobody talks so consistently about God as those who insist there is no God.

157

A Few Timid Suggestions

Government is not reason, it is not eloquence—it is force! Like fire, it is a dangerous servant and a fearful master; never for a moment should it be left to irresponsible action.

- George Washington

If society insists that government solutions are better than market ones, despite all the problems, distorted incentives, and inevitable negative consequences, there are a few flaw-reducing offsets. First, federal government solutions should always be the last alternative. Decisions should take place at the local level whenever possible since local governments have to compete. The smaller and more local the government, the more likely it is that people can "vote with their feet." And because they can, local governments, on balance, are more cost-conscious and service-responsive. Second, to streamline the systemic problems of bureaucracies, several bureaucracies should supply the same service. Invariably the resulting competition will improve efficiency. Another workable idea might be to set a limit on annual spending and back it with automatic cuts if the ceiling is not met. Term limits, the line item veto and other legislative rules might also limit the power of special interest groups.

By terminating all corporate welfare, ending low-priority domestic programs, devolving all welfare programs to the states and private charities, and seriously challenging the constitutionality of all federal spending programs not designated by the Constitution, many of the remaining functions of government would be candidates for privatization.

Privatization

> Government has no other end but the preservation
> of property.
>
> -John Locke

Technology is reinforcing the worldwide move to markets and capitalism as the most powerful force for change. Everybody takes for granted the ability of automatic-teller-machines to spew out money anytime and anywhere in the world in seconds. Drive into an automated gas station, insert your plastic card, and in minutes you are back on the road. Soon, the e-customer is going to become the e-voter. Citizens are going to expect the convenience and service they get in other areas of their lives. In short, people will not tolerate poor service and regimentation. Citizens will demand that government service be either outsourced or e-governed to business-like efficiencies. As the information/technological age continues to lubricate markets and drive transaction costs to zero, most people will prefer that every function of government be privatized and returned to the market. Citizens who call on government to supply them with security and favors from cradle to grave, only encourage more government. If their pleas are successful, they might lose their freedom and gain no security in exchange.

Should government always provide the schooling for the nation's young? The answer is no. Choice, vouchers and competition in the marketplace will eventually break the government monopoly on schooling. And now, with the Internet, an entire school or even a great library will one day reside in the student's laptop computer.

Will government operate the prisons? No. Prisons will be either privatized or run more efficiently by having many of their functions outsourced. What about public roads and bridges? Those who use will pay. The private sector will eventually both build and run prisons, roads, and bridges.

Although the running of government lighthouses has always been a government activity, that idea is antiquated. With advanced communications, ships can be tracked and guided privately. Every boat will have its own "lighthouse."

Are government railroads run efficiently? Sometimes. But government trains already have cost taxpayers $9 billion. It would have been cheaper to buy an economy ticket on a commercial airline for the people who ride these trains than to continue the Amtrak boondoggle. Tonight Show host Jay Leno has been chiding Amtrak for its safety record for years. He's introduced an actor covered with bandages as the Amtrak president and shown what he calls "Amtrak footage," a clip from an old black-and-white movie showing two steam engine trains exploding in a head-on collision. Recently he said "Amtrak could eliminate 600 jobs, not by firing employees, but by sending them on a train trip."

What about airports? Privatize them. Great Britain, Burbank in California, Westchester County in New York, and many others are lightening the tax burdens of their citizens, lowering the costs of operation and turning airports into a profitable operation. What about private air traffic control? Canada and 16 other nations have created a nonprofit, user-fee-based corporation to handle air traffic control. The U.S. Congress has already allowed some 200 smaller control towers—from Flagstaff, Arizona to Martha's Vineyard, Massachusetts—to be run by private companies. As the number of airline passengers grows from 733 million in the year 2000 to 1.2 billion passengers in 2012, there is no possible way that the technologically backward Federal Aviation Administration can cope with that kind of growth.

That's why countries from Britain to New Zealand have abandoned government micromanagement and have instituted user-fee-based air traffic control systems.

But for safety considerations, isn't it necessary that government run air traffic control? Most observers would argue that air traffic control would be both cheaper and safer if private, profit-making operators were in charge. The average cost of operating and maintaining a Level I Tower (the lowest FAA rating in terms of volume of traffic) is three times as high for government towers, which use less of the latest technology, as it is for private ones.

Removing the air traffic control system from the auspices of the Federal Aviation Administration and making it a private, non-profit corporation controlled by a diversified user board of directors would take it out of the hands of politicians and the vagaries of Washington control. Capital spending for up-to-date equipment would be market determined. It has been estimated that if LaGuardia Airport had the most modern technology, air traffic there could be boosted by 10%—and when current prototypes were used, such as in Australia, New Zealand, the United Kingdom and German traffic could be boosted by as much as 50%. It's an idea whose time has come.

Private fire departments are happening. Rural/Metro Corporation is the private fire department that services my hometown of Scottsdale, Arizona. Compared to government fire fighting, the protection in Scottsdale is cheaper, faster, and more effective. The main reasons are that Rural/Metro constantly pushes for fire prevention with special attention to making every home safe from fire. In addition, these private fire fighters use four-inch fire hoses instead of the standard two-and a half-inch hoses used by most government-operated fire departments. Isn't it amazing how much more water you can get on a fire with a bigger hose?

Many city governments own airports, hospitals, golf courses, museums, and even classical music radio stations. They subsidize education, real estate, day care centers, and dozens of different businesses, always calling on the taxpayer for money. But they can't keep their streets clean, provide adequate police protection, and teach children how to read. Government is doing what it should not do and not doing what it should. Nothing is less productive than to make more efficient that which should not be done at all. Streamlining services that government should not be doing in the first place is a waste of time and money.

The issue is not for government to become efficient, but to decide whether or not to leave certain activities in the hands of government at all. As my friend John Fund of the *Wall Street Journal* has said, "If government were a consumer product on a store shelf, it would be removed for being defective and sued for false advertising."

During the 2000 presidential debates and discussions, many people asked what government is going to do for them. "We have needs," said one young man. "What might government do to take care of us?" Democratic candidate Al Gore had government solutions for every problem. Health care for everybody, food stamps for the needy, grants for aspiring artists, loans for promising business ventures, subsidized housing for impoverished home seekers, and, of course, a lock-box for Social Security. Allowing people to control part of their pension funds and invest in the market was just "too risky."

In a pleasant way, candidate George W. Bush responded—and I paraphrase—just a minute, government is not the answer to your problems: you are. Government is not a sugar daddy. Get a life. This is America, a do-it-yourself society. Talk to your minister, see a priest, consult with your wife. You can do it. When personal responsibility goes, everything goes. Self reliance is a virtue that has made this country great.

Bush is a religious man who holds the belief that God, and not man, shapes personal destinies. Having an anti-utopian mindset, he holds realistic views about the role of government. Taking many small steps against poverty, like faith-based initiatives and better economic incentives, he refuses the traditional Lyndon Johnson grandiose schemes of declaring war on poverty. His modest views of himself and government recognize that both have some power to do certain things well. He agrees with Abraham Lincoln:

> You cannot strengthen the weak by weakening the strong. You cannot build character and courage by taking away man's initiative and independence. You cannot help man permanently by doing for them what they could and should do for themselves.

What happens when government taxes Peter to help Paul? At least three main problems emerge: first, Peter becomes a Paul-bearer. Second, Paul becomes an immovable object. When you pay people not to work, they don't work. And third, piggyback replaces baseball as the national pastime.

Government cannot do anything for you that it did not do to you first. You've heard it before, but let me refresh your memory. The three biggest lies are (1) "Your check is in the mail," (2) "I'll respect you in the morning," and (3) "I'm from the Federal Government and I'm here to help you."

Privatization, free markets, and the triumph of the individual will eventually win the day. If the power of the state is measured by the power that its citizens surrender to it, privatization is a move in the right direction. The last end of the state is not to dominate men, nor restrain them, but rather to set people free so that they may live and act with full security and without injury to themselves. The end of state intervention is the beginning of real freedom.

As we enter the twenty-first century, the efficiency of markets and the onrush of global capitalism are making government obsolete in much of what it does. Very few people care about what government is doing. Government is no longer central in people's lives. Only when important policies misfire does the economy take a nose-dive. Raising taxes, prohibiting free trade, instituting excessive interest rate hikes, restricting new electric plants and precluding the development of new oil and gas fields are the things that government can and will do to create problems.

Anti-trust suits like the one government brings against Microsoft are so misguided and pose such magnanimous threats to the economy they must be understood for what they are and the havoc they wreak in a market economy.

CHAPTER 7

The Microsoft Debacle

Breaking Windows

This is a story of highs and lows
About the Microsoft Company and Bill Gates' woes.
They invented Windows
A hydraulic of the mind
Freeing us from the drudgery
Of the daily information grind.

Microns of switches on a silicon slice
Thinner than the dots on a pair of dice.
A window to the world with the click of a mouse
A bank, a school, a store, and more.
All in your house.

The way to produce it Microsoft perceived
Cost less than their competitors would ever believe.
And not just process, this handy organizer
Could access any window from all web browsers.
The price of the device, the company thundered
The miniscule sum of under a hundred (dollars, that is).

Praise and plaudits, riches and fame
All associated with Bill Gates' name.
Millions got rich, but envy too
The world is full of that myopic view.

The Best Is Yet To Come

But isn't it amazing
How quickly fame flies?
Gates so respected today
Tomorrow the Justice Department tries.

Gates paid little attention to what the lawyers were doing.
Everything's fine with Microsoft, thought he.
Everything's fine with the company thought he?
Bill reckoned not with fate.
Government got into his business big-time
His political response too late.

So off to the Potomac, Washington DC
Gates went because he must.
It was time for a friendly chat
With the folks at anti-trust.

"Constitutional law in modern times," they argued,
"Has proved to be quite broken.
We much prefer 1910 type law
It gave Standard Oil quite a-soakin."

So here are the horns of your dilemma
The rules and laws you can count on.
Like the bull on the ranch
Government comes to serve you.
Relax rancher Gates. Don't feel so lied on.

When your price is too high, that is not good
We'll say with repetition.
But when your price is too low, that's even worse
Because that would be unfair competition.

The Microsoft Perspective

Another point we want to make
To avoid piratical illusion.
Never, never charge the same price
Since that would be collusion.

So put your hand on the throttle, but
Your foot on the brake.
Which action you ask should it be?
Well unless you set price to barely suffice
We'll charge you with counts on all three.

With all your price fixin'
And unfair competition
E-gad you priced your browsers for free.
Are you clueless in battle? Or sleepless in Seattle?
Just admit, monopoly!

"Oh Justice, Oh Justice," Gates angrily replied,
"I lowered my prices and produced better software each day.
Oh Justice, Oh Justice, I implore you to tell me, please
What exactly does your Department say?"

Ah, from their legal lair
This problem was no puzzle.
Their answer here was crystal clear
"Monopolists need a muzzle."

Then Bill replied from the company side:
"Windows and browsers and Microsoft Word
Is what competition is all about.
Beating our rivals with much better prices
Harms only our competitors, no doubt."

The Best Is Yet To Come

But in the halls of Justice
Special interests held no sway.
Creative laws were concocted
And trust busters saved the day.

And so throughout this land of ours
Where computer laws are made.
All users are protected by government.
Only freedom has decayed.

Nevertheless, we really should give credit
To Justice when its due.
They really stuck it to Mr. Gates
And all members of his crew.

Judge Jackson proved they quashed innovation
More inventions should have taken place.
They even tried to kill old Netscape
Now suing, and unable to keep the pace.

So the company was finally broken, in two
Never again to give away things for free.
Justice is now into Windows full time
Producing software for just a small fee.

Yes, it's true, the product is priced at ten thousand
But users pay just a hundred.
The rest is covered by a levy on income
Now only the taxpayer gets plundered.

But Microsoft is only the opening foray
More anti-trust suits and SEC actions will be filed each day.
Alarmed at B2B exchanges, telecom mergers, and E-Bay's price
Government now monitors and controls and regulates
And, of course, takes its slice.

Wrestling the whole global community to stop consolidation
They make sure all prices are fit.
Nothing new can happen anytime, anywhere
Without Washington's finger prints on it.

The Pioneers Always Take the Arrows

The idea of imposing restrictions on a free economy
to assure freedom of competition is like breaking a
man's leg to make him run faster.

- Morris R. Sayre

What are the problems in America: education in its inner city schools? Twenty million elderly without health insurance? Crime in its cities? A social security system going insolvent? What about technology? Is computer software fast enough? When working on your computer, what is the bottleneck, the computer, the software, or you? Is America experiencing enough productivity increases? Do we generate enough millionaires? Are most people better off?

Underlying all the fabulous economic news of the last two decades, what about technology? Hasn't it been driving productivity up and inflation down for almost two decades?

So our government chooses to meddle *where*? It files an anti-trust suit against Microsoft. I'm not kidding—Microsoft!

The only power corporations have, whether they be large or small, is the right to stand in the marketplace and cry their wares. If customers like their products, they will buy, and the company will prosper. If they do not, the company will be sitting on the curbstone, forlorn, and perhaps broke. But government anti-trust poses another problem.[1]

Read the words of Judge Jackson in U.S. vs. Microsoft, No. 98-1233 (TPJ) (D.D.C. Nov. 5, 1999) (findings of fact) paragraph 65, and his charges of monopoly pricing, but be forewarned: Jackson's a dull guy. When he wakes up from a nap, there's a tag on his toe. He couldn't be the life of the party in a coma ward. Note his words—comport, probative, incipient—excuse me?

> It is not possible with the available data to determine with any level of confidence whether the price that a profit-maximizing firm with monopoly power would charge for Windows 98 comports with the price that Microsoft actually charges. Even if it could be determined that Microsoft charges less than the profit-maximizing monopoly price, though, that would not be probative of a lack of monopoly power, for Microsoft could be charging what seems like a low short-term price in order to maximize its profits in the future for reasons unrelated to underselling any incipient competitors.

Judge Jackson admits that it is not possible to tell whether Microsoft is, in fact, charging a monopoly price. Yet he dismisses this lack of evidence as irrelevant because Microsoft could simply be using low prices today in order to "capture the market" and charge exorbitant prices at some future date. It seems that the government hasn't considered the idea of waiting until Microsoft actually *does* charge monopoly prices, and then bringing action under law. Rather, the U.S. will try Microsoft for a crime it *might* commit in the future. How would you react if a police officer knocked on your door and gave you a speeding ticket because he was sure you were going to exceed the speed limit tomorrow?

Consider Jackson's charge of price-setting. If a business sets a price above the prices of its rivals, it can be charged with the intent to monopolize. If it sets a price below those of rivals, it can be charged with predatory pricing or unfair competition or restraint of trade. If it charges a price similar to those of rivals, it can be charged with "collusion and joining a conspiracy to fix prices." In short, the minute you go into business, whatever price policy you adopt, you violate the antitrust laws. As Joseph Heller's protagonist, Yossarian, put it, "That's some catch, that Catch-22." The wide discretion and limitless capacity to attack any business at any time gives the trust busters enormous power.

When Microsoft created new technology to compete with its rivals, Judge Jackson described the company's motivation as "fear and alarm." When Microsoft offered incentives to its business partners, Jackson decried this as "quashing" and "stifling" of rivals. When Microsoft licensed its products only under conditions favorable to its long-term success, Jackson described these actions as "threat and force." When Microsoft ingeniously melded its technological and business strategies to convince customers that it was the best, Judge Jackson viewed it all as seizing control and trying to capture the market.

What, then, are Justice standards for prosecutorial action? Is his a subjective judgment on excessive pricing power or contacting powers? Or, is it a subjective judgment on excessive profits? What about excessive market share? Has there been an objective charge yet? And why do they want to break up the company? Is antitrust law a form of industrial policy masquerading as law enforcement? How do they take a law that cannot be explained and apply it to a case in which there is no clear, direct precedent? Do Microsoft shareholders have any rights? What do they mean when they say Microsoft was trying to make its office applications work well with its operating system? Don't users want their Microsoft products to work well together? What would you say if you heard Jackson accuse the company of making its office applications work well with its operating system? Would your answer be "so?" Recall the story of the five-year-old girl answering her friend's question of when she was going to be six. Her answer: "On my birthday, duh."

David Becomes Goliath: Stone Him

In 1974, Gates began with a big idea in a small garage. He sought to create a powerful, affordable operating system for personal computers, not unlike Hewlett-Packard. IBM and DEC were the giants of the time. Only large organizations could afford their computers and operating systems; only highly skilled professionals could make them work. Gates faced almost insurmountable odds. But he did it. And then, just when his business was booming and the cash was rolling in, he directed the development of a new product, Windows, which replaced his principal source of revenues, DOS, and made it completely obsolete.

Since then, he has been adding feature after feature to his Windows system, making it much easier to use than its direct predecessor, DOS. And the river of money coming from customers turned into a flood of Biblical proportions. He got rich. Everyone benefited. If you have any doubts about that, go to a museum of computer technology, and have them boot up a MS-DOS PC, vintage 1985, with an Intel 286 microprocessor. What you will see is a blank, black screen, with only the dreaded C: prompt in the upper left corner—C:\. Now all you have to do is type in some simple commands, such as: \CD\PROGS\APPLIC\SSHTS\LOTUS <ENTER> and LOTUS123 <ENTER>, being careful not to misspell even one letter or add one extra space, and you'll be up and running. Easy as 1-2-3? Yeah, right. Millions of people bought Windows, and gleefully, gladly ripped out DOS, and lived happily ever after. All was well. Well, not really.

Trustbusters took on Microsoft not because it was a "price-gouger," but because its web browser was priced free. Stop a second, take a deep breath, and absorb this concept. Your government wants to protect you from getting something for free! Something you can really use. Isn't it nice to know they're looking out for your interests? And spending your money to do it.

Microsoft was not exploiting its workers. Many were becoming multi-millionaires. Microsoft was not exploiting you: it was making your life easier and more productive. Microsoft was not making too much money on its browsers. It's hard to make big bucks when you give your product away. The Justice Department has found no dead bodies, no wrecked companies, and the software industry had grown by leaps and bounds. So what's the problem?

Judge Jackson says that Microsoft wasn't innovative. Pardon

me? If Microsoft isn't innovative, and that's a legal problem, then Exxon, U. S. Steel, Schick Razors, and about 20,000 other companies might as well close up shop right now. Even a lawyer could not make that stick. The company did spend $1 billion to create the latest version of Windows and a test by ZDnet Labs ran it for 90 days without it crashing, compared to two days for the previous version. Not innovative? And the system still manages to be backwards-compatible with thousands of programs created for previous versions. Not innovative? That kind of innovation does not come out of a garage. What incredible chutzpah from an institution (the courts) that still uses Latin and has bailiffs (who predate Robin Hood). Let's see, the latest development in courtroom technology would be—what—the gavel?

What would have happened if Microsoft didn't possess a so-called monopoly? Judge Jackson and the Justice Department say more innovation would have occurred. But is that plausible? Dozens of companies try to write software making compatible their hundreds of different disk drives to create corporate data centers. Thousands of programmers labor incessantly to try to translate their companies' data for 30-odd versions of Unix operating systems. In the mainframe world, every time you want to exchange data from one custom-written software application to another, you have to write a third piece of custom software, an interchange program. And that program works only for those two pieces of software and is useless for any other. Every one of them would prefer working to the Microsoft standard. Why write a piece of software over and over for hundreds of different standards when you can write it only once and use your resources to be innovative? That is why companies have been ripping out mainframes and replacing them with PC networks as fast as they can convert their applications programs.

174

The Microsoft Perspective

The Justice Department determined that the Microsoft Corporation should be broken into pieces as a "remedy" under the antitrust laws. It wants to split the company into two: one to make the Windows operating system and the other to develop the specific software applications to run the system. This means that the federal government is taking it upon itself to seize one of the world's largest corporations and to restructure the entire computer industry. And this is going on at the same time that Exxon, which formerly gobbled up Humble Oil, is merging with Mobil to recreate an appreciable facsimile of the Standard Oil Trust that the trustbusters broke up in 1910. But that development hasn't excited a flicker of interest from the Justice Department. Perhaps Bill Gates should pay OPEC to announce that they're going into the software business.

The myth that fewer competitors always translates into high prices permeates this antitrust suit. But, in fact, many capital-intensive industries are characterized by competition among only a few firms. Boeing and Airbus now dominate airplane manufacturing, yet few complain about the high prices and low quality of planes. The declining price and rising computing power of micro processors have literally created the information age, yet production is concentrated largely in two firms, Intel and Advanced Micro Devices.

What are the damages the Department of Justice hopes to remedy? Are you hurt because Microsoft gave you their browser for free? Are you hurt because it is integrated with the Windows Operating Systems, thus making it easier to install and use? Are you hurt because the browser you got for free makes it easier to link your applications and data to the Internet, and vice-versa? To paraphrase Cuba Gooding, Jr.'s line in the movie *Jerry Maguire*, "Show me the damages!" Judge Jackson says Microsoft has created an unspecified confusion among consumers. It adds

175

new features (so?). It causes computers to run more slowly (really?). On top of all this—as they integrate a browser into Windows it makes it harder for employees to keep their workers from surfing the web.

And, incidentally, it makes it harder for Netscape to keep selling a non-integrated browser. The company we could charge with not innovating is Netscape. True, its first browser was a huge breakthrough. But what since? In the Internet age, you can't sit on your laurels even for a second. If Microsoft is making a better browser, and one that is integrated with the operating system to boot (no pun intended), then Netscape needs to produce another major innovation, one so compelling that customers will seek it out in preference to Microsoft's. Microsoft killed Netscape not by aborting the Internet revolution, but by spending more than Netscape could have dreamed of spending to make the Internet revolution happen faster and putting it on everyone's desktop. And whatever Microsoft invests to keep Windows indispensable, it's nickels and dimes compared to the billions that corporations and households have invested in their existing applications and data.

For some reason, the Judge believed that somewhere along the line, Netscape or Sun or Oracle should have taken the lead from Microsoft. But they didn't. Somehow Gates defied the rules of the marketplace. But it seems that Judge Jackson was unhappy because Gates defied the judgment of bureaucrats who think they have the right to dictate what the market *ought* to do. Even Michael Dell, President of one of Microsoft's big competitors explained to the politicians, "We don't want people in the government designing software. Buyers don't shop for the latest chip, the latest version of Windows, the latest edition of Office, they buy the latest package of all these things."

Microsoft competes in the marketplace. Microsoft spends

enormous sums on research and development. Microsoft produced a browser capable of matching Netscape's. Microsoft offered better customer service. Microsoft integrated Internet functions into its Windows. And for all this what do they get? Antitrust.

If you are going to practice honest antitrust, you have to ask why there isn't a competitor to Windows? In fact, customers can buy Linux, which only recently got an easy-to-use graphical interface and doesn't run much of the existing software. Customers can buy a Macintosh, which is a nearly perfect substitute if you're interested in the killer applications of the Internet age, web browsing and e-mail. Or, customers can buy anyone of the 31 flavors of Unix. Then there is Java, Sun's Microsoft "killer." The Department of Justice complains about Windows being the "only" choice, but the virtues that make it the "only" choice wouldn't exist unless consumers agreed that it was, indeed, the best choice.

Nobody needs the 25,000 existing Windows applications developed by Microsoft, says Judge Jackson. They supposedly constitute the "applications barrier to entry" that Microsoft exploits to protect its "monopoly." But many people, especially corporate users, do vitally need two or three of these programs that are indispensable to their businesses. What the lawsuit fails to understand is that most of these programs would never have been written, or would have been much more expensive, if there had not been a single standard common to a large audience of potential customers. Further, if they weren't written to a single standard, they'd all work differently, and corporations and individuals would have to spend large sums on training to be able to use all these incompatible programs.

Without Microsoft's "monopoly," the world would be

177

poorer in choices, not richer. You would still have the drawbacks of Macintosh, Unix, Linux, and who knows how many incompatible alternatives. The only choice you wouldn't have is of an operating system so ubiquitous that every piece of software that's written is also written for it.

Notice, then, the Department of Justice's attack. They seek out and charge antitrust against the biggest, the most distinct, the most successful, the most profitable, the most widely advertised, and the most frequently patronized firm in the world today. Moral indignation is, in most cases, two percent moral, 48 percent indignation, and 50 percent envy. No passion is so strongly rooted in the human mind as envy. Maybe the new old saying should be, "Those who succeed get sued." Envy is hatred without a cure. If greed is the natural vice of those who have more, envy is the natural vice of those who have less. Envy marches under the banner of justice and equality, but is, in fact, a vice masquerading as a virtue.[2]

The antitrust advocates call it leveling the playing field but it's really the leveling of the ability, the skills, and the rewards of the players on the field. Microsoft is being assaulted because it's the most widely recognized company on the planet. It is being hounded because its chairman is a young multi-billionaire and the world's wealthiest man. When Judge Jackson asked whether Gates was trying to show contempt for his court, Gates might have replied, "No, your Honor. I'm trying to hide it." Microsoft is accused of being a monopoly because it has thousands of millionaire employees and because its stock had soared before the anti-trust charges. Microsoft has risen above all competitors, not through force or fraud, but through voluntary exchange and with no favors or handouts from government. In business, success goes to the person who convinces the world, not to the person who had the idea first. Gates' customers are convinced.

In short, Microsoft is in the process of being lynched. In a world without walls or fences, who needs Windows and Gates, says the Department of Justice. But isn't justice about punishing the bad for being bad and rewarding the good for being good? Doesn't objectivity require the rule of law? Why would a top antitrust official himself, a man by the name of Lowell Mason, who once headed the Federal Trade Commission, call these laws "a system of tyranny?" And now that the Clinton Justice Department has broken the back of technology's ablest competitor, they wonder why the stock market tanked and individuals in the American economy are trillions of dollars poorer.

Who gets the last laugh?

As the Department of Justice breaks Microsoft in two, Bill Gates might get the last laugh. IBM's long anti-trust trial, which resulted in IBM having to give up its punch card monopoly, also resulted in making the company mainframe computer giant. When the Rockefellers and Standard Oil were broken up, it forced them to leave their staple kerosene business and become a gasoline company. Ten years after the breakup, Rockefeller's fortune was ten times larger than before. Will history repeat itself with Microsoft and Bill Gates?

I've often wondered why Bill Gates doesn't go on television and answer his critics. Here's what I imagine he'd say:

> I'm the reason you have computers on your desk right now. I'm the reason you can connect to the world and rant your infantile bumblings. I've earned

every dime I've made. I didn't inherit any of it. I've benefited millions of customers, thousands of employees, and made many people millionaires. The reason I've done so well, is that I've produced what people want. I've not held a gun to anyone's head and said, "Give me your money."

You, government, on the other hand, confiscate what you want through taxation and then charge *me* with monopoly? Enough of this nonsense. What business doesn't want to get rid of its competition? The issue is whether you succeed by giving people what they want and produce what they'll use, or employ goons and thugs to shut down the other guy's store. Microsoft doesn't employ goons and thugs. But I'll tell you who does. You do.

Government thinks it should watch us, inspect us, spy on us, direct us, legislate over us, preach at us, and control us. It constantly seeks to assess, censor, command, and indoctrinate. In my opinion, government hasn't the right—or the wisdom, or the virtue—to do all that. What presumption to think that everyone should be noted, registered, taxed, stamped, licensed, authorized, admonished, prevented, reformed, and corrected. Only if you are a slave should you be exploited, extorted, pressured, and robbed. Well, America has no slaves.

Thank you. And God bless America.

Antitrust: A Lawyers Paradise

He works on a contingency basis. That's an old gold mining term meaning he gets the gold and you get the shaft.
-Robert Orben

The most unfortunate implication of antitrust laws is the extent to which government protects competitors rather than the competitive process. Says economist Thomas J. Dilorenzo:

> As a general rule, some ninety percent of all anti-trust suits are litigated by the private antitrust bar. As a rule, whenever one company sues a rival, it is because the rival is charging lower prices or providing superior products and services. Antitrust lawsuits are meant throw a monkey-wrench into the smoothly-functioning gears of the competitive process, and are therefore inherently anti-competitive.

The general public has been deluded into believing that monopoly is a free-market problem and that the government, through antitrust enforcement, is on the side of the 'angels.' The facts are entirely the opposite. Antitrust, whatever its intent, has served as convenient cover for an insidious process of monopolization in the marketplace by protecting the alleged monopolists' competitors. Such is the deeper and subtle meaning of antitrust policy. Economic evidence reveals that antitrust policy actually shelters inefficient enterprises and offers a hunting license for lawyers, with the tripling of damages the reward for successful suits.

A brief history of twentieth century antitrust suits in Appendix B reveals that whenever one company gets government to bring a suit against its rival, that company is usually charging lower prices or providing superior products and services.[3] There is one thing about the future, however, that is certain: the federal regulatory dragon will not be killed. The problem of trying to tame government sufficiently to keep it from destroying markets and market efficiency is endless.

PART III

Turbocharging Work and Business

If there is a country in the world where cooperation could be least expected, it is America. Made up as it is of people from different nations, accustomed to different languages, modes of worship and lifestyle, America's potential for wealth creation would appear to be limited. Yet, because America chose to embrace freedom and limited government, these difficulties disappear and our country has been producing prosperity in cordial unison for over 200 years. Because freedom encourages differentiation, not uniformity, and taps the genius of everybody, America's intellectual capital now produces more goods and services than any nation on earth.

The Internet is just one of the latest of the many technological breakthroughs that turn entrepreneurial efforts into a veritable economic hurricane. Businesses are rushing toward a world in which virtually any jot of data and every piece of knowledge on the planet will be instantly accessible. Since economic growth depends to a great extent on the speed, number and quality of connections between individuals and their ideas, the so-called Information Age takes unlimited wealth from a mere possibility to a high probability. As humans eliminate geographical constraints and improve technology, the pace of prosperity shifts into overdrive.

What will future work look like? As the Internet breaks boundaries, lubricates markets, drives transaction costs to zero and turbo-charges frictionless capitalism, how should individuals and business adjust? Will there be enough jobs? What should companies do? How will they compete? And, why is it called rush hour when nothing moves?

The Best Is Yet To Come

CHAPTER 8

Jobs that Work

"I lost my job. No, not really. I know where my job is. It's just that when I go there, a new guy is doing it."

-Bobcat Goldthwait

The New Meaning of Joblessness

How can the average person prepare for the twenty-first century? Will there be enough jobs? Will the nature of work be different in the new economy? Or, would it be easier to answer the question: what would a chair look like if your knees bent the other way?

Today, it is productive work that matters, not jobs. If jobs were the key to high incomes, a nation could easily create as many jobs as it wanted. Everybody could be given the job of digging holes one day and the joy of filling them up the next. Everyone would have a "job," but everyone would also be exceedingly poor. We do not need more jobs. We do not need more people being idly busy. We need more productive work and more productive workers. As we engage machinery and workers that add more value, each worker will produce more output.

Defining today's work as a job at a place often boxes a person in. This static approach to work reduces incentives, discourages accountability, and rewards people, not for getting the necessary work done, but for showing up and doing their assigned job. It allows people to say, "That's not my job!" A defined job at a fixed place is a rigid solution to an elastic problem. When the work that needs doing is changing constantly, we cannot afford the inflexibility of written job descriptions or even the time it takes to write them. Today's marketplace demands far more from everybody.

Yesterday's jobs were about establishing boundaries and setting rules for operating inside the company. A job was just one piece of the organizational puzzle: management, marketing, budgets, rules, job descriptions, salary, and supervision were all part of the hierarchical lines that defined, measured, and described "the job." Jobs in an industrial economy were not that dissimilar to jobs in a planned economy. Hierarchical and top down, the boss ruled. That's over. Shout goodbye to the job paradigm where:

- An employee was part of a vertical hierarchy, with responsibility to the person above him and exercising power over those below him.

- Everybody had a job—sales, finance, accounting, marketing—and a particular kind of task to do, over and over and over. The message was: you'll never skid if you stay in a rut.

- Job descriptions defined responsibilities and were used to measure, evaluate, and promote. Often there were no reasons given. It was just policy.

- Everyone's job was to reach for the job above him by aspiring to greater responsibilities and financial rewards through the organizational hierarchy.

As the economic landscape's tectonic plates shift, work life changes with them. The shift from an assembly line to work moving at the speed of thought, from crunching stuff to connecting it, and from producing lots of stuff to producing lots of the right stuff, is a powershift of major proportion. The

186

intellectual dimension ascends as the importance of muscle recedes. Brains are replacing BTUs. Information is replacing raw materials. When brains are needed, muscles won't help. Through the second half of the twentieth century, the U.S. tripled the value of its output with no increase in the weight of the materials produced. It did so by replacing alloys for basic materials, fiber optics and wireless for copper, diesel fuel for coal, and telecommuting for hours in traffic. In each case, knowledge was the substitute for mass and effort. Yogi Berra was ahead of his time (and himself) when he said, "Ninety percent of what we do is half mental, and the other 10 percent doesn't matter."

The Internet Blitzkrieg

When land was scarce, nations fought over it. Now, the battle is for talented people who best use technology to get their work done. The new rule of business in the twenty-first century is the Internet. When asked where it ranks in priority for today's economy, Jack Welch, CEO of General Electric, answered, "It's number 1, 2, 3, and 4." The Internet will be the tool—e-mail, e-service, e-commerce, e-files, e-business, e-this and e-that. And, the biggest *"e"* of all: economic opportunity.

Internet technologies are altering the way companies deal with their customers, employees, partners, and suppliers. Failure to understand this may not be fatal, but failure to change the way companies do business might be. Though not every company currently uses the Internet for every detail, some day soon a corporate Web site will enable all customers, suppliers, and employees to interact. The Web will replace the telephone and physical address of the business as the place of interaction.

The Best Is Yet To Come

Tomorrow's work will use sophisticated telecommunications, personal computers, wireless digital gadgets and the Internet every day, all day and for most work. Why? Because buyers and sellers will have the technological skills and tools to be connected, and e-mail will become the most common method of communication in business and homes. Since most communication among business, consumers, and government will be self-service digital paperless transactions, work in the future will be information rich, high value added work. Clerk-like tasks will be obliterated. Ideas, creativity and innovation will supersede brute force. The twenty-first century will be a time for machines to work and for people to think, create, and do.

Work will be Web-based and global. Telecommunication technologies will create intense, worldwide competition for business where the planet becomes the relevant market. Soon, competition for every job and every piece of business will come from practically anywhere on earth. Portable digital devices will soon make us wonder why we called a place rather than a person; why we thought our decision had to be made alone when we could have used the electronic tools to get the insights of the entire team and the benefit of everyone's thinking; why we made our customer wait for the decision; or why we couldn't react faster to a particular problem. The Web allows everyone to act big and act fast. It can assemble talent, do a project, and in much less time.

Employees and employers will have to adapt: you either change the rules or somebody else will. The only thing permanent is change. Change is inevitable, except perhaps from a change machine. Those who adapt successfully will thrive; those who resist change will not.

e-lancer

This new era of work will have a different center of gravity. It's called customization, the "studio approach." Yes, Hollywood studios do employ people to handle the marketing, finance, and distribution side of their businesses. But, the creative side of the business—actors, producers, directors, script writers, costume people, and hundreds more—all come together and make the movie. When it is finished, they move on to the next project. And while the next project may be similar to the last, there are always unique problems, new twists and new demands from an increasingly sophisticated and informed public. This will require fresh and innovative thinking from every member of the newly assembled project team.

Authors Thomas Malone and Robert Laubacher say:

> The fundamental unit of the new economy is not the corporation, but the individual. Tasks are not assigned and controlled through a stable chain of command but are carried out by independent contractors, e-lancers, who join together in fluid and temporary networks to sell goods and services. When the job is done, the network dissolves and its members become independent again, circulating through the economy, seeking the next assignment.

Today, temporary and contract workers make up just under 10 percent of the workforce. But their numbers are growing rapidly as companies outsource non-core competencies. In Silicon Valley, for example, over half of the programmers in information system departments are contractors who complete a specific project, then move on.

No longer a traditional employee, today's contract worker must manage his or her career like that of an external vendor. Independent contractors have to think of the future. They don't let what they can't do stop them from doing what they can. And they don't let doing what they can today stop them from learning what they'll need to know tomorrow.

Because most work will be done by project teams made up of contract workers from different functional backgrounds, everyone will have to shift focus rapidly from one task to another, working with different people across functional lines. Bosses will no longer boss, they will coordinate. Vague job descriptions and working on more than one project at a time will be the norm. In the traditional job world, the boss told you what to do and instituted controls to make sure you did it. Now the boss may not even understand what you do. Her job is to make sure that you have what you need in order to do what you know how to do. She supplies resources and then gets out of the way. Eschewing the title of "boss," she prefers the description Navigator on the Sea of Confusion.

A friend of mine, 20 years my junior, went to college, got an MBA at UCLA, went to work for a large brokerage firm, and has never made less than a million dollars a year in salary and bonuses. Talented young people don't expect to wait for their turn. In a world where minds are more important than muscles, they are not trainees. They are often authorities. The relentless rise of the quasi-adolescents who wield the technological tools are reshaping the world. Those who grew up in the 60s and 70s were the generation that wanted to change the world. The current generation wants to *own* it. They are the most entrepreneurial generation in American history. In their language, "cool" and "awesome" are interspersed with "seamless integration" and "real-time data feeds." Not to mention their bumper stickers, which read: "The Internet Changes Everything," "Think Outside the Box," "Imagine the Future." Immature? Perhaps. Productive? Absolutely.

e-gone

Today, supermarkets have become banks, bookstores have become cafes, and computer terminals have become e-commerce shop windows. On Madison Avenue, the Maytag repairman is facetiously hailed as the loneliest guy in town. He's going to get plenty of company. As product quality rises and prices plummet, many physical goods simply are not worth fixing. Telephones do not break very often and when they do, out they go. The same with automobile tires and television picture tubes. Remote diagnostics will be so prevalent in the future that whatever the ailment, customers can hook the faulty appliance into a digital network for a speedy diagnosis of the problem. Often the repair will be a software patch that can be transmitted back to the appliance over the Internet. So, while customer service is still important, the job of many repairmen will become obsolete.

Now that customers can deal directly with manufacturers and service providers, there is little value added in simply transferring goods or information. It probably means the death of the middleman because the value of a "pass-through" middleman is falling to zero. Travel agents who simply quote plane fares, for example, will disappear. This kind of high-volume, low-value transaction is perfect for a self-service Internet travel reservation site. Only those travel agents who provide highly personalized tours of Europe or the National Parks, for example, will still be in demand. As for book sellers, Amazon.com, the new "middleman" of the book business, offers a selection from literally thousands of publishers, including hard-to-find self-publishers, along with recent information, book reviews from readers, suggestions of related or similar books and reminders tailored to your individual tastes. All this is delivered efficiently, rapidly and at minimal cost.

The New Customer Service

Most occupations will be a combination of Internet interactions and personal contact. It's not a matter of either/or. John Naisbit, author of *Megatrends,* got it right 20 years ago when he spoke of "high-tech/high-touch." The Internet belongs on the marketing-sales-service spectrum, part of the high-tech and the high-touch. Combining Internet services and personal contact gives everyone the benefit of both kinds of customized interaction.

Most companies will move pure transactions to the Internet and use their online capabilities for information sharing and routine communication. They will reserve person-to-person interaction for the aspects of the transaction that add the most value. For example, people will use the Internet to make reservations, place product orders, gather information, assess product values and check the order status of their shipment. These are rather straight-forward tasks that do not usually demand one-on-one relationships. Ray Lane of Oracle believes that "changes in business processes will emphasize self-service. Your costs as a business go down and perceived service goes up because customers are conducting it themselves."

There was a short vaudeville bit played in front of an Alpine set. A man would yodel. An echo would repeat the yodel. The man would say "Hellooo!" The echo would answer "Hellooo!"

All kinds of versions of this act were used in different movies and always got a laugh. Modernizing the skit the for the global age the man yells out "Hellooo!" The echo answers, "Press one for a customized greeting, press two for the yodel, press three if you want to leave a message at the tone . . ."

With smart systems in place, companies can shift people from repetitive, non-thinking work to more productive, high-value activities. Using software to handle routine data chores allows the human touch where it really matters. It's incredibly valuable to have a person working with a customer who is unhappy or who has special needs. Customers will tolerate occasional mistakes as long as the organization fixes the problem quickly and efficiently at no additional cost to the customer. Consumers come back to the company that lives by the creed: "Customer service first."

In a hotel, for instance, smart software can dramatically shorten check-in and check-out time and solicit routine feedback. This frees up staff to act as facilitators, greeters, information dispensers, and friendly concierges rather than just clerks. Let the clicking do the clerking and personal service do the extra things that make for an enjoyable and repeatable stay for guests. An acquaintance of mine works at the front desk of a Arizona convention hotel where he prides himself on making guests feel special. When someone arrived at the reception desk, credit card in hand, he would sneak a peek at it and address the guest by name. Once, during a particularly busy check-in time, one of the guests presented a corporate credit card. "Welcome to Scottsdale, Mr. Bell," my friend said. "Oh, please," the man replied, "just call me Taco."

"The Ritz-Carlton Experience enlivens the senses, instills well-being and fulfills even the unexpressed wishes and needs of the guest," says the Ritz Carlton Credo. Why does Ritz position itself in the service business? Because management knows that

193

it's fairly easy to imitate a Ritz hotel, but much harder to emulate its service. There are only two kinds of competitive advantage: those that are based on offering customers something truly wonderful and unique and those that aren't. The future belongs to those who see possibilities before they become obvious.

Surprise and Delight

The service challenge is to exceed customers' expectations: be customer obsessed and be consumer-centric. Products and services must go beyond people's expectations. Customers no longer want to just talk about how a product works or discuss its outstanding features. They either say "I love it," or they don't. If they don't, you're done.

My personal example of outstanding service is a true story I have shared with hundreds of audiences. I am flying from Phoenix to Dallas on American Airlines. The air is rougher than I have ever experienced. Everyone is getting sick, including me.

Seated in an aisle seat in row two, I notice a woman in a front row bulkhead window seat get white as a sheet. Gagging, she pops her seat belt to step across the man next to her to go to the bathroom. As she takes her first step, she throws up on his lap.

The flight attendant immediately gets up and helps the lady into the bathroom. The attendant quickly gathers some wet towels and goes to help the man clean his lap. As the flight attendant bends down to help the poor guy, she too gags. Wham. His lap is heaved on again. I mean, its the funniest thing I've ever seen in my life. Two throw-ups in one lap in less than a minute.

The man unbuckles his seat belt, stands up, turns around and says to everybody in first class, "Would anyone else?" (like to throw up on my lap).

194

It was a stitch.

Later, I gave him my business card and told him I would be interested in investing in his company. Anyone who has a sense of humor when everybody is losing their lunch on his lap is my kind of guy.

A month later, he writes to tell me about his company, and in a last paragraph incidentally notes that American Airlines gave him money for a new suit and two free first class air tickets to any destination.

Now, that's what I call surprise, delight, and exceptional customer service.

Most companies are catching on: be consumer-centric; get in the consumer's shoes. "Don't tell me about your grass seed. Tell me about my lawn."

The interesting thing about the service economy is that often there is nothing tangible. You can't demonstrate it, inspect it, warehouse it, recall it, or store it. As Charles Revlon once said, "We manufacture perfume in the factory, but we sell hope in the store." Charles Ritz was reported to have said, "The guest is always right. The guest is always right. Even if you have to throw him out of the hotel, the guest is always right."

Markets are about the changing tastes and preferences of customers. Of course, there's no way to know what people will want in the future. Or is there? Succeeding means leading customers where they want to go before even they *know* where they want to go. Who knew people would want a microwave oven, a cell phone, or an ATM before someone invented them and brought them to the market? Now, just try to live without them. The market is dynamic and spontaneous and leaves no room for preconceived boundaries. It is about creativity on the fly. Companies should be idea led and consumer informed. So should every person in business.

Change Brings Problems Which Present Opportunities

The phrase "supply chain" implies a linear relationship. Viewed along a continuum of vendors, manufacturers, distributors, and sales, each could believe that the others had to be tolerated and were not really partners in the whole effort. But today in a connected, Web-linked, "we're all in this together" world, worldly partnerships are forged and dissolved every day. Anyone in the network can choose to interact, suggest and make the process work better for customers. Unless you add value or touch the customer in a meaningful way you are not needed. The idea is to always use information for better supplier relationships, better inventory management, better response times, and better real time collaboration. Every change creates new needs and new opportunities.

Opportunities are always found within the problem. Customers tomorrow are going to have a mind-boggling array of perceived needs and available options. If you cannot provide what they want when they want it, save them time and simplify their lives, the twenty-first century is going to be difficult. If all you can see is change destroying old opportunities, and bringing bad news, then change is going to be your enemy. But if you can see that change simply relocates the opportunity by changing customers' wants and preferences, presenting another need to be filled and a place to add value, then change is your friend.

We have all driven through a rainstorm listening to some radio announcer in a windowless room telling us what a sunny day it is. Look for yourself. Understand your customers. Follow your customers. Change with your customers.

Income or Wealth?

> All I ask is the chance to prove that money cannot make me happy.
>
> -Manhattan stock broker

Workers must focus less on salary and more on wealth. A salary by itself never made anyone rich. Consider it walking around money and concentrate instead on your whole asset portfolio. That is why stock options and incentive programs are becoming the payment of choice, desired by both parties of the voluntary exchange. The source of future wealth is shifting from earned money to money that works for you—from earned to returned. Your nest egg is your investment egg; 401(k)s and IRAs are just two of the many possibilities for building your future. Today's salary is not nearly important as building tomorrow's wealth. The old chestnut, "I have enough money to last me the rest of my life—if I don't buy anything," is more wisdom than cliché. Money is of little use to people if they spend it as fast as they make it. All they have left are bills and the reputation for being a fool. You can't have everything anyway. Where would you put it all?

Workers must act as though they are in business for themselves by maintaining a plan for career-long self-development. They can start by taking primary responsibility for investing in health insurance and retirement funds, and by renegotiating compensation arrangements with the organization when and if their needs change.

No matter how workers take control of their financial futures—by restructuring their work with their existing company, by becoming a contract employee, or even by starting a new company—they begin to realize that they really work for themselves regardless of their business arrangement. This new focus must weight the relationship between effort and equity, between wages and wealth, and between income and investments. Effort, wages, and income are about the short term. Equity, wealth, and investments are about the future. Don't buy the house; buy the neighborhood. The best kind of work emphasizes your skills, talents, and future wealth rather than what it pays right now. It's always wise to be more concerned with skill enhancement and wealth than with consumption and income.

I've never been poor, only broke. While poor is a frame of mind, a demotivator, broke is only temporary. Remember that to really enjoy the better things in life, you first must experience the things they are better than. I will admit, however, that while poverty is not a disgrace, it is terribly inconvenient.

Improvement Begins With "I"

Those who add value stay around. Those who don't, don't. It's your contribution that counts, not the hours you put in or how busy you are. Never mistake motion for action. We've all seen people who stay busy, who even work hard, without adding any real value. They make the mistake of thinking that effort should earn them a paycheck. We buy art not by how much paint the artist layered onto the canvas, but by how pleasingly the paint was arranged. If there is nothing special or interesting or noticeable about your work, no matter how hard you apply yourself, you won't get recognized, and that probably means you won't get paid much either. Think of yourself as an artist.

Leadership is action, not position. It is a performance. A decision is the action a leader must take when the information they have is so incomplete that the answer does not automatically suggest itself. And the problem is if you don't risk anything, you'll probably risk even more. It is a consciousness about your actions because others are watching. It is about awakening possibilities in other people. Worldwide connectivity that allows information sharing, e-commerce, and synergistic collaboration only increases the size of your audience. It can all be done anywhere, anytime.

The Web makes anything possible, and it makes it possible faster. Every resume that comes to Lucent via the Web gets answered in 30 minutes or less. Leadership emphasizes doing and being proactive. But keep in mind that not to act is to act, and not to decide is to decide. Even a mosquito doesn't wait for an opening—it makes one. Perfect aim is useless unless you pull the trigger. Don't bog down in endless preparation trying to get things perfect before you make a move. Yes, high quality is crucial, but it must come quickly. Patience is the art of waiting in a hurry. You can't sacrifice speed. Learn to fail fast, fix it, and go on. Living with more ragged edges is the order of the day.

A sense of the value of time is now crucial. Finding the best way to divide one's time into one's various activities is an essential preliminary to efficient work, and is probably the only method of avoiding hurry.

Less Shirk Means Less Irk in Work

If you can tickle yourself, can't you laugh when you please? Why should upper management be responsible for your morale? Some of us think they should. If attitudes go sour, the boss gets the blame. Everyone makes mistakes, but the seeds of failure are sown when you start blaming others for those mistakes. When you blame others, you are trying to excuse yourself. It's a lot easier to be critical than to be correct. If employees are mentally down and out, the company is expected to provide emotional hand-holding until its people are happy again. This attitude won't work any longer and does not really help anyone. Isn't it interesting that some people would die for the liberty of the world, but they would not make the little sacrifice that is needed to free themselves from their own individual bondage of bad attitude and blame?

Putting someone else in charge of your morale really disempowers you and when you blame upper management for your problems, you only hurt yourself. You are much better off taking personal responsibility for attitude control. And yes, attitude does determine altitude: dispense enthusiasm and you'll reach new heights.

The marketplace doesn't care how old you are. Its focus is on energy level. Don't let low morale drain away precious energy, destroy your self-confidence, or damage your attractiveness as a job candidate. Organizations want employees who can cope with change without breaking stride. So take charge of your moods. Act upbeat, and you start to feel better. Show resilience rather than allowing yourself to wallow in negative emotions such as anger, depression or bitterness.

Both problems and opportunities are the natural offspring of change. The rest of your work life will be filled with them. If you become a problem-solver and an opportunity-taker, you'll be a valuable person to have around. Companies need people who can create solutions, not merely point out problems. Complaining is not a constructive act. Every minute spent complaining is a minute spent not doing. Identifying problems in an accusing, blaming fashion does little to improve things. So, instead of being a finger-pointer, and rather than trying to single out somebody to blame, assume ownership of problems. Let the solutions start with you. Never identify a problem without also creating a solution—or at least a process that will lead your team to a solution.

As a former ballplayer once said, "If fans don't come to the ballpark there is nothing we can do to stop them." He's right. The game involves constant change, little stability, and minimal customer loyalty. Yes, some people think this is rotten. And yes, many job situations are difficult. The only one who really likes change is a wet baby. "Where in heaven's sake did all those good jobs go?" you ask. "Overseas competition is sucking the good jobs right out of the country," many lament. "There aren't any jobs out there," a few moan. "This would be a great job if it were not for the customers," many complain. "There's nothing to do except live off unemployment benefits and hope to hit it big in the lottery," a few believe. "I could never learn to use the Internet," say the fearful. "Just because you're paranoid doesn't mean they're not out to get you," says the sorry soul. In fact, these thoughts are debilitating and unhelpful. We waste precious energy if we resist, get angry, or give in to grief over all that's (supposedly) being lost. You may be disappointed if you fail, but you are doomed if you don't try. Either find a way or make one. To reach a goal you have never attained, expect to do things you have never done before.

Lance Morrow's *Time* magazine article called "*The Temping of America,*" along with a response by Tom Peters, presents two distinct views. Morrow writes of "the great corporate clearances of the '90s, the ruthless restructuring efficiencies, and the millions of Americans being evicted from the working world that used to sustain them." He talks of the sense of "betrayal" among American workers, comparing it to that felt by our troops in Vietnam. Tom Peters, in turn, belittles Morrow's argument and responds to his hand-wringing with a rebuttal full of upbeat talk about the exciting possibilities that an entrepreneurial work force and the contract society have created.

Each side of this argument is articulating an important half-truth. The organization experts and the economists are right when they say that these changes are coming, whether we want them or not. And they are right in pointing out that there are real opportunities. But it is also true that this shift undermines people's sense of security and takes away the core of their identity. When people lose things of such magnitude, they can lose hope too.

But facts are facts. Whether the stone bumps the jug or the jug bumps the stone, it is always bad for the jug. You can't sit on the lid of progress. If you do you will be blown to pieces. The world doesn't care about our feelings. The issue is not our opinion of the changing world but our response to it. Success awaits those of us who catch on to what's happening and invest energy in finding and seizing the opportunities brought about by change. What are you going to do about change? Excuses won't work. If "ifs" and "buts" were candy and nuts, we'd all have a Merry Christmas.

Perpetual Motion/Ambiguous Work

In the new world of work, the emphasis is always on the *new*—using your brain to generate creative ideas and paying careful attention to what the customer really wants, not just today, but tomorrow and even years from now.

Managing work means managing perpetual motion. Mario Andretti, the three-time Indianapolis 500 winner, said, "If things seem under control, you're just not going fast enough." If everything seems to be going well, you probably don't know what is going on. Anyone can hold the helm when the sea is calm, but the modern world now rides mostly rough seas. Just as the ship's captain makes constant maneuvers to negotiate the changing conditions, businesses must be continually improving and changing its core to survive the fiercely competitive environment. Everyone must be willing to quickly adjust. Better three hours too soon than one minute too late.

If you cannot act with haste when the company changes, you probably should quit. It's best for you and best for your employer. Strong job commitment benefits your employer and it makes your work far more satisfying. It's therapeutic and an excellent antidote for stress. Commitment is a gift you should give to yourself. Michelangelo puts it positively: "The greatest danger for most of us is not that our aim is too high and we miss it, but that it is too low and we reach it."

Pinning down needed work is like trying to nail Jell-O to the wall. You're constantly faced with new expectations, shifting priorities and different reporting relationships. Roles may be vaguely defined and assignments are continually changing. Work today is not about wearing one hat, but many: the sales hat, the marketing hat, the planning hat, the customer service hat, the time management hat, the how-to hat, and many others. In this kind of work environment there are usually more questions than answers. And even when some questions cannot be answered, decisions still must be made. There is not enough time to be perfect. People who have a high need for structure simply hate this kind of situation. It even eats on employees who have a high tolerance for ambiguity and uncertainty because, sooner or later, people like closure. They grow weary of having to endure open-ended issues, unanswered questions and a fluid set of responsibilities. One pundit said, "We live in a world with too many moving parts." Many times it will feel like driving in a fog

203

at midnight: you can't see much, but you'll see enough to get there. And the upside is that you're going to travel to new, different and exciting places.

Nine Promises to Yourself. Plus One.

A variation of Coach John Wooden's nine promises that can bring you happiness and success might read like this:

1) Promise yourself that you will talk health, happiness, and prosperity as often as possible. It's not what we have, but what we use; it's not what we see, but what we choose. These make up human happiness. Happiness always sneaks through a door you didn't know was open.

2) Promise yourself to make plans as fantastic as you can, because 25 years from now, they will seem average and mediocre. Make your plans 10 times as great as you first planned and 25 years from now you will wonder why you didn't make them 50 times as great. Aim high! It is no harder on your gun to shoot the feathers off an eagle than to shoot the fur off of a skunk.

3) Promise to think only of the best, to work only for the best, and to expect only the best of yourself and others. Even if your daily route is temporarily detoured, look forward to the great scenery. Beware of the soft bed of habit: easy to get in, hard to get out.

4) Promise to be as enthusiastic about the success of others as you are about your own. Light yourself with the fire of enthusiasm and people will stand in line to watch you burn. Nothing is as contagious as enthusiasm. A fire loses none of its flame in lighting another.

5) Promise yourself a purpose. It is the eternal condition of success. If you don't know where you are going, you are at the mercy of those who do. If you chase two rabbits, both will escape. One of the strongest characteristics of genius is the power of lighting your own fire.

6) Promise to forget the mistakes of the past and press on to greater achievements in the future. A mistake is a lesson on its way to be learned. If your dreams turn to dust, vacuum.

7) Promise to wear a cheerful appearance at all times and give every person you meet a smile. Even when you feel you're walking up a gangplank with no ship, there is a reason to be expectant. Remember the lowest ebb is the turn of the tide.

8) Promise to give so much time to improving yourself that you have no time to criticize others. Putting out another's candle does not brighten your flame. Now is the watchword of the wise. Excellence is not an act but a habit.

9) Promise to be too large for worry, too noble for anger, too strong for fear, and too happy to permit trouble to press on you. If you want to test your memory, try to remember the things that worried you yesterday. Most worries are re-runs anyway.

Just in case you feel digitally impaired, promise yourself that you will get a PC Internet tutor. Even Jack Welch, President and CEO of General Electric Company, found himself a mentor to learn the basics. Anyone can do it. Everyone must learn to "drive" this new machine. If you think education on the Internet is tough, just try ignorance of the Internet. The doors of opportunity are open and everyone must be equipped to walk through them.

Practice hands-on usage. Learn to use e-mail and other electronic tools to get familiar with the new way of doing things. Look at creative Web sites. Listen and learn. You can observe a lot by just watching. Ask a lot of questions. Ask friends and acquaintances for their favorite Internet sites and shortcuts. Become an Internet user and consumer. Buy some books and arrange travel over the Internet and see what it's like. In short, familiarize yourself with the Internet. Study the Internet. You'll begin to feel comfortable with this new technology and understand that anyone who continues to upgrade and improve their human capital will prosper. That is my promise to you.

CHAPTER 9

Globalism and the Internet

The Internet is an amazing communication tool bringing the whole world together. I mean, you sit down to sign on to America Online in your hometown, and its just staggering to think at the same moment, half the way around the world, in China, someone you've never met is sitting at their computer, hearing the exact same busy signal that you are hearing.

-Dennis Miller

An idea, born when its time truly has come, can sweep across society like a virus that has no antidote. Unstoppable, it affects everything and everyone. We divide much of human history by the dates such ideas emerge: the nation-state, democracy, Newtonian mechanics, the assembly line, electricity, fission, private property, digitization. Today, it is globalism—a process of international social and economic integration that is probably irreversible. Globalism now equals capitalism practiced worldwide. Great ideas have changed us many times before and this one surely will also.

The slow, stable and divided Cold War system that dominated international affairs since 1945 has been replaced by a dynamic and interconnected system where economics and trade supersede war and territory. Globalism is no longer tied to a nation-state, but is driven by people who know they can work for anyone, anywhere in the world and can invest their money the same way. It involves the inexorable integration of markets, nation-states, and technologies to a degree never known before. Globalism, an integration of the world economy that will change the way people live and work, has the potential to restructure class, culture and tradition.

The first decade of the twenty-first century will bring a tidal wave of change. The traditional bureaucratic structures of business mentioned in the last chapter will give way to an Internet-driven, brand-owning, customer-focused globalized economy. The e-business revolution will either invigorate every shop, every manufacturer, and every service company, or else sweep it away. Either the supply chain will be streamlined, top to bottom, with tremendous efficiencies gained, or it will be caught in what Joseph Schumpeter called "creative destruction," a storm that takes no prisoners. The inevitable outcome will produce more haves and have-nots: the haves will be a part of a global capital market that will produce incredible prosperity. The have nots will be those who do not live under freedom, did not foresee the coming Internet-driven world, and worse yet, still do not have deeded property rights.

When parts of the planet were isolated physically from one another, global Gross Domestic Product barely grew. Then, with the invention of the telegraph and the railroad in the nineteenth century and the car, telephones and airplane in the twentieth century, ideas began to circulate and combine in ways no one had thought possible. While unprecedented growth took place, it will be dwarfed by the intellect and imagination that capitalism driven by the Internet will spawn.

Is it happening everywhere? No. Japan is still caught in a decade-long slump. Europe is hamstrung by restrictive labor policies that hamper corporate change and is still very slow to abandon age-bound traditions of apprenticeships and corporate paternalism. Most people in developing countries have never touched a telephone, much less been connected to the world through the Internet. But, their time will come. Poverty delivers a strong message. It might not be PCs in every room, but it will surely be pocket wireless devices that permit not only endless audio (and eventually video) chats but also economic and information connections to the planet. Everyone, especially the young, will eventually be given a chance to participate in the global economy.

Global markets, which are growing at more than twice the rate of domestic markets, intensify the pressure to expand production, cut costs, and strive for efficiencies. The digital age has greatly lowered the barriers to entry, driving down production costs, transportation costs and transaction costs. Competition and opportunity now come from everywhere. As global markets widen, knowledge exchange makes people smarter, faster, connected, and richer.

The arrival of freer capital markets, powerful desktop computers and the Internet has enabled small companies and even individuals to compete with their bigger rivals. The spread of free trade means that start-ups can break into markets without setting up expensive offices or having to cultivate cozy relationships with local politicians. Anyone can mix and match ideas from around the world and turn himself into a knowledge broker. The Internet brings people together who might not otherwise meet: Italian designers and Japanese computer wizards, for example, or Taiwanese advertisers and German chemists.

Everything about global capital markets seems to be breaking records these days. The amount of capital in circulation is greater than ever before. The speed of movement is faster, the ratio of capital to traded goods bigger, and the consequences of a mistake more devastating. Like an invading army finding a crack in the fortress, businesses and entrepreneurs are scaling walls of new opportunities, seeking the mutual benefits of voluntary exchange. The value of imported and exported world manufactured goods, which was $2 trillion in 1986, has ballooned to over $8.5 trillion just a decade and a half later. By 2000, the number of transnational corporations, as measured by the United Nations Conference on Trade and Development (UNCTAD), had increased to about 70,000 from 7,000 in the 1960s. Multinationals started acting like integrated global organizations rather than like loose affiliations of national companies and nation-states.

The Contract Economy

Globalism is a move away from buildings and more toward relationships and the customer. The signature office buildings of large corporations will give way to technologically connected spaces: cars, small offices, and homes. Subdivisions of companies will be free to buy services or products from each other or from outsiders. The Internet will help customers find the best deal they can. Consumers will easily jump from one retail Web site to another to find the best prices on many goods, or they will ask a shopping robot to do the search for them. Rather than being shielded from outside competitive pressures, each subdivision of a company will become part of the marketplace. Much work will be outsourced. The process of bringing an outside market into the firm will not be limited to large units of major companies. Subdivisions of subdivisions will also be forced to compete. Since the smallest subdivision is the individual, eventually we will reach a point where there is very little difference between an employee and an independent contractor. Our hierarchical business world will be replaced by a

210

contractual society in which every individual will either run his own business or run a business within the business he works for.

For example, in any business that has a marketing department, the president faces all of the problems of the traditional business manager: how to motivate, how to spur creativity, how to make personal goals consistent with corporate goals, how to increase sales with less budget. In a business that contracts out for marketing services, however, the manager deals with different problems. Most likely, numerous competitors approach the manager periodically with ideas on how to better market the company's products. So, in a business that handles marketing internally, the manager asks: "How can I get other people to solve my problems?" The manager of a company that contracts out the marketing function asks: "How do I choose among many competitors, each of whom desperately wants to solve my problems?" In one case, employee behavior is a problem requiring management skills because employees are shielded from competition. In the other case, most of the traditional management problems have vanished, precisely because there is competition. Now the management skill required is to be a smart shopper and to choose the service that most effectively meets the business need. Instead of hiring permanent or part-time workers, business will hire contingent workers—contract workers whose hiring is contingent on the results that the organization wants to achieve. Market forces will drive the system.[1]

Internet Driven e-Commerce

> Ideas go booming through the world louder than a
> cannon. Thoughts are mightier than armies.
> Principles have achieved more victories than
> horsemen or chariots.
>
> -Will Paxton

The world has seen four main waves of innovation sparked by capitalism's entrepreneurs. The first, from the 1780s to the 1840s, was the industrial revolution in Britain, fueled by steam power; the second, from the 1840s to the 1890s, was the railway age; the third, from the 1890s to the 1950s, was driven by electric power and the car. The fourth is the age of globalism, driven by high technologies such as communications, satellite and cable infrastructures, television, and the giant of them all, the Internet: a global brain detached from human bodies where everybody is connected and nobody is in charge.

In scientific terms, the Internet may not be as significant as the printing press, the telegraph, or electricity, but it will have a bigger impact on creating prosperity. The cost of communicating via the Internet has plummeted far more steeply than did the cost of using any previous technology, allowing it to be used more widely and deeply throughout the economy. An invention that remains expensive, as the electric telegraph did, is bound to have a lesser effect. While the printing press made us all readers, the electric telegraph all communicators, and the television all viewers, the Internet makes us all producers. Manufacturing costs, and transaction costs are all being driven down. As costs fall, the cost of starting a new business collapses. Author Kevin Maney of *USA Today* writes of how IBM

212

recognizes that the strength of the wolf is the pack and the strength of the pack is the wolf:

> A group of computer programmers at Tsinghua University in Beijing is writing software using Java technology. At the end of each day, they send their work over the Internet to an IBM facility in Seattle. There, programmers build on it and use the Internet to zap it 5,222 miles to the Institute of Computer Science in Belarus and the Software House Group in Latvia. From there, the work is sent east to India's Tata Group, which bypasses the software back to Tsinghua by morning in Beijing, back to Seattle, and so on in a great global relay that never ceases until the job is done. It's like a forty-eight hour day through the Internet.

To give just minimal detail, the Internet is an extension of a computer network originally formed in the United States during the 1960s by the Advanced Research Projects Agency. Since then, it has expanded into a global computer network linking thousands of individual and corporate computers via existing telephone and wireless connections. Some computers on the Internet are restricted only to authorized sets of users, such as those within a single company. These machines are collectively referred to as an Intranet. The Internet consists of software standards that allow for e-mail and file transfers, and search engines and browsers that allow us to find, retrieve and view needed information from every library, business, data file and customer. The network is powerful because it is simple and the devices that attach to it are intelligent. Combine digital technology with advanced software and powerful microprocessors; lay optical fiber strands at a pace of some 4,000 miles a day with almost 30 million strand miles in the United

States alone; expand wireless bandwidth; and you are on the way to achieving seamless, universal connectivity. The Internet is becoming the world's major commercial thoroughfare and the means for conducting life in the twenty-first century.

While most of the traffic on the Internet has been e-mail and file transfers, new search engines can now find information much more easily, thus permitting all organizations to put their information on Web sites accessible to the world. Every day tens of thousands of new users log on to a reliable and inexpensive global outreach tool known as the World Wide Web. Using the Internet and Web browsers, the Web's resources can bring together world companies and libraries of information of every kind. For the price of a local phone call, individuals can do deals, buy stocks, choose a vacation site, buy a pair of shoes, or communicate with someone 12,000 miles away. The Internet is the best decision support system ever conceived because it not only utilizes the wealth of billions of human organic containers (human minds) but it also acts synergistically with the unlimited ceramic, sand, and light of technological machinery that never tires and works at the speed of thought. The Internet is eliminating obstacles to production, trade and exchange at a pace never expected or even dreamed of in centuries past.[2]

The New World Network will merge the Internet with telecom's high-speed fiber optic, cable, and wireless systems. The Internet will be everything: the World Wide Web; the phone lines; the conveyor and purveyor of music and video; and more. Thousands of new devices and gizmos will combine worldwide phone service with worldwide e-commerce capabilities, the Web, video and e-mail, which will merge markets from everywhere. The Internet, because it makes everything compatible, will be *the* conduit. Text, image and sound will all metamorphose into bits communicating every language going anywhere and flowing easily into a variety of old gadgets and ones yet to be invented. Digital devices in telephones, portable sound systems, and desktop computers will translate voice into digital bits and back again through the network.

Wireless Internet is now the benchmark for consumer adoption of the new technology. The introduction of technologies such as mobile phones, personal digital assistants, voice mail, text messaging and paging have truly moved the world to a 24/7 environment—anytime, anyplace, anywhere. It happened because of the convergence of four traditionally separate technologies. First, is the Internet itself, which provides access to an unprecedented amount of information 24 hours a day. Second, is the deployment of third-generation wireless networks that enable high-speed mobile data access. Third, is the emergence of next generation mobile appliances compatible with these networks. Fourth, is the integration of secure transaction technology into these systems, the same technology that makes the stock exchanges, automatic teller machines, and electronic fund transfer networks work so effectively today.

The mobile user, eventually all of us, will demand a full range of wireless Internet solutions. The global model of the Internet will be ubiquitous and borderless. Networks that integrate mobile voice with Internet data will all inter-operate with voice mail, prepaid calling, phone/calling card services, home location registers, local number portability, intelligent devices and peripherals, call-processing services, and 800 telemarketing services.

A good gauge of the pace of technological change is how quickly the cost of the technology declines. Over the past three decades, the real price of computer processing power has fallen by 99.99 percent, an average decline of 35 percent a year. The cost of a telephone call has declined more slowly, but over a longer period. In 1930, a three minute call from New York to London cost more than $300 in today's prices; the same call now costs less than 20 cents—an annual decline of around 10 percent.

AT&T, as just one example, has spent more than $20 billion over its 116 years of existence on brand development. Its logo, its dial tone, and its customer service is well known and well deserved. But in the last decade, the falling prices just mentioned have wiped out 80% of their core revenue stream. Neither the famous brand, the fabulous reputation, nor its excellent CEO could stop the fiber-optic revolution that literally changed the core of its business. Who could have been prepared for that kind of "creative destruction?"

Why Is the Internet So Powerful?

Several features make the Internet a powerful tool. First, it is pervasive. It can boost efficiency in almost everything everyone does: design, marketing, accounting, manufacturing, communications, everything. While the productivity gains of steam, electricity and railways were seen mainly in the manufacture and distribution of goods, the Internet is the first technological revolution to also boost productivity in services, from health care and education to finance and government. That is no small matter since services account for nearly three-fifths of America's annual output.

Second, by increasing access to information, the Internet also helps markets to work more efficiently. Many economists suggest that the new economy should really be called the "nude economy" because the Internet exposes and makes everything more transparent. Thankfully, you don't have to get undressed to log on. The Internet allows consumers to seek the lowest price and helps firms to get quotes from all suppliers. If the secret to selling is to just let people know what's available, the Internet is it.

Another great feature is that the Internet reduces transaction costs and barriers to entry. It moves the economy closer to the textbook model of perfect competition, which assumes abundant information, many buyers and sellers, zero transaction costs and no barriers to entry. For hundreds of years, these were only far-fetched assumptions that economists dreamed about. Today, they are reality.

Better-informed markets also lead to the most productive use of resources. Farmers can get instant information on weather, prices and crop conditions in other regions. Manufacturers can track changes in demand more closely via direct links to electronic scanners in shops and retail stores. The technology of the Internet makes it easier and cheaper to process large amounts of data while reducing the time it takes to design new products. More and more knowledge can be stored as a string of zeros and ones and sent anywhere in the world at negligible cost. By reducing the cost of communication, the Internet has helped to globalize design, production, and capital markets which spurs competition and innovation. The speed and diffusion of new technology increases trade, investment and productivity.

Number-crunching tasks that once took a week can now be done in seconds. Today, a Ford Taurus contains more computing power than the multi-million-dollar mainframe computers used in the Apollo space program. Cheaper processing power allows people to use computers for more and more purposes. In 1985, it cost Ford $60,000 each time it crashed a car into a wall to find out what would happen in an accident. Now, auto manufacturers can simulate a collision by computer for around $100. BP Amoco uses computer-enhanced seismic exploration technology to prospect for oil, cutting the cost of finding oil from nearly $10 a barrel in 1991 to only $1 today.

American Airlines spends less than 10¢ to create an e-ticket, compared with $12 for a paper version. By ordering supplies, from pumps to pipes, on-line, the construction giant Bechtel saves at least 40 percent on each transaction. More than 40 percent of Charles Schwab's $961 billion in customer assets are in on-line accounts.

In 1970, it would have cost $187 to transmit *Encyclopedia Britannica* as an electronic data file coast to coast in America because transmission speeds were slow and long-distance calls expensive. Today, the entire contents of the Library of Congress could be sent across America for just $40. And as bandwidth expands, costs will fall even further. Within 10 years, international phone calls could, in effect, be free, with telecom firms charging a monthly fee for unlimited calls and deriving most of their revenue from video and other services.

As communications costs plunge, the benefit of being on-line increases exponentially with the number of connections. According to Metcalfe's Law, attributed to Robert Metcalfe, a pioneer of computer networking, the value of a network grows roughly in line with the square of the number of users. The Internet got its turbo boost with the invention of the World Wide Web in 1990 and the browser in 1993. Already, the number of users worldwide has climbed to more than 350 million, and will reach a billion within a few years.

Business-to-business e-commerce, for example, can cut firms' costs in many ways. It reduces procurement costs, both by making it easier to find the cheapest supplier and through efficiency gains. A report by Goldman Sachs, an investment bank, estimates that on-line purchasing could save firms anywhere from 2 percent in the coal industry to, perhaps, 40 percent in electronic components. It is now much cheaper to place an order on-line and there are likely to be fewer errors in orders and invoicing. Cisco Systems reports that it used to have to rework a quarter of its orders because of errors in its phone and fax ordering system. When it switched to online ordering, the error rate fell to 2 percent, saving the company $400 million.[3] British Telecom claims that buying goods and services on-line reduces the cost of processing a transaction by 90 percent and cuts the direct costs of goods and services it buys by 11 percent.

Another saving is from much lower distribution costs for goods and services such as financial services, software, and music. The marginal cost to a bank of a transaction over the Internet is a mere cent, compared with 27¢ via a cash machine, 52¢ by telephone and $1.14 by bank teller. On-line commerce also allows more efficient supply-chain management, cutting out layers of middlemen.

Better information also reduces the need for firms to keep large stocks. Dell Computer's build-to-order model, which completely eliminates inventories, is being widely copied. Car, steel, construction, and aerospace firms are setting up B2B exchanges, which will provide a more efficient marketplace for buyers and sellers to exchange products. Such exchanges are likely to spring up in most industries. GM, Ford, Daimler-Chrysler and Renault-Nissan plan to move all their business to a joint electronic exchange with a turnover of $250 billion and 60,000 suppliers. According to one estimate, when all suppliers eventually go on-line, the cost of making a car could be reduced by 14 percent.

Because of the pace of today's business decisions,

organizations have reduced their chain of command, flattened their hierarchies, and handed the authority for many decisions to front-line employees. Because organizations want to unburden themselves of big, slow-moving inventories, they shift to just-in-time systems of materials handling driven by demand-pull—which changes procedures and processes throughout the organization. Smart companies see inventories as evil. Big inventories often indicate that you don't know what your customers will want to buy tomorrow or next week. The less inventory, the more working capital available to drive revenue-generating activities. The closer you get to predicting demand for your product, the closer you get to zero inventory. More information means less inventory, and less information means more.

Because many organizations want to involve their suppliers more closely in operations, they put suppliers (and even customers) on their product development teams—which, incidentally, now are also peopled with individuals from different functions who have never worked together before. Again, a major shift for everyone is involved. Suppliers, and all the new team members, will need to figure out not just what the company wants today, but what the consumer will want tomorrow. A sophisticated, demanding customer will insist on higher quality, new features, and better service, all at lower prices.

Most companies will use process control systems for everything: meeting customers' changing orders; integrating manufacturing plans; keeping production data-ordering inventory; shipping product; billing; accounting; and mowing the lawn in front of the headquarters. Common order entry with inventory and scheduling software will be widespread. Everything used internally from Post-It notes and paper clips to raw materials will be ordered automatically. Vendors will have access to a company's purchasing database to plan more efficient deliveries.

Customers will have Web access for checking product availability and placing orders. Just recently, my friend Karen needed a sleeping bag for a 10-day wilderness expedition. She accessed a site that allowed her to put in various preferences, such as temperature; bag style; waterproofing; cost; manufacturer; and so on. Finally, it gave her three hypothetical choices and asked her to rank them by the probability that she would buy them; then it recommended several bags and told us where and for how much we could purchase them. The whole transaction took about five minutes. Karen's comment? "Cool." The Internet is all about providing faster, friendlier, and more personal customer service. Everyone in the value chain will have access to the kinds of information they need to be innovative and more responsive to felt needs. The more information businesses have, the better able they are to meet customers' needs and add value to the firm.

In retail, brick-and-mortar companies such as Gap, Best Buy, Wal-Mart, and Land's End are using the Internet as another way to reach customers. By offering a physical and an on-line store, retailers provide consumers with multiple ways to shop and research products. It even opens up new sales possibilities. K-Mart, through its on-line division Bluelight.com, is now selling big-screen TVs, an inventory that, before Bluelight.com, was unthinkable.

The Internet also changes the relationship every company has with its products. Whirlpool, for example, now stays in constant contact with the products they sell to make them better, to understand how they are performing, and to download upgrades and service/maintenance information. Wireless diagnostics are the new order of the day and will do more to change customers relationships with their products than any other single thing.

221

The Old Economy

What do you call an airline that serves peanuts for breakfast, lunch and dinner, has bunny-costumed flight attendants popping out of overhead compartments, and announces that those wishing to smoke should "file out to our lounge on the wing, where you can enjoy our feature film, Gone With the Wind?" A rip-roaring success, that's what! Dallas-based Southwest Airlines Company.

-Fred Wierseman

In a few years, there will be no more talk of the old economy and new economy. The companies left standing in the midst of the Internet tsunami will have synthesized the best of both. They will be organizations that use their size, operational excellence, and global infrastructure to fly by their competition. They will rely on service, speed, imagination and rule-busting strategies. Initially the Internet was about thousands of employees, customers, and partners getting wired into the system. The next step was key business processes getting linked to the net and a critical mass of customers coming on-line. The creation of e-business and e-commerce systems basically formed that critical foundation. But now the net is primed for its next evolution—not so much about you working the Web, but about the Internet working for you.

The future will be about the mass proliferation of e-services. E-services to solve problems, complete transactions, and make life easier. Some will be available on Web sites, some on your

222

telephone, some will be delivered through your TV, pager, car, e-mail in-box, or virtually anything with a microchip in it. Most of the time you will not have to go to a Web site to trigger an e-service. Some common services today are the UPS package tracking service; MapQuest's driving direction service; Schwab's stock trading services, and your bank's checking account services. Push a button on your car dash and an e-service could find the information you're looking for. Speak into a PDA and an e-service could book your hotel. Some e-services will be triggered automatically, such as low on gas, turn off the lights, the refrigerator needs milk.

Lou Gerstner, head of IBM, likes to describe the new "dot.com" firms as "fireflies before the storm—all stirred up, throwing off sparks." In other words, dot.toast. According to Gerstner, the impending storm will arrive "when the thousands and thousands of institutions that exist today seize the power of this global computing and communications infrastructure and use it to transform themselves."

IBM has used the Internet to cut the average time it takes to order supplies from vendors from 65 days to 23 days. All of its human resources functions, from health insurance to retirement, have moved on-line. IBM has already saved about $7 billion from Internet efficiencies since 1995. "We're only at the 2 percent mark of our journey. The real revolution is yet to come," says Gerstner.

Jack Welch of General Electric agrees. He says the dot.coms start with no revenue and lots of expenses for advertisement, warehouses, and more. So their break-even is—where? Who knows? They are totally revenue-dependent. Contrast that with "the old companies," whose businesses already have sales and expenses. Now, when you digitize those and move toward the Internet, costs fall, sales climb, margins climb, and the profits just pour in. For example, GE's 1999 auction transactions amounted to $200 million and over $5 billion in the year 2000. In 1999, transactions cost GE $50 each; on-line the cost is now $5. Welch has issued a challenge to each of GE's more than 20 big businesses to "destroyyourbusiness.com," that is, reinvent yourself before some upstart does it for you. All 600 top managers were told to find an internal Internet mentor who could tutor them in the ways of the Web revolution. When Welch says that GE wants to create "an effervescent culture just sparkling with creativity," he means it.

John Chambers, CEO of Cisco, has grown sales from $1.2 billion in 1995 to $20 billion in fiscal 2000. How? By directing enormous amounts of information technology toward customer service. Chambers more than quadrupled the company's spending on IT. By doing things its competitors could not do, Cisco now handles 80 percent of the monthly four million customer requests for information via the Web, not only serving customers better, but also saving the company an estimated $250 million a year. In fact, Cisco handles 87 percent of sales on the Web.

Consider Cisco Systems' automated purchase process. Since 70 percent of its customers place orders via the Web, there is no need for a traditional sales force. Cisco has more than 120 partners in its Internet router production process who act together—procuring, producing, shipping, repairing—as a single, virtual company. Customers place orders directly into an "Electronic Retrieval Process" system that selects suppliers and assemblers. Even the engineering function is integrated into the system. When a customer designs a router, Cisco's design department uses its database of customer-developed specifications to fit the product to his or her needs. The companies that use this platform join Cisco's partnership and become, in effect, part of the corporate nervous system.

In an auto plant, the assembly line is centered around a car. As a car moves down the line, new parts are added at each station, and inventory moves from the loading dock to replenish the work stations. At Cisco, the process is centered around the customer's order, but now each department, worker, outside contractor, and subcontractor can work on the order simultaneously, rather than waiting for all the "stations" to finish their task. From the customers' perspective, the process is seamless. Whether a router is made by Cisco or by a partner company makes no difference to them. But it is Cisco's computers that test all finished products in order to protect the brand name. This process saves Cisco $450 million per year.

In short, the company that makes routers and switches that speed communications and direct traffic on the Internet should lead the rapid growth of the emerging intelligent network. But, can you count on Cisco to collect profits like a "toll collector" on the information superhighway? Or will it be caught in Schumpeter's "creative destruction"? The company that made the Internet possible is being squeezed by fiber optics from above and by microchips from below. Since neither is Cisco's core competency, can they remake the company in the image of a new all-optical network?

Carly Fiorina, CEO of Hewlett Packard, was spurring the company into the Internet age even before her official duties began. Filming a video to be played a few days before she arrived, Fiorina urged HP to reinvent itself by interjecting Internet strategies to sharpen vision, focus, and execution. Pushing the whole company strongly toward the Internet has paid off. Expenses are down, growth and market share is up, and HP stock will surely rise significantly. Fiorina agrees with Gertsner, Welch, and Chambers that the old established companies are going to be the big winners using the Internet. She already has saved $75 million by moving personnel functions onto an internal web site.

Hewlett-Packard sees three trends for the e-services model to take hold. First, the proliferation of ready applications (apps-on-tap). Many companies will take full advantage of pay-as-you-go software for many key functions, such as accounting, payment systems, payroll, purchasing, etc. Second, will come the birth of new e-service portals: vertical portals like Open Skies in the travel industry; horizontal portals such as Ariba.com's procurement portal; and loyalty portals. Third, the dynamic brokering of e-services when consumers and businesses send out requests for services via the net. E-services will bid to fulfill those requests, giving companies the opportunity to reach customers where they are. The mix and match of e-services will only be limited by the imagination. Global position servicing will link with a traffic routing service to provide real time traffic information. E-services can be rapidly customized to meet a specific need.

Leo Mullins, CEO of Delta Airlines since 1997, early on found that Delta had the worst technology in the business. Some Wall Street analysts even questioned the company's long term survival. Mullins decided to transform technology from a nightmare into a profit engine, even though the technology was not Delta's. By turning over all distressed inventory, i.e., unsold seats, to Internet-based discounter Priceline.com, he generated some $1.4 billion, or 10 percent of Delta's annual revenue online. The Priceline deal encouraged Mullins to do more on the Net. Delta now has about 40 Internet related programs touching every aspect of the company's business.

Another example of the old becoming new again is Nordstrom. J. Daniel Nordstrom, the founder's great-great grandson and current President of Nordstrom.com, boasts the largest online shoe store in the world, offering 30 million pairs of shoes to choose from. Revenues, including catalog sales, will exceed $250 million in 2000. Not bad for a company that came late to the Net.

Mark Hogan's presidency of GM Brazil was interrupted when he was asked to head up e-GM. Hogan took over an umbrella unit created in 1999 to oversee the automaker's on-line efforts, and his OnStar dashboard communication system is now in over a million vehicles. For $40 a month, drivers can choose to be linked to the Internet for road directions, restaurant and gas station locations, and dozens of other helpful items. e-GM is projecting a billion-dollar-a-year business from its eventual 10 million subscribers. It's good for GM, and good for you, but don't try to get out of a speeding ticket by explaining you were reading your e-mail. That gives a whole new meaning to the term, "speed reading." Hogan is also luring shoppers into showrooms via the GM BuyPower Web site and is spending $50 million a year on Web partnerships. This is but one of GM's efforts to regain market share and serve the customer.

Wal-Mart, the #1 retailer in the world, achieved that rank by creating a discount store with a wide array of merchandise and friendly service, and by connecting real-time to all stores, suppliers, headquarters, and even customers. By diversifying into groceries, gasoline, and adding international operations and membership warehouse clubs by using lots of technology to do its business and maintain minimal inventories, Wal-Mart is now using the power of the Internet to expand its business. Through data mining, Wal-Mart focuses on the value of gathering and analyzing information. Now that it has gained control over distribution and understands retail patterns, the past is prologue for Wal-Mart. Watch out!

Oracle's Larry Ellison proclaims that "the Internet changes everything" and Intel's Andy Grove warns that in five years' time "all companies will be Internet companies or they won't be companies at all." Things might not change as quickly as corporate chiefs and technologists hope. But change they will. History indicates that most people exaggerate the short-run impact of technological change and underestimate its long-run impact. This is what happened with the spread of electricity, and the invention of the horseless carriage, and it will probably happen again with the Internet.

The culmination of four decades of creative ideas, all pulling and synergistically reacting with each other, the Internet makes distance irrelevant. In today's world, everybody is connected and nobody is in charge. The time and distance that have kept people from trading and talking with each other are being removed. By reducing the obstacles to trade, more trade takes place, and individuals everywhere become more efficient and prosperous.

Twenty-first century superstar companies will travel a wide range of innovative pathways. Few of those will contain one iota of nostalgia for yesterday's core businesses. Core will change again and again. But that does not mean that core is unimportant. Quite the contrary. The odds of success for businesses stretched far from their strong core are low. And yet, no opportunity will be out of bounds. Oftentimes an in-house entrepreneurial idea will gain independent status totally outside the company and will be left to prosper on its own. Shareholders will no longer be concerned only with the market value of the parent company, but also with the total returns from both parent and spin-offs.

Of course, the reverse will also happen, when parent companies buy young companies with great ideas whose products and services can be sold by the parent. By continually renewing their "core," parent businesses sidestep the ever-present problem of disruptive technologies putting them out of business. The question is always how much of the innovation occurring outside the company can be successfully purchased, integrated, and then leveraged by the parent.

Obviously, every company has multiple opportunities to use its existing talent to find potential businesses that lie in its white spaces. When Quaker State moved from just drilling and selling oil to actually servicing the ongoing lubrication needs of a car (Q-Lube), they saw in that move profitable "white spaces." Today, Charles Schwab handles our securities trading, but tomorrow it will also manage our estate and tax planning, bill paying, and other financial transactions quickly and efficiently. Great companies will pursue value and a strengthened core. Getting the full profit potential from your core is critical. The Los Angeles Lakers, for example, would benefit more from a 20 percent improvement in Shaquille O'Neal's free-throw game than from a 75 percent improvement in the 12th player on the bench.

In reality, the Internet Age is not defined so much by the speed of time to market or even the speed of time between new products and services as it is the speed of constant transformation to new cores. One pathway will not do. To thrive, people and organizations must be multi-faceted, multi-trained, and multi-tasked, highly versatile, and adaptive. Many pathways utilizing size and speed and innovation and intellectual capital will help informed organizations to win again and again in a permanently disruptive world. Companies will be built to last because they are being rebuilt to change. Companies that embrace the Internet must now mirror the Internet. The idea is not to survive the Internet, but to be the Internet.

"Why Not?" The Slogan for the Twenty-First Century

Who could have imagined the possibility of turning every written or spoken word, every picture and every number into zeros and ones and moving them across a satellite system or through a fiber optic cable at the speed of light? Who looked far enough ahead to see that all the world's communication systems, from telephones, radio, and TV, to satellite systems and wireless gadgets, would converge into a single giant global communications system?

From the time that the radio was first introduced, it took 38 years for 50 million people on the face of the earth to get one. However, it took only 16 years for the first 50 million people to get a television, and 13 years for 50 million people to get a personal computer. It took only four years for the first 50 million users of the Internet—that is why the phrase 'Internet speed' was introduced. When we look at the adoption rates for wireless Internet, we are looking at less than a year for the first 50 million users.

Who would have thought that everyone on the planet would have access to a common global postal system in which we can all send each other mail and never have to lick a stamp? That we can all access a common global shopping center in which everybody can buy and sell and never have to circle the parking lot looking for a place to park. That we can all be part of a common global university where we can go to take classes and not be distracted by the guy next to you cracking his knuckles. Who could have imagined a common global library where we can all go to find the information we need and never have to pay an overdue fine? Who would have thought that consumers could have whatever they want, whenever and wherever they want it?

Increasingly, we must all use the word impossible with the greatest of caution. Nothing is impossible except skiing through a revolving door.

Business is about giving customers attention, solutions, and outstanding service. Consumers don't want Net advertising or mass content: they want attention. Take Federal Express, for example. Customers don't care what kind of airplanes they use. They don't care that Fed Ex has a great brand name. They care about their package number 7088792. That's what is important. There's where they get value added. If Fed Ex can pick it up, deliver it, allow the customer to track it, and do it fast, efficiently, and at a low price, that is what matters. If a company uses lots of technology to do all that, fine. But a customer's main concern is his package.

Television comedian Steven Wright quips:

> I went down the street to a 24-hour grocery. When I got there, the guy was locking the front door. I said, "Hey, the sign says you're open 24 hours." He said, "Yes, but not in a row."

We can joke, but it's clear that 24/7 customer service will be the new benchmark.

Who would have thought that customers could custom-order products from a manufacturer, send an e-mail to ask technical support questions, and visit on-line gathering places to sift, weigh, and inquire about a trade or topic of interest? Because the system is interactive, customers do not just get what they want. They get *exactly* what they want.

Who would have thought that consumers would control the supply chain and that global producers would follow their customers' lead? With the Internet acting as a continuously updated full-color catalogue of ideas, opportunities, trading potentials, critiques and attitudes, consumers can truly rule. Customer satisfaction is no longer a mere slogan, but a science. Recognizing that market-perceived quality is the customer's opinion of your products (or services) compared to those of your competitors, it is clear that customer service must be bench-marked against your best competitors and then improved from there. As more and more companies move to the Internet, consumers will constantly get improved products and services, lower costs and more choices, and a renewed attentiveness to their complaints.

Who would have believed that globalism would leverage the under-utilized human capital of developing countries so that entrepreneurs in Lima, Calcutta, Cairo, and Taipei could be integrated worldwide, making location irrelevant? Infrastructures such as roads, railroads, and seaports, though important, will become less so because all can be partially overcome by the electronic infrastructure. Consumers will increasingly demand universal paging, instant wireless access to e-mail, phone calls that can be made and received anywhere, anyplace, anytime and for any length. The new dynamic silicon of wireless devices being developed to meet the low-energy requirements of mobile technology and based on all-optical switches will be an even bigger revolution than the personal computer. Hang onto your hats. It's a small world, but I would not want to wire it.

PART IV

Limited Government/Unlimited Wealth

The twenty-first century will be as different from the twentieth as night is to day. The speed at which wealth is produced is primarily determined by the speed at which humans exchange and process information. As millions of scientists and entrepreneurs working on millions of projects can now access each other's work and breakthroughs immediately through the Internet, the multiplier effect of prosperity and growth is magnified greatly. It's the difference between an arithmetic progression: $2 + 2 = 4$; $4 + 4 = 8$; $8 + 8 = 16$; and an exponential progression: $2^2 = 4$; $4^2 = 16$; $16^2 = 256$. In other words, the world has barely scratched the surface of what is possible and what is about to become possible.

In addition, the 2000 American presidential election portends a return to market oriented public policies. Policies on welfare, education, health care, social security and energy are in a very real sense a continuation of the U-turn toward capitalism discussed in an earlier chapter. Planning is out, competition is in. Market solutions are replacing political ones. Taxes must be cut, not increased. Government must become smaller, not larger. Capitalism's institutions of private property and economic freedom suggest that social needs will be solved with private solutions. Markets inevitably squeeze out waste, efficiently communicate information, reward innovation and provide the services that everybody wants.

As government control fades and markets ascend, history suggests that both individuals and countries will prosper. Never before could it be said that the future holds "unlimited wealth." Never before could it be said that the political model will be replaced by the market model. The following chapters will continue to explain why.

The Best Is Yet To Come

CHAPTER 10

American Policy and Free Market Reforms

Welfare – Education – Health Care – Social Security – Energy

Welfare

Welfare reform in the mid 1990s, formulated by the Republicans for over two decades, and thankfully signed by President Bill Clinton, has freed people from a government driven system that promised freedom from economic wants but penalized all market-based economic activity. It was a system that said if you want a check from the U.S. government, then you must not work; you must not own anything; and you must not get married, particularly to a man who is working. The welfare system, not surprisingly, broke up families, subsidized illegitimacy, inhibited the formation of families, punished work, punished savings, and punished the spirit of enterprise. The compassionate safety net, designed with good intentions, became a snare, trapping people in poverty. Helping people to become helpless was not an act of kindness. The welfare state was about profligacy, waste and cultural destruction. Often one pays most for the things one gets for nothing.

Replacing the Aid to Families with Dependent Children (AFDC) program with Temporary Assistance to Needy Families (TANF) has been effective. It converted welfare from an entitlement that paid mostly cash benefits to needy parents into a combined cash benefit work program with a benefit contingent on meeting work requirements. The whole idea is to help people prepare for and find jobs rather than just receive checks. The program works. By the end of 1999, the national welfare caseload had declined by more than 50 percent from the 1994 peak, and welfare rolls have declined for five consecutive years.

235

The market-based welfare reforms enacted during the last decade by Wisconsin Governor Tommy Thompson, now the Secretary of Health, Education, and Human Services for President Bush, tend toward reducing welfare and increasing the opportunities of the poor. Asked to contribute to the lives of others through special services, welfare recipients interestingly improve their own lives as well. Individual dignity is being recognized. Hope and ambition are being emphasized and reborn. Accountability for jobs and family is being stressed. Personal responsibility will be valued over victimization.

The recipe for America's enormously successful pre-1965 anti-poverty program was capitalism. Minimizing both incentive reducing taxes and government regulation to encourage everyone to provide for themselves through their own work and entrepreneurship, the self-reliant family was to be the nation's main anti-poverty program. A minimal safety net of public and private support would be provided, of course, to those families who were unable or unwilling to provide for themselves. It appears that America wants to re-institute that program.

Education

Education, for whatever reason, has become the established church of the United States. It is one religion that Americans believe in. It has its own orthodoxy, its pontiffs, and its noble buildings.

-Michael Sadlier

Education is the biggest business in America. It has the

largest number of producers and customers, the most extensive and costly physical plant, and without question, impacts our most valuable raw materials. It consumes our greatest investment of taxpayers' money with the exception of national defense, and has the greatest influence on what America will be tomorrow. No wonder education is the focus of almost every political campaign. But, alas, something is very wrong. It's now understood that we no longer have the three R's in America. Instead, we have the six Rs; remedial readin,' remedial 'ritin, and remedial 'rithmetic.

The American political left is very concerned about education. Read what some of them have to say.[1]

Martin Luther King III, President of the Southern Christian Leadership Conference, tells us:

> We must continue the work my father began. Education is the key to freedom and opportunity. We basically have one supplier, the public education system, and it has become a huge bureaucracy. This bureaucracy has to be challenged. Fairness demands that every child, not just the rich, has access to an education that will help them achieve their dreams.

Dr. Dorothy Height, chair and president emeritus of the National Council of Negro Women, expresses this view:

> No parent should have to forsake their child's education for the sake of a system. No child can afford to wait even one year for a quality education. The child does not exist to serve the system—the system should serve the child.

Says the Honorable John B. Breaux, U.S. Senator (D) from Louisiana:

> I have always believed that parents should be in charge of their children's education. If parents can't choose which schools their children go to, or what subjects they are taught, or who teaches them, then what exactly are they in charge of?

And in remarks before the Senate Government Affairs Committee in 1997, Senator Joseph Lieberman made clear his position on the state of public education in Washington, DC:

> There are some who dismiss suggestions of school choice programs and charter schools out of hand, direly predicting that these approaches will 'ruin' the public schools. The undeniable reality is that the system is already in ruins.

The American political right is also concerned about education. Now let's see what some of them have to say: [2]

The Honorable Henry A. Kissinger, Chairman of Kissinger Associates, says:

> I totally believe in public education. Yet somewhere along the line we have some who equate our hugely important commitment to public education—or what we might more accurately call 'educating the public'—with a single supplier government monopoly model. As we all know, monopolies have always produced bad products at a high price. The education monopoly is no different.

238

General Colin L. Powell, U.S. Army (Ret.), former Chairman of the Joint Chiefs of Staff and currently President Bush's Secretary of State, tells us:

> I've also seen too many schools that are failing. They are trapped in fossilized bureaucracies—let's use innovation and competition to help give our children the best education possible.

And, finally, the Honorable John McCain, U.S. Senator (R) from Arizona, says:

> Freedom and self-governance are about making choices. The greatness of our free enterprise system is based on the undeniable principle that competition produces excellence. It's time that competition be allowed to work its wonders in the educational arena.

As these quotes suggest, almost everyone agrees there is something seriously wrong with America's public education system. Our children are actually worse off when they leave the system than when they enter it. In fourth grade, they were among the best performing students in the world in math and science. But by eighth grade, they're barely keeping even. And by 12th grade, they trail every other industrialized nation except Lithuania, Cyprus, and South Africa. Study after study shows that fewer than half of U.S. high school graduates can locate information in a news article, follow directions on a map, or balance a checkbook.

One American teacher asked a student, "How many wars has

the U.S. fought in its history?" The student answered, "Eight." "Please name them for me," requested the teacher. The student answered, "One, two, three, four, five, six, seven, eight." Okay, so I'm joking. But stories not much less shocking than this one are common in our schools.

What is the answer? Well, it certainly isn't money. Since 1960, public education spending has increased by over 300 percent, yet student achievement has declined in virtually every discipline. While education budgets rise, student performance levels fall. America spends more money per student than any other country in the world and paradoxically, public education flourishes because it fails to educate effectively. Falling scores only increase the demand for more money.

The often repeated scenario of "give us more money and we will do a better job" reached its climax when the Kansas City government school system under court order plowed almost unlimited amounts of tax money into its system—into magnet schools, into countless educational programs, and into the finest physical plant that money can buy. The system spent a billion dollars over and above the normal school budget, an extra $36,000 for each of the system's 36,000 students. Not surprisingly, the Kansas City school experiment reports that in terms of scope, programs, and quality of physical facilities, Kansas City's schools are the best in the world. A near doubling of property tax rates to pay for such amenities as Olympic-size swimming pools, a planetarium, greenhouses, and a working farm made Kansas City the highest per pupil spending district of the nation's 280 largest districts. But after 13 years the experiment was ended (1999) after a judge found its schools still failing and even less integrated than before. What's the problem?

The National Education Association (NEA) and the American Federation of Teachers (AFT), the unions of the education establishment, constantly cry out for more government spending. The Kansas City experiment and many others demonstrate clearly that more money is not the solution.

Show Me the Numbers

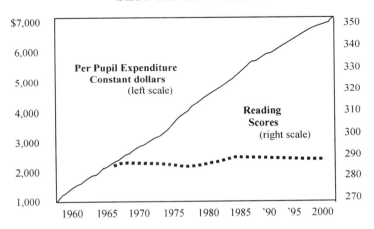

The numbers on the graph tell the story. Eric Hanushek, senior research fellow at the Hoover Institution, shows that for three decades American taxpayers have obediently coughed up increasing amounts of money for education.[3] As you can see, while funds devoted to public education have trebled, student performance has languished. While the thin black line of per pupil expenditures streaks upward, the dotted line score on reading tests remains flat. Scores on math, science, and writing reveal the same depressing result. The only possible conclusion? Kids today are dumber than they used to be. Well, maybe. Or maybe kids just got lost in huge classes. Indeed, the National Education Association argues that class sizes are too big.

241

However, the facts are that some of that increased spending has gone to lowering student-teacher ratios. Student-teacher ratios were lowered from 25.8 in 1960 to 17.3 in 1995. And what was the payoff? Overall student performance has not improved, nor have U.S. students shown any improvement in international achievement tests.

If it's not the spending, not the kids, not the class sizes, not the teachers, then what is it? In one word: monopoly. The K-12 education system in the U.S. is now literally devoid of any competitive discipline that might encourage efficiency. Most states work under a centralized school-funding policy that determines how much each of the 16,500 government school districts will get. The government has conferred state monopoly on public schools by funding them with taxpayer money, apportioning them one to an area, and then directing a steady stream of students to them according to student's residential location. Parents pay taxes to the state and have virtually no say over the operation. Parents have a difficult time abandoning poor schools or getting rid of bad teachers. They cannot select the school that is best for their child, they cannot determine the level of spending, and they cannot select the curriculum approach that best suits their child. Moving to a new school district is obviously expensive for some and out of the question for others. Enrolling their children in a private school forces the parents to pay twice. All the current escape valves are simply not practical for the average family.

Monopolies are always a problem. Monopolists serve themselves, not their customers: administrators and teachers first, students and parents last. Monopolists know that the only realistic choice for most parents is to have their kids educated by their monopoly school.

Today's government school structure is a top-down, bureaucratic, noncompetitive system. Monopolistic competitors grow inefficient because there is no threat of organizational survival. In many inner-city schools, the principal is assigned to the school, the curriculum is determined in detail by the central bureaucracy, the teachers are assigned to the school, and the students are required to attend. Everything about the school is dictatorial. Nobody has made a *choice*. And making matters even worse are iron-clad tenure laws and a pay system that rewards seniority rather than performance.

When standard achievement tests show that children are not learning much in schools, the common answer is, "We aren't paying teachers enough." Of course, the teachers' union doesn't explain how higher pay to the same teachers, in the same overcrowded schools, with the same old textbooks and the same politicized curriculum will solve students' learning problems. Now don't get me wrong—I like teachers. My wife taught for 10 years and I was a professor for 15. Higher pay for teachers was our Eleventh Commandment. So pay teachers more. But don't be surprised when that step alone doesn't stop the decline in test scores in the public schools.

Author Lewis J. Perelman states:

> In essence, the public school is America's collective farm. Innovation and productivity are lacking in American education for basically the reasons they are scarce in Soviet agriculture: absence of competition and market forces.

Even the late AFT President Albert Shanker admitted that:

Public education operates like a planned economy, a bureaucratic system in which everybody's role is spelled out in advance and there are few incentives for innovation and productivity. It's no surprise that our school system does not improve. It more resembles the communist economy than our own market economy."[4]

It has been said that public schools have become a place of detention for children placed in the care of teachers who are afraid of the principal, principals who are afraid of the school board, school boards who are afraid of the parents, parents who are afraid of the children, and children who are afraid of nobody. Where do we begin to repair this mixed-up "chain of command?" With the parents.

Until parents are in charge of their kids' education and can choose from a variety of schools, the problem is not going to go away. When the system is allowed to be competitive, new options will emerge, and education will begin to prosper the way the rest of America has. It's not a matter of left vs. right; it's a matter of right vs. wrong. Providing inner city parents the right to choose the school they would like their children to attend would have the effect of immediately shutting down schools that are no more than day-care prisons protected by their monopoly franchise. The NEA should be ashamed of defending an education monopoly that denies millions of kids a fair start in life.

Choice/Voucher

While the twenty-first century answer to education is choice, the concept of parental choice has about as many meanings as there are interested parties. Even the education establishment talks about choice in schools as long as parents and students are permitted to choose only from traditional government schools whose survival and budgetary support remain guaranteed. Indeed, teachers unions have offered advocates of serious reform merely token choice (e.g., the Milwaukee experiment that applies to a minuscule portion of the school system's students) in order to deflect demands for a thorough-going competitive overhaul.

So-called choice plans that fail to offer real alternative education models from which to choose—public schools, non-profit schools, and private for-profit schools—will never bring the benefits of competitive rivalry. An analogy would be a situation in which government food stamps could be spent only in government grocery stores. One supplier, fewer choices, and inevitably non-competition and non-consumer responsiveness. A politically driven system in which schools are not allowed to emerge spontaneously in response to what parents and students want precludes educational reform.

Suppose the government said to you: "If you relieve us from the expense of schooling your child, you will be given a voucher, a piece of paper redeemable for designated sum of money, if and only if, you use it to pay the cost of schooling your child." The sum of money might range between $2,000 and $4,000 and be enough to give parents freedom of choice. This step would reintroduce competition into the system. The stipend for each student could be used at any school the parent feels is compatible with his or her child's needs.

The major objective of educational vouchers is to drag

education out of the nineteenth century—where it has been mired for far too long—and into the twenty-first century by introducing competition on a broad scale. Free-market competition can do for education what it has done already for other areas, such as agriculture, transportation, power, communication, and, most recently, computers and the Internet.

Evidence continues to mount that vouchers do work for kids who use them. A new study of students in Washington, New York and Dayton, Ohio, conducted by researchers at Harvard, Georgetown, and the University of Wisconsin indicated that after two years, the average performance of black students who switched to private schools was 6 percent higher than that of students who stayed in public schools. The only way to uncouple poor kids from lousy schools is to give poor kids vouchers to enable their parents to have choice. Only a truly competitive education industry can empower the ultimate consumers of education services—parents and their children. Instead of schools choosing students, as they do now for the 90 percent of students who go to government schools, students and their parents would choose the school.

Choice would undoubtedly offer new paths to learning. Scientific Learning, for example, has a set of computerized programs that increase reading levels from one to three years after just six weeks of intensive effort. Could you imagine how quickly a market-driven education system would transfer this technology to their current school remedial programs? The emphasis would be "results" and not how many unionized language teachers are hired. New methods of teaching would replace old, and costs would go down just as surely as quality would go up. This happened when parcel and message delivery was opened up to competition, when the telephone monopoly was dismembered, when air travel was deregulated, when Japanese competition forced the U.S. automobile industry to change its ways, and on and on. Government schools would have to compete or close up shop. This approach has been in use in the Netherlands for 80 years, and is now used in New Zealand. It has produced academic progress, a system structured for particular students' needs, and a high level of parental satisfaction in those countries.

Public opinion polls indicate that a majority of Americans support the concept of educational choice. This is especially true among poor Americans and racial minorities, who are often trapped, without choice, in collapsing urban school systems. For years, national polls have shown that two-thirds of those surveyed favor allowing parents greater control over where their children attend school and what is taught there, and notable majorities approve descriptions of specific provisions and programs to accomplish this. A May 2000 poll conducted by the *Washington Post* revealed that 64 percent of registered voters nationwide favor education reform that would "provide parents with more alternatives such as private or charter schools if they don't want to send their child to a traditional public school." A national opinion poll recently conducted by the Joint Center for Political and Economic Studies found that 57 percent of blacks support vouchers.

Education choice would create powerful disincentives for bureaucratic growth and powerful incentives for empowerment of professionals at the school level. In a marketplace where parent and student satisfaction are crucial to a school's longevity, schools must respond to diverse family wants and needs. This can be accomplished only if the people closest to parents and students, namely, teachers and principals have ample authority.

This is not just a matter of theoretical speculation. The New York City public schools, for example, employ more than 6,000

central office personnel—an administrator/student ratio of 1 to
150. The Catholic schools of the Archdiocese of New York, a
smaller system than its public counterpart, but nevertheless the
12th largest school system in the country, employs only 30 central
office personnel—a ratio of 1 to 4,000. Political control of
schools costs more money and produces students with lower
performance; choice reverses that. The numbers are clear. On
the whole, private schools offer better education and superior
performance for less money. Consider this: currently the cost of
public school per pupil averages $7,316, or about double what
private school costs. Yet public schools, on average, deliver a
lower quality education than private schools, as evidenced by
scores on standardized achievement tests.

Competition Produces Quality

The most compelling statistics about school choice and
related reforms, however, are those that tell the tale of how many
children can and do benefit from actual programs. In less than a
decade since the first privately funded voucher programs was
formed, some 1,700 others have opened in 34 states and the
District of Columbia. And, in cities like Milwaukee, Cleveland,
Indianapolis, Phoenix, and Tampa, where school choice programs
have flourished, private individuals providing scholarships
have empowered thousands of parents to place their children in
better schools and encouraged thousands more to place their
children on waiting lists to do the same.

The first state-funded voucher program was the Ohio
legislature authorized Cleveland Scholarship and Tutoring
program. Prospering and popular, six thousand parents applied
for the original 2,000 openings for students. Have academics

improved?   A Harvard study of a thousand parents whose children were accepted into the program with a thousand parents of children who were not, is revealing.   Over two-thirds of the voucher parents were "very satisfied" versus one-third of the public school parents who said that they were "very satisfied." One-fifth of the voucher pupils showed significant gains in reading and math compared to national averages.

But is it cost-efficient?   The scholarships provided up to 90 percent of tuition costs or $2,250, about one-third of the per-pupil cost of Cleveland's public schools.   The overwhelming satisfaction with school safety, school discipline and the teaching of moral values make voucher programs the popular choice for low income and minority parents.

The issue is not public vs. private.   It is choice vs. lack of choice; voluntary association vs. legal coercion.   Americans have long enjoyed the variety of goods and services that spring from competition and the private sector.   Do you think Ford and General Motors would have improved their cars in the 1980s like they did without competition from Japan?   Do you think the computer and semi-conductor business would have driven down the costs and vastly improved the speed and quality of its products without competition?   Do you think that you would be able to buy the food, clothing and other consumer goods you do at the price you can afford if there was only one source of supply?   And yet, we have but one source of supply in public education, the government, who try to convince us there is just one "best" product for all students.   Don't different children need to be educated differently?   Don't we need schools that specialize in mathematics, in science and the arts?   Shouldn't education be an industry in which a thousand flowers bloom?   Isn't it time for thousands of free choices to be made by millions of free people in a free society?   To cross the bridge or to burn the bridge, that is the question for the National Education Association and those opposing choice.

Social Security

> With all its alluring promise that someone else will guarantee for the rainy day, Social Security can never replace the program that man's future is, after all, a matter of individual responsibility.

> -Dr. Harold Stonier

Almost 70 years ago, in 1935, government devised a system for providing an old age pension. Society Security, officially known as Old Age Survivors, Disability, and Health Insurance (OASDHI), created by the U.S. Congress, is an insurance and welfare program funded by payroll taxes on behalf of the American people. This mishmash of a "pay-as-you-go" system is a fraudulent pyramid scheme, where government forces everyone to participate. There are no trust funds accumulating the specific annuities that would be associated with a private program. Social Security is simply a system of taxing those currently in the labor force for the benefit of the system's recipients. Perhaps the greatest Ponzi scheme ever conceived, government combines an unacceptable tax with an unacceptable benefit and calls it Social Security.

Whether you're a teacher or a waitress, a bus driver or an accountant, a large part of your earnings goes to the Social Security payroll tax every pay period. If you work for somebody else, part of the tax is withheld from your paycheck, and your employer pays an equal amount on your behalf. If you work for yourself, you pay both parts. The government keeps a record of what you've paid in, but the payroll taxes you are paying now are not held by the government in an account with your name on it. Most of the money goes back out again to pay the Social Security benefits of retired people. Not only is there no trust fund building up an asset base compounding annually, but the system also perpetuates the myth that the employer pays half of the Social Security tax. When the employer pays Social Security taxes, most of that money is not available for wages, salaries, and other fringe benefits. In other words, the worker is actually paying both halves of the payroll tax.

The system has worked this way from the time President Franklin D. Roosevelt signed the legislation in 1935 and the first benefit check was issued in 1940. But things have changed since 1940, when, for each person receiving Social Security payments, there were 42 people working. By the middle of the twenty-first century, there will be only two workers for each person drawing Social Security benefits. Because of this demographic fact, payroll taxes paid will be insufficient to pay the promised benefits.

When Social Security was first established, life expectancy in the U.S. was 62 years. Since Social Security benefits didn't start until age 65, that was a smoking deal for government. Everyone was expected to die before they received their first retirement check. But now life expectancy is 76, which means we add 14 years of liability for every beneficiary in the system. Currently, the 45 million beneficiaries mean that we have added more than a half-billion years of financial liability to the system. In dollar terms, the problem is stark. If we were to take the present value of the future benefits to be paid out in Social Security and subtract from that the amount we are going to collect in Social Security payroll taxes, we are $11 trillion short.

Sometime in the not too distant future—the best estimate now is about 2015, when the baby boomers will be retiring—Social Security will begin paying out more in benefits than it is collecting in payroll taxes. Social Security's revenues will fall short of outlays by $7 trillion in 2015, ballooning to a deficit of more than $300 trillion in 2039. As a result, Social Security will face a daunting challenge: how to collect an ever-increasing tax burden just to pay benefits already promised to citizens.

When compared with private retirement plans, the Social Security program falls short on all counts. Private plans are tailored to individual preferences and lifestyles. Social Security, however, has but one plan. Strings and restrictions attached to Social Security are numerous and often arbitrary. The system limits outside earned income; it pays benefits on a monthly basis; widows lose survivorship benefits if they remarry; ad infinitum. Is it any wonder that federal employees choose to remain outside the Social Security system? Shouldn't all Americans be allowed to opt out of this rigid, inefficient and morally repugnant government-enforced monopoly and channel their hundreds of billions of dollars into private savings and new capital formation programs? Any politician who says we don't need such fundamental reform is seriously irresponsible.

If the Camel Once Gets His Nose in a Tent, His Body Will Soon Follow

Personal retirement accounts are working all over the world. Great Britain made the transition with the help of Margaret Thatcher.[5] More than 75 percent of eligible British workers have now chosen to invest their payroll taxes in private stocks and equities, and have averaged a 13 percent return on their private investments. Britain's pension pool, now worth over U.S. $1 trillion, is larger than the pension funds of all other European countries combined.

On November 6, 1981, Chile also created a system of personal retirement accounts and financed the transition without tax increases or benefit cuts. Chile also eased people's concerns by giving them the freedom to choose between the old and new systems. In the first month alone, one out of four eligible Chilean workers chose the new system. Today, more than 95 percent of eligible Chilean workers participate in the new system.

José Piñera, one of the University of Chicago-trained economists mentioned in Chapter 3, was the architect of Chile's inspiring effort to save Social Security. As he puts it:

> The new pension system gives Chileans a personal stake in the economy. A typical Chilean worker is not indifferent to the stock market or interest rates. When workers feel that they own a part of the country, not through party bosses or a Politburo, they are much more attached to the free market and a free society.

Isn't that what Americans would want also? Or, are there some among us who think the whole scheme too risky?

A worker's rate of return is based on three factors: the amount of money paid into the system, the worker's monthly benefit, and the worker's life expectancy. In general, workers born before World War II paid significantly less in taxes than they will receive in benefits— and, as a result, can expect a higher rate of return than subsequent generations. By contrast, baby boomers can expect a rate of return of less than 2 percent, and Generation Xers can expect less than 1 percent. Children born today can expect a rate of return from Social Security of almost zero, assuming that the program can pay full promised benefits.

Almost everyone has a personal stake in Social Security. Suppose you're a 35-year-old male construction worker. If your earnings are similar to those of other construction workers, you can expect a Social Security benefit of $1,351 per month in today's dollars during your retirement. Assuming you live a normal life-span, the real rate of return on the payroll taxes you and your employer paid for 46 years will be only 1.2 percent.

Now, consider what would happen if those same payroll taxes had been regularly invested, say 60 percent in stocks and 40 percent in bonds. Based on the historical performance of the markets, you could expect to retire with a $6,607 monthly benefit—an increase of $5,256 per month, or more than $64,000 per year. In this case, the real rate of return on your contributions would be 4.8 percent.

During the next 10 years, Social Security receipts are estimated to exceed payments to Social Security recipients by $2.4 trillion. President George W. Bush proposes to use about $1 trillion of that sum to finance personal retirement accounts for young workers. Does that, as Al Gore contended, "undermine Social Security" by promising "the same $1 trillion of Social Security to younger workers and the elderly at the same time?" Not at all.

Under current law, government borrows and issues special non-negotiable government bonds in return. Those bonds constitute assets of the "trust fund," counted on to finance future payments. They can be converted to cash only by collecting new taxes or borrowing. Under President Bush's plan, $1 trillion of those assets will instead be held in the form of securities in personal retirement accounts. Does replacing government IOUs with private securities weaken Social Security? Quite the opposite. The Bush plan does not affect the benefits promised to current retirees. For younger workers, the account will finance part of what otherwise would be an obligation of the trust fund. In addition, the higher yield on the personal retirement accounts will benefit both the retirees and the Social Security trust fund. In effect, the establishment of personal retirement accounts would convert a non-funded liability of $1 trillion into a fully funded liability, which strengthens rather than weakens Social Security.

Despite the recent volatility of the market, both historical experience and the logic of economic growth indicate that markets go up in the long term. Even if stocks continue to yield 7 percent a year, which is their historical average, for over 100 years, the Dow will be over 50,000 by 2025. Reducing the historic antagonism between the investor class and the working class would be greatly reduced if the investor class came to include everyone.

Nevertheless, politicians are reluctant to give up the power that goes with a government-dependent pay-as-you-go system. Even though current system retirees can expect a meager return of less than 2 percent, do not have a claim to the main part of their life long contributions, and will undoubtedly face extended retirement dates and reduced benefits, privatization is still an idea to be resisted, especially by bureaucrats.

Although Alan Greenspan has been one of the strongest opponents of privatizing Social Security, he has reversed field. Now he not only supports it, but even has a specific plan to implement it with a two-tiered approach. First, younger workers would move to a new semi-privatized plan where they would be permitted to earmark a portion of their Social Security payroll tax for investment in stocks and bonds. Meanwhile, older workers could continue in the existing plan as is. Thus, over time, all workers would be covered. Greenspan says, "A privatized defined contribution plan would, by definition, convert our Social Security system into a fully funded plan." In other words, he supports President Bush's plan.

Perhaps the next step of the Bush/Greenspan plan to allow just young workers to finance their personal retirement accounts would be a variation of Steve Forbes' plan for *all* workers. Here is his plan in a nutshell:[6]

- You would be free to choose to stay in the current system, or invest part—and eventually the lion's share—of your Social Security payroll taxes in your own personal retirement account, similar to an IRA or 401(k) plan.
- You—not the government—would own this account. It couldn't be taken away from you. In your will, you could leave your assets to your spouse, children, relatives, or even your favorite charities.
- Married couples would share benefits equally. Half your money would go into your own account, and half would go into your spouse's account. In the case of separation or divorce, you would not have to go to court to fight over the assets. They would already be yours.
- A small portion of your money would go to purchase your own private disability insurance and life insurance. Again, you—not the government—would own these insurance policies.
- You would be free to choose an investment company, and, if you want, to change investment companies. All companies would be licensed by the Securities and Exchange Commission. The system must be safe and secure.

256

- You would be free to choose your investment options from a menu of sound fiscal choices. The menu could include stock index funds, mutual funds, U.S. Treasury bonds, other forms of bonds, and bank certificates of deposit. You would be free to change investment options as you see fit. Some basic guidelines would be established to protect your economic security. Obviously, investing in Honduran racehorses or Asian derivatives is not going to be part of this new system.
- You would receive a periodic printed statement detailing the performance of your account. The Internet would allow you to check the status of your account on-line—day or night—with your own secure password.
- You—not the government—would choose your retirement age. You could work with a financial planner to figure out how much money you would like to retire on, set your own personal goals, and know that all your hard work was really building toward something special.
- The assets you build up in your personal retirement account would not be subject to federal income tax. The federal tax on capital gains would be eliminated to help maximize the return on your money. The "death" tax would be abolished so that your spouse and children could inherit your assets without suffering financially at the hands of the federal government. Most people do not realize that under current law, your Individual Retirement Account can be taxed at rates upwards of 85 percent. How is this possible? When you die, your IRA becomes subject to estate taxes that can run as high as 55 percent. When your children try to withdraw the money in the IRA, it is subject to personal income taxes. All that nonsense would disappear under this new plan.

- Undergirding the entire system would be the assurance that the federal government would guarantee you a minimum benefit. A safety net is absolutely essential. If the stock market crashes—or if, for some other reason, the money in your account when you retire does not meet the guaranteed minimum—the federal government would make up the difference.

And now here's the big secret. A partial privatization of Social Security, our retirement funds, is already going on in the United States at a furious rate. In 1985, private pension plans, IRA's, and 401(k) plans had total account balances of $3.8 trillion dollars. By the year 2000, these balances had grown to nearly $14 trillion dollars. In the decade of the 90s, these balances grew by an impressive 10% per year. The accounts are self-managed and directly funded by the individual. IRAs and 401(k's) grew by a stunning 19% and 14% per year over that same period. Presently, 44 million American families have at least one IRA account, and another 48 million have a 401(k) account (although there is overlap, as 33% of the IRA account holders also have a 401(k).

Clearly, Americans are taking matters into their own hands. A survey by the Investment Company Institute, in 1990, of 1,366 households who had a 401(k) account revealed that 44% expected their 401(k) account to be the primary source of income during their retirement. Another 26% thought that a traditional pension plan, or their own savings and investments outside the 401(k) plan, would be their mainstay. Only a mere 6% indicated that they intended to rely on Social Security for their primary income in retirement.

Stock options and 401(k) plans have made thousands of ordinary workers millionaires during the past five years. Let there be no doubt: the stock market pays off best for those who are in it for the long run and not for short term speculation.

The performance of private retirement plans has been so stunning for the last 15 to 20 years that we could just announce that Social Security was finished, pay off all the present liabilities as they come due, and close it down, except for one main problem. Not all Americans have IRA or 401(k) plans. In the simplest way of thinking about it, privatizing Social Security is really about extending the proven results of America's private retirement plans to all Americans, and providing everyone with the opportunity to earn money compounding at 6 to 8 percent or even more a year compared to the 1 or 2 percent of Social Security.

The arguments for privatization, whether the Bush plan, the Forbes plan, or something similar, will eventually carry the day. Not only would they provide a retirement income two to three times higher than Social Security, but they would also increase the savings in the economy, broaden stock ownership, and give individuals the opportunity to control their own retirement.

While Social Security is a complex issue, government rhetoric should not discourage the interested citizen from trying to understand or get involved in the issue. For help in dispelling the fog and the myths about Social Security and Social Security reform, visit the National Center for Policy Analysis' Web site at http://www.mysocialsecurity.com. There, you can plug in a few pieces of personal, job, and financial information and compare for yourself the financial differences resulting from market investments and those from relying on the current Social Security system.

Health Care/Insurance

The thesis of this section is simple and comes from the President of the National Center for Policy Analysis (NCPA), John Goodman: "If we want to solve the nation's health care crisis, we must apply the same common-sense principles to medical care that we apply to other goods and services."[7] Goodman has been making that argument to Congress for almost 20 years.

In a recent *New York Times/CBS News* poll, almost 80 percent of the respondents agreed that the American "health care system is headed toward a crisis because of rising costs." The irony is that health care costs are rising because, for individual patients, medical care is cheap, not expensive.

On the average, patients pay only 5¢ out-of-pocket for every dollar they spend in hospitals. The remainder is paid by private and public health insurance. Patients pay less than 19¢ out-of-pocket for every dollar they spend on physicians' services, and they pay less than 24¢ out of every dollar they spend on health care of all types. Patients, therefore, have an incentive to purchase hospital services until, at the margin, they're worth only 5¢ on the dollar and to purchase physicians' services until they are worth only 19¢ on the dollar. The wonder is that we don't spend even more than we do.

Health care is often said to be a necessity. However, there are other necessities such as food, clothing, housing, and transportation. If we paid for any of these items the way we pay for health care, we would face a similar crisis. If we paid only 5¢ on the dollar for food, clothing, or housing, for example, costs would explode in each of those markets.

If we are to control health care costs, we must be prepared to make tough decisions about how much to spend on medical care vs. other goods and services. So far, we have avoided such choices, confident that health care spending can be determined by "needs," rather than by choices among competing alternatives. In this respect, the U.S. health care system is unique. The United States is the only country in the world where people can consume medical care almost without limit, unconstrained by market prices or by government rationing.

The medical marketplace today is far from normal. In a normal market, producers search for ways to satisfy consumer needs at a price consumers are willing to pay. Demand is a given. The problem for producers is to reduce the costs of meeting that demand. In health care, the opposite is true. All too often, consumer preferences are regarded as irrelevant. Producers decide what their costs are going to be and then wrestle with getting consumers to pay those costs—through out-of-pocket payments, through employers and insurance companies, or through the government.

In a normal market, increases in sales are universally regarded as good. The more consumers buy, the more their needs are being met. If domestic automobile sales increased each year as a percent of our gross national product, most people would cheer. In health care the opposite is true. The annual increase in health care services is viewed not as a benefit, but as a burden.

In the topsy-turvy world of health care, what would normally be viewed as "good" is considered "bad," and vice versa. Thus, in order to truly understand the medical marketplace, we have to discover all of the ways in which government has undermined normal market forces.

The potential demand for health care is virtually unlimited. Even if there were a limit to what medical science can do (which, over time, there isn't), there is an almost endless list of ailments that can motivate our desire to spend. About 83 million people suffer from insomnia, 70 million from severe headaches, 32 million from arthritis, 23 million from allergies, and 16 million from bad backs. Even when the illnesses are not real, our minds have incredible power to convince us that they are.

If the only way to control health care costs is to have someone choose between health care and money (that is, choosing between spending money on health care vs. on other goods and services), who should that someone be? There are only two fundamental alternatives: the patients themselves or a health care bureaucracy that is ultimately answerable to government. If the best is yet to come, the solution must start with consumers.

Patient Power

The United States of America was founded on the proposition that individuals possess "unalienable" rights. These are not favors granted by government, but rights of action derived from individual membership in the human community—or, as our Founders called them, "God-given." Individuals cannot be used against their will to satisfy the wants and needs of others.

Unfortunately, our current health care mess is a complete abandonment of these moral principles, and a wholly opposite view of rights has come to prevail. Today, individuals are entitled to make demands on others. Our government has legislated the "right" to medical treatment, thus enslaving those who are required to contribute to the health care costs of others.

What really happens when government takes from Sue and gives to Dwight?

If Sue's dues are Dwight's rights, is liberty for belles really what it's cracked up to be?

> When a law bestows a right,
> It rightfully should be,
> Enjoyed by every single soul,
> that's equality.
>
> But when the law grants privilege,
> It's time for you to fret,
> If you're the one who's got to give,
> While others git to get.
>
> Take health care by the government.
> When these accrue to Dwight,
> And bills for same are sent to Sue,
> That's not an equal right.
>
> Such laws should be repealed at once,
> Legislatively.
> In search of equal rights for Sue,
> Let's E R A s e[8]

But we cannot erase the fact that about 44 million Americans do not have health insurance and their number has been rising. How did that happen?

Health insurance coverage in the U.S., whether provided by the employer or the state, has had the side effect of making all responsible parties of health care indifferent to the cost of service. When you try to protect people from the costs of care, neither consumers or providers have incentives to lower those costs. For example, even typical and minor medical expenses in the U.S., such as treating cuts or a cold, are insured. From an economist's point of view, such comprehensive insurance is not actually insurance at all but rather an expensive form of price illusion. There's no end to the demand for something when someone else is paying for it. This puts great pressure on the system, driving unit costs of health care provision up, thus making insurance for the uninsured even further out of reach.

Government makes the situation even worse by responding to the problems of the uninsured by expanding insurance coverage still further. Then, they try to contain the inevitable price spiral by rationing services and adopting so-called managed care systems. Putting health care in the hands of bureaucrats and accountants, instead of doctors and health care professionals, is hardly the model for the future.

At least two government policies have contributed to this problem and made it much worse than it needs to be. The first is the tax law. Most people who work for large companies receive health insurance as a fringe benefit. Because the health insurance premiums are deductible expenses for employers, many workers effectively avoid a 28 percent income tax, a 15.3 percent tax for Social Security (half of which is paid by employers), and a state and local income tax. Thus, as much as 50 cents of every dollar spent on health insurance through employers is effectively paid by government. Economics teaches that we get what we subsidize. About 90 percent of the people who have private health insurance obtain it through an employer.

In contrast, the unemployed, the self-employed, and most employees of small businesses get little or no tax subsidy. If they do have health insurance they must first pay taxes and then purchase the insurance with what is left over. Isn't it interesting that 34 million people who have no health insurance pay higher tax rates to fund the $60 billion annual tax break for those who do have employer-provided insurance?

A second source of the problem is state government regulations—specifically, laws that mandate what is covered under health insurance plans. Examples of mandated coverage include alcoholism, drug abuse, AIDS, mental illness, acupuncture, and in vitro fertilization. In 1970, there were only 30 mandated health insurance benefit laws in the United States. Today, there are at least one thousand. Coverage for heart transplants is mandated in Georgia, and for liver transplants in Illinois. Minnesota mandates coverage for hairpieces for bald people. Mandates cover marriage counseling in California, pastoral counseling in Vermont, and deposits to a sperm bank in Massachusetts.

There are more than 240 health-related professions in the United States, ranging from chiropractors and naturopaths to athletic trainers. Every year, these special interest groups descend upon state legislatures demanding more and more regulations—and more and more mandated coverage. These regulations drive the cost of health insurance even higher. The NCPA estimates that as many as one out of every four people who lack health insurance has been priced out of the market by these costly regulations.

A primary reason health care costs are rising is that most spending on health care is done with someone else's money rather than the patient's. As a result, patients avoid making tough choices between health care and other goods and services. The most wasteful kind of health insurance is insurance for small medical bills. These are the expenses over which patients exercise the most discretion and for which opportunities for waste and abuse are greatest. By the time an insurance company and all third party interests get through processing a twenty-five dollar physician's bill, the cost will be fifty dollars—thus doubling the cost of medical care.

Besides being very costly, the way we do health insurance is also strange. The company bets that you'll stay well; you bet that you won't. So, you invest your money and hope that they win. But if you win, you live long enough to grow into a feeble prisoner of your own age or a nursing home inmate who cannot leave, who hates the bad food, who is shoved around by stressed-out attendants, sedated by vegetative drugs, and more often than not, confused with the criminally insane. Go figure.

Medical Savings Accounts: The Solution

The alternative to third-party insurance is individual self-insurance. The alternative to having third parties pay every medical bill is to have people pay most medical bills with their own money. From an economist's viewpoint, American health care policy is in a completely predictable cost-and-service death spiral. People who should be making decisions, patients and doctors, aren't. Rationing and managed care solutions are doomed to failure because they require the provider to be antagonistic to the consumer.

The National Center for Policy Analysis, for nearly two decades, has conducted studies and concluded that insurance should be provided for catastrophic medical costs and that 80-85 percent of the rest should be transacted with the medical profession on a cash or quasi-cash basis.[9] Automobile casualty insurance works that way. Car owners do not go to their insurers for minor repairs, or to fill their gas tanks, or to get an oil change. They pay these costs out of pocket. However, they do go to their insurance company when they have an accident and significant costs are incurred.

In the same way, medical savings accounts would give consumers a special tax-protected account out of which they could pay for out-of-pocket health care costs. The alternative to having large bureaucracies limit spending decisions with arbitrary rules and regulations is to let people make their own decisions. Many economists who have studied the health insurance market believe that allowing people to choose a high-deductible insurance policy and put the savings (from lower premiums) in individual medical savings accounts would be the best way to make the system competitive and, thus, lower health costs. The vast majority of people would have, fairly quickly, accumulated savings far in excess of the annual deductible. If they did not spend all these savings, they could use the funds for post-retirement medical expenses or as a supplement to retirement pensions. The way to control health care costs is to give employees incentives to economize and be disciplined shoppers.

Singapore is an example of a city-state that has built its entire health care system around individual self-insurance. Singapore's workers are required to put 6 percent of their income into medical savings accounts every year. The share of gross domestic product in Singapore that goes to health care is just 25 percent of what the U.S. spends, without significant differences in the quality of health care. In fact, they specifically try to avoid the American system, seeking "to avoid unrestricted and open ended medical insurance, which leads to the provision of unnecessary medical services and escalating premiums." Hong Kong has adopted the same approach to containing its health care costs.

Self-insurance through medical savings accounts would be the most important first step we could take to reduce the numbers of the uninsured. Driving medical costs down through competition is critical. The other complementary policy is to drive costs down by improving the whole information system.

Health Information System

> The doctor was busy and it took hours to check all of his patients. Down to Mr. Smith, the doctor apologized to the old man saying, "I hope you didn't mind waiting so long." Mr. Smith said, "No problem. But it is a shame you couldn't see my illness in its early stages."
>
> - Milton Berle

In Bill Gates' book, *Business at the Speed of Thought*, he tells of a new Microsoft employee who was called home because his mother had suffered a mild stroke. When she was well enough to leave the hospital, Mrs. Jones (not her real name) stayed with her sister while her son completed arrangements to move her to Seattle to be near him. While Mrs. Jones largely recovered, she was never able to live on her own again, and her periods of good health were filled with additional hospital stays treating increasingly acute problems.

The medical events of the last two years of Mrs. Jones's life demonstrate the best and the worst aspects of American health care. She received good care, including a number of state-of-the-art procedures, from three different hospitals and from more than a dozen physicians in two different states. As her physical abilities declined, her middle-class family was able to find decent facilities providing greater degrees of care. While Medicare and her private insurance paid most of the bills, the family agreed to pay the rest. Her many doctors, nurses, and other caregivers were professional, kind, and Mrs. Jones retained her dignity until her death.

The American health care system, however, did not work very well for the Jones' situation. When Mrs. Jones left the first hospital for her sister's hometown 30 miles away, a lapse of communication between doctors led to her medication being kept at full strength when she should have been on a declining dosage. By the time she arrived at her sister's house, side effects of the high dosage required her to be hospitalized immediately. But unfortunately, her records didn't come with her, and a number of expensive tests had to be redone. While her final three-week hospital stay did not involve any surgical procedures, the brief period cost another $25,000.

These and other problems went on even though Mrs. Jones had family members working on her behalf. Her son and daughter-in-law spent dozens of hours standing in line at one agency or on the phone with another. And it took a year before they could convince one hospital to stop billing them for services that had been paid in full.

Because of the many hospitals, physicians, clinics, pharmacies, care facilities, and public and private agencies involved, the amount of paperwork was unbelievable. Reconciling bills was a whole procedure to itself. Using colored Post-it notes, blue if a bill had been submitted to Medicare, yellow if it had gone through Medicare and been submitted to a private insurance company, red if the bill had been returned because of errors, and green if the bill had gone all the way through the system and was ready to be paid.[10]

Who would want to count the number of people and all the paperwork involved in Mrs. Jones's case? For every doctor, nurse, or some type of health practitioner involved with her, there must have been a dozen others doing the billing for the hospital, the doctor's office, Medicare, the insurance company, the pharmacy, and others. Experts have estimated that 25 percent of our nation's total medical costs are wrapped up in documentation and paperwork. Doctors openly admit that the fun of medicine is gone because of paperwork, excessive documentation and the constant threat of lawsuits. If we simply reduced the overhead of paperwork in health care from 25 percent to 15 percent, projected drug benefit costs could be paid for the next decade. Better health information systems will reduce costs and improve quality.

Until all doctors, labs, blood banks, pharmacists, hospitals, radiologists, and other health professionals can write, obtain, and share the medical information necessary to prescribe, monitor, chart, and bill for procedures and other services, costs will only go up. When caregivers begin to take advantage of recently developed technologies, costs will drop significantly. Health care will not only become better and more efficient, but the nurse's familiar phrase, "the doctor is in" will also become, "Please stand closer to your computer—the doctor is in." Many futurists are saying that "health kiosks" at the local mall, able to measure vital signs and diagnose problems, may replace many of our visits to the doctor in the near future.

Health data, information and knowledge in the future will not only be in the doctor's organic container (his/her mind), but will be found in the entire system's ceramic container (health care information stored in computer systems around the world). The practice of health care will be revolutionized when all health care professionals invest in digital information systems that will analyze, track, and make available all the needed information. Everyone wins. When everyone has access to an entire data base of medical knowledge, costs will fall, health care will improve, and society will be the winner.

One demographic trend of many is cited here as to why something must be done soon. Children under the age of 5, on average, receive eight prescription drugs per year. That trend, then, declines for the next 40 years down to four. However, at age 45, the trend reverses, and from that point on, for the rest of a person's life, the amount of prescription drugs used every year accelerates. The trend peaks at age 76 and older, where people average 18 prescription drugs per year. The U.S., demographically, is about to enter its high-health needs decades. The system must be fixed.

The fundamental problem, however, is more than just medical savings accounts and information. The question is whether and how much government should be involved in medicine. It is one thing to protect the rising costs of health care and quite another to think that an institutionalized government system would reduce them. It is one thing to demonize the pharmaceutical companies as excessively profitable as Senator Clinton and former Vice President Al Gore incessantly do, and quite another to think that government will ensure the quality of medicine we have come to enjoy.

Read what Dr. Gunnar Biörck, an eminent Swedish professor of medicine and head of the department of medicine at a major Swedish hospital has to say:

> The setting in which medicine has been practiced during thousands of years has been one in which the patient has been the client and employer of the physician. Today the State, in one manifestation or the other, claims to be the employer and, thus, the one to prescribe the conditions under which the physician has to carry out his work. These conditions may not—and will eventually not—be

restricted to working hours, salaries and certified drugs; they may invade the whole territory of the patient-physician relationship. If the battle of today is not fought and not won, there will be no battle to fight tomorrow.[11]

Energy

Every source of energy has its critics: electricity is fine, but not if you have to use coal or water or nuclear to generate it; windmills kill birds; oil spills, and it, like coal, is high in carbon content and dirty; solar takes up too much land; natural gas is fine, but don't drill near me and for heaven's sake don't send a pipeline through my backyard. Don't even think about mentioning nuclear. Nevertheless, America now consumes almost 100 quadrillion British Thermal Units of energy a year. Automobiles, factories, airplanes, tractors, computers, kidney machines, radios, and DVD's are just a fraction of the items needing energy to work. By 2020, America will consume 125 quads of energy, a 25 percent shortfall from the current supply. Where will we get it? And how?

Unfortunately, America's energy infrastructure is woefully inadequate. We must modernize it by repairing and expanding the outdated network of transmission lines, refineries, and pipelines now in place. We need more electrical generation. Almost 50 refineries have been closed since 1992 and no new ones have been built for 25 years. By keeping an iron grip on the nations interstate pipeline system, the Federal Energy Regulatory Commission, FERC, has discouraged companies like El Paso from adding the capacity needed to handle times of peak demand. Pipeline operators have had little incentive to add capacity since the 1992 imposition of price caps, which replaced a time when companies could charge rates that would earn them a fair rate of return on invested capital. Price caps and controls in whatever

272

form, turn energy problems into disaster and then catastrophe.

The California energy blackouts resulted, in part, from government putting caps on the price of retail electricity and setting rates for alternative energy below cost. The operators simply closed down, the export of power out of California rose 85 percent, electricity supply in the state fell 3,000 megawatts, and the artificially low prices created no incentive whatsoever to conserve. The result: brownouts, rolling blackouts and turning intersections into demolition derbies.

While deregulation of electricity in California did not work because of price controls and other regulations imposed by government, it has worked in other parts of the country. Regional markets were created that matched supply and demand, competitive energy exchanges were created that included all of the power plants in a multi-state region, and new power producers multiplied like rabbits. Trading electricity into and out of the region was encouraged. As deregulation makes markets more efficient, a suite of Internet tools provide the up-to-the-minute pricing information so that informed business decisions can be made. The transaction from production to consumption of electricity happens at the speed of light. Putting real market information in the hands of all decision makers is crucial. The Internet does just that. Markets work.

The common-sense path forward for America's energy future is enhanced energy efficiency, a realistic conservation effort, and most important, enhanced domestic production using an entire array of supply alternatives: gas, oil, coal, hydroelectric, hydrogen, photovoltaics, and perhaps even nuclear.

Interestingly, natural gas will be the main fuel for the next few decades. Electrical generation will increasingly be fired by natural gas; the fuel of the hydrogen economy for transportation (the fuel cell economy) will be extracted from natural gas or propane; and all the other normal uses for natural gas will make gas America's main fuel.

The Best Is Yet To Come

Natural gas should meet all the reasonable wishes of environmental groups and users. The amount of carbon emissions from the straight combustion of natural gas is half that of oil and coal for the same energy output. It is cheap and abundant. The energy content of a standard unit of gas (thousand standard cubic feet, Mscf) is about one-sixth of the energy content in a barrel of oil, while its price has historically been one-eighth the price of oil or less. The source of this gas will come from the massive gas reserves in deep offshore Gulf of Mexico or the very large known gas supplies in Alaska that can either be liquified or brought directly by pipeline that connects to the continuously expanding Canadian pipeline system.

Although innovative technologies such as fuel cell vehicles, hydrogen, distributed energy, and photovoltaics will all come on like gangbusters in the 21st century, it is my guess that the petroleum industry will not only play a big part in the new century, but it will prosper.

The two potential energy sources for the long term future will probably be nuclear fission and fusion for stationary energy (i.e. electrical power), and hydrogen for moveable energy (i.e. transportation fuel). Hydrogen, propelled into the world economy as a hydrocarbon-derived fuel during the early part of the century will eventually have to originate from non-hydrocarbons, mainly water. Such a transition will require incredible technological developments. Akin to the shift from steam to internal combustion engines in the last century, the ongoing shift to natural gas, and then hydrogen, will result in sweeping changes to virtually all physical infrastructure and all associated economic and social norms.

In the meantime, we are not running out of oil. We are not running out of gas. Hydrocarbons can continue to provide the robust interim energy solutions toward the hydrogen based economy for another two hundred years. Thankfully, the transition will take less than a hundred.

CHAPTER 11

The Best Is Yet To Come

Famous Yale economist, Irving Fischer, a week before the 1929 stock market crash that led to the Great Depression said, "Stocks have reached what looks like a permanently high plateau."

- Encyclopedia Britannica

Economists, including myself, have found that forecasting is very difficult—especially if it's about the future. In fact, the moment you forecast you know that you are going to be wrong—you just don't know when and in which direction. Eventually we learn that those who live by the crystal ball must learn to eat cracked glass. Nevertheless, we always like to make our projections to the nearest tenth of a percentage point to prove we have a sense of humor. My motto these past years has been, "Give them a number or give them a date, but never give them both." And never underestimate the power of a platitude when explaining your forecast. More than one person has told me to stop: for if you forecast wrong, nobody will forget it, but if you forecast right, nobody will remember it. Nevertheless, it is my dad's comment that keeps me encouraged (and humbled): "Your guess, I guess, is liable to be as good a guess as somebody else's guess."

You've heard the story of Albert Einstein dying, going to heaven and meeting St. Peter at the gate: Unfortunately, the Einstein mansion was not quite completed and St. Peter told him that he would have to live with three roommates for a couple of months.

The first roommate introduced himself by saying that he had an IQ of 180. Einstein returned the greeting by assuring the fellow they would have a great time talking about the theory of relativity.

The second roommate was quick to boast that he had an IQ of 120. Einstein replied, "Terrific, we can discuss the quantum theory of mechanics and examine some mathematical equations."

The third roommate sheepishly made his way up to Einstein and told him his IQ was only 80.

Einstein paused, gave him a long look and asked, "Where do you think interest rates will be going this year?"

So here goes. But remember, you will always find some Eskimo ready to instruct the Saharans on how to cope with heat waves.

The Forecast

As this is written, (Summer, 2001), the stock market's irrational exuberance and the dot-com meltdown are behind us. But, the energy problems in California, high energy costs for the country, and the monetary liposuction performed on the economy by the Federal Reserve System in 2000-2001 in response to the post Y2K computer glitch problem, are still playing themselves out. As long as the Fed assumes there is an inflation threat while prices are plummeting everywhere and the Democrats in Congress think that tax cuts cost money, the economy is caught between the dog and the fire hydrant.

Stock market agonies, however, reflect only a minor part of

what is occurring in the digital economy. The Internet revolution has just begun. While companies have restructured, flattening hierarchies and customizing products, the new, niche markets necessitate innovation at an even faster pace. The three million digital switches that exist for every human on the planet and the half-billion PCs, one for every 13 people, is just the opening salvo. Hundreds of millions of mobile phone users will soon number a billion, which will only enhance the ongoing globalization. Anytime one paradigm replaces another, hunter and gatherer with agriculture, agriculture with the industrial age, and now the industrial with the technological age, the existing power structures fight for their disappearing lives.

The turbulence is reflected in the rising tide of envy towards America (globalization equals capitalism equals America), the mounting opposition to free trade by the unions, environmentalists and the anti-growth crowd, the fear of traditionalists with the upcoming breakthroughs in genetics, modified food manufacturing, the regeneration of human organs and the social and moral dangers of genetic manipulation. Information have nots and want nots are angry about the polarization of wealth; the fears of the digital divide are widely held; and the natural resistance of the speed of change going on in economies, finance, family life, resource use and religion seems to be constantly upsetting.

The convergence of the Internet and digital technology with biotechnology and its bio-digital capabilities will make the biological revolution an integral part of the ongoing turbulence. Pharmaceuticals as chemistry will eventually be replaced with pharmaceuticals as biology—your biology. And, information technology itself in the form of bio-chips or even DNA based computing will reform communication technologies again and again.

The first decade of the twenty-first century won't even begin

277

to clarify the massive changes dramatically affecting the future of human history. We are bound to be surprised by the reversals, breakthroughs, upsets, volatile swings, and even luck and chance. For now, though, we can say this.

Productivity growth, the fundamental driver of prosperity, is high. The U.S. continues to be number one in the world in technology, health care, financial services, knowledge creation, biotechnology, computers, dynamic silicon, commercial banking, the Internet, pharmaceuticals, media, waste treatment and manufacturing efficiency, among many other things. These will drive our economy for years to come. With fewer new entrants into the labor force, unemployment is unlikely to rise as much as in past downturns and the demographic changes to be mentioned will continue to boost the pool of our investment savings.

While the pain of the trillions of dollars lost in the stock market cannot be overlooked, the benefits should not be underestimated. The U.S. is currently in the process of feverish adjustment with a flurry of bankruptcies, restructuring, mergers and buyouts, all of which will positively reshape the economic landscape again. It is the risk element in our capitalistic system which produces prosperity. Risk always brings out the ingenuity and resourcefulness of entrepreneurs, which insure the success of enough ventures to keep the economy growing. The stock market difficulties in 2000 and 2001 will shake out the flakier firms and business models, and will leave the stronger firms to lead a new phase of wealth creation. Growth will be robust.

Interestingly, while there are no other world competitive powers on the horizon, opportunities for U.S. companies to invest and operate in Japan and other countries are numerous. The world is opening up. Both China and India are lowering tariffs. Latin American is poised to be an economic miracle.

278

Both Western and Eastern Europe are set to cast off the debilitating socialist policies that so menaced and destroyed their economies. World investment and trade opportunities will proliferate. The golden age of American agriculture is yet to come.

Capitalism will produce more wealth in the next twenty-five years than all the people who have ever lived produced in the last two thousand five hundred years. Gross world product will increase from just under $30 trillion in 2001 to over $60 trillion in 2025. Twenty-five years from now the Dow Jones will be considerably higher than 50,000, per capita income in the U.S. will have surpassed $60,000 and America's government, currency, language and economic system will be emulated by scores of countries throughout the world. As machines work and people think, as technological change accelerates, and as wealth has more to do with ideas than it does with raw materials, there is at least one obvious conclusion: When wealth is connected to ideas and ideas are synergistic and unlimited, the amount of wealth the world can produce has no topside.

The Triumph of Capitalism

Capitalism has been as unmistakable a success as socialism has been a failure. But here is the part that is hard to swallow. It has been the Friedmans, Hayeks, von Mises who have maintained that capitalism would flourish and that socialism would develop incurable ailments. All three have regarded capitalism as the "natural" system of free men; all have maintained that left to its own devices capitalism would achieve material growth more successfully than any other system. From this admittedly impressionistic and incomplete sampling

279

I draw the following discomforting generalization: The farther to the right one looks, the more prescient has been the historical foresight; the farther to the left, the less so.

- Leftist Professor Robert Heilbroner

The dawn of the twenty-first century finds the State in a defensive and contracting role. The world is beginning to understand freedom, markets without boundaries and the need for a reduced role for government. The sharp challenge to statism, starting over twenty years ago with Thatcher and Reagan, is now a common theme. A resurgent capitalism and the dramatic arrival of new technologies are laying a fresh base for prosperity. The planet is moving away from the political model to the market model. Privatization and deregulation have become the preferred policies for stabilizing a government's finances and creating a platform for prosperity. Information has always been the main ingredient of power, but it was always the kings, queens, presidents, and generals who had it. With decentralized information, however, comes decentralized power. CNN, Fox News, the Internet, the World Wide Web, and hundreds of millions of telephone calls each hour shift power from government authorities to individuals. Microelectronics is pulling decision making downward and outward from central authorities of all kinds—hence, a huge thrust toward market solutions and away from political ones. The enlightened self-interest of human beings does not have to be managed, planned or controlled. Most people realize that the market is. Gravity is. Markets happen. Markets work. And because they do, the new century will be characterized by wealth production of unimaginable proportions.

The Best Is Yet To Come

As the commanding heights of ownership and control are transferred country by country from government to free markets; as the cords of poverty are broken by the victory of freedom and unleashed dynamic capitalism; as homes are titled, crops are deeded, and businesses get articles of incorporation in places where capitalism gets its first opportunity; and as free trade and entrepreneurs become the main drivers of the system, prosperity throughout the world is inevitable and mutually beneficial.

Capitalism works because markets work. Capitalism works because even selfish people can make a contribution because they, like everybody else, must deliver something that others want to buy. Mutual gains from voluntary exchange happen in capitalism because it is in everybody's self-interest to make it happen.

Capitalism distinguishes itself from all other methods of organizing production in that it acts as a check on plunder by elevating the mutual benefits of trade. Voluntary exchanges create wealth even when nothing new is produced. A math book traded from the shelf of a non-mathematician to someone who can use it, for even a dollar, benefits both parties. The world is now slightly richer because there were positive consequences of that trade which depended little on the benevolence of the book buyer or book seller. Self-interest and the benefits accruing from exchange moves things forward productively.

Bill Gates, billionaire founder of Microsoft, could be the most selfish or the most altruistic person in the world—but unless he produces the right product at the right price and delivers it to the right place and at the right time, he will not be successful regardless of his heart.

Adam Smith, the first and probably the best economist ever, can be paraphrased this way: the butcher does not slaughter, slice, package, refrigerate, and then sell the beef because he loves you. Indeed, he might love just himself. The customer, however, ends up being the main beneficiary of that whole process. "Even though a person intends only his own gain, he is led as if by an invisible hand to promote an end which was no part of his intention," said Smith. When it comes to economics and prosperity, that statement is probably the most important truth ever written.

Think about it. Capitalism is an economic system that efficiently produces wealth, often using as its main tool a very selfish human being. It works for both sinners and saints. Yes, heart attitudes and faith are all determining when it comes to salvation and an overall enjoyment of this life and a chance for the next. But capitalism does not depend on the redeemed or altruist heart to do its work. Under capitalism, even the egotist must shift his focus away from himself and ask, "What can I do to serve you? What can I produce to make you happy?" A capitalist must spend almost every waking minute thinking about what they can do for someone else. A successful entrepreneur must be able to see needs and meet them.

No wonder capitalism has emerged as the system of choice throughout the world to produce wealth and higher standards of living. It naturally creates incentives to productively use everybody, regardless of their religion, their race, their education, and their idiosyncrasies. Because the impersonal market of capitalism separates economic activities from political views, it protects all of us from being discriminated against for reasons that have nothing to do with our productivity.

While capitalism seldom produces the managed, neat and tidy system that bureaucrats like to envision, it always produces dynamic innovation and constant change. When mistakes are made, its markets are self-correcting. Competitive capitalism is a great "flushing system," a perpetual cycle of destroying the old and inefficient way of doing things with something better. Innovation replaces tradition. The present replaces the past and looks to the future.

The historical debate is over. Capitalism has no rivals. The ideas of Marx, Engels, Lenin, and Mussolini—and the centrally planned alternatives of communism, socialism, and fascism—all self-destructed for one main reason: they did not work. The planned economy turned out to be an idea where everything is included in the plans except economy. It was built on a faulty premise of public ownership and no personal freedom. The history of every conceivable alternative for producing wealth leaves us with only one viable conclusion: freedom and free markets. When freedom proceeds, prosperity follows. When freedom leads, the mutually beneficial exchanges of capitalism relentlessly move nations forward. The spontaneous order, described by Adam Smith, F.A. Hayek, and Milton Friedman, produce a marketplace in which cooperation and competition coexist peacefully to produce progress. As countries become freer, they inevitably become wealthier. The 20 percent of the world's countries with the largest amount of economic freedom produce, on average, over ten times as much wealth per capita as the 20 percent with the least economic freedom. The twenty-first century will make prosperity, rather than poverty, the natural condition.

Demographics: A Choice Already Happened

Early in 2001, the United Nations Population Division released highlights of a major new report on world population prospects for the next half century. Who would have guessed?

The United States will be in the demographic catbird seat for the next fifty years.

While a global surge in the number of older people is now occurring because of a worldwide health care explosion, not every country suffers equally. In 2050, more than a third of China's citizens will be 60 or older; in Japan almost one-half will be 60 or older. But the United States, which is favorably disposed to immigration and will probably take half of all the newcomers absorbed by developed countries, will remain distinctively young compared to the West and most developed countries. The UNPD estimates that, in 2050, the median age in the U.S. will be 41 (it is currently 36), compared with 49 in the rest of the developed countries. No other now-developed country would have such a young population.

Today, there are two Americans for every Russian. In 2050, the ratio will be four to one; there will be a four-to-one ratio with Japan. To the extent that population matters in international affairs, America's demographic prospects would seem to support an even greater U.S. global influence in the years ahead.

Another important demographic fact is that the largest generation of births in American history, the baby boomers, are nearing their peak in earning and spending power. Nearly 75 million people between the ages of 35 and 55 will have a dramatic impact on the economy and bring with it another boom. As many demographers have noted, an economy's growth is strongly predetermined by its birth numbers: the greater the numbers, the greater the generation's effect. The creative skills and financial assets of these "boomer entrepreneurs" will propel the economy to new heights.

Trade Multiplies Choice

Few things in this world are as inimical to the progress of people, particularly the poor, as protectionism. To achieve economic growth and avoid moving backward, people need the chance to sell their services and goods as much as possible. The primary rationale for free trade is not that exporters should gain larger markets, but that consumers should have more choice. Of course, the former is a consequence of the latter.

Gradually, most countries are lowering tariffs and moving toward free trade. The mutual gains from voluntary exchange represent a win/win idea that is becoming widely accepted. Specializing in comparative advantage and seeking trade opportunities, the entrepreneurs of the world will produce enormous wealth. When wealth is connected more to ideas than to resources, where mind work supersedes muscle work, and where the Internet is spreading at dizzying speeds to the whole developing world, there is no conceivable end to the ideas and prosperity generated.

Just a few decades ago Hong Kong, Singapore and Taiwan were very poor. Today, they have some of the highest per capita incomes in the world. Any country can choose prosperity if it wants to. But no country can get there without free trade and freedom.

The world will not retreat to the statist, closed economies of the past. Even if communist countries like China wanted to, the mere existence of the Internet has made it nearly impossible for the Chinese government to isolate its people from the ideas and ideals of freedom. Attempts to control a population are doomed to fail. The technological revolution is breaking the natural barriers of time, distance and place. As trade barriers are reduced, more trade occurs and standards of living rise.

Technology Expands Choice

The technological/Internet age will be a second industrial revolution times ten because, this time, it will touch *every* person: "everybody connected, nobody in charge" is one definition of the Internet. The digital age is a shift from the old physics to the new, from the macrocosm to the microcosm, where Quantum Theory physics makes things better as they get smaller, cooler as they operate faster, and cheaper as they become more valuable. Computers are a hydraulic of the mind that frees us from the drudgery of information processing much like bulldozers free us from the drudgery of dirt processing. As information replaces raw materials and brains replace BTUs, economic power has shifted to the individual. It is all about intellectual capital and the liberation of human minds.

Low Inflation and Interest Rates Enhance Wealth

The Chicago School and Milton Friedman taught the world more about inflation and its causes than any institution or person on the planet. As a result, finance ministers throughout the world, as well as our Fed, knows how to stop inflation. And they have. The result is a market system that can effectively function without distortion. Prices, wages, interest rates, profits, and losses are the signals of a market system that misfire and make no sense when inflation runs rampant. Stable price levels mean lower interest rates—and that means higher growth. The double- and triple-digit inflation characterizing most of the twentieth century, in most countries, will be less likely in the new one. As the century enfolds, American-like prosperity will emerge on every continent and that is good news for everybody.

286

Lower Taxes Create Incentive and Choice

There are just two natural equilibrium's for the welfare state: one in which the majority benefits at the expense of the minority and the other is where the minority benefits at the expense of the majority. As the late economist and defense official G. Warren Nutter has told us, "Once the welfare state reaches a certain relative size, both equilibrium's become untenable, leaving the borderline situation where half of the population tries to gain from the other half. That situation weakens government and imperils democracy as well."

Think of our present political situation. One half of the voters by and large represent the producers of wealth. The other half by and large represent the recipients of governmental favors. With a divided government, one party wants lower taxes and the other wants bigger government. What does it get us? With the automatic tax increases that come from moving into higher tax brackets, 1999 tax receipts hit a peacetime record of 20 percent of the total economy, the highest ever. Individual income taxes account for more than half of all federal revenues, up to 50 percent from just 40 percent in 1993. Even middle-class families now pay a marginal tax rate of at least 28 percent and many pay 36 percent or more. This tax bracket creep is the main reason that overall federal taxes now soak up nearly 21 percent of the gross domestic product, the highest level ever since the 20.9 percent in 1944 when WWII was in full swing. Somehow the trend must be reversed.

The Administration of George W. Bush brings us good news on the tax front. It appears they will push hard for an income tax rate reduction and perhaps an increase in the current income threshold for each tax rate. To restore taxpayer confidence in the whole system, Bush will hopefully:

- Lower all graduated rates across the board.
- Eliminate the bulk of special preferences, thereby broadening the tax base.
- Focus on tax return simplification, eliminating all complexities within reasonable revenue costs.
- Repeal the alternative minimum tax for individuals and corporations, off-setting the tax base enlargement.
- Expand tax-free savings incentives. IRAs and 401(k)s should be liberalized by raising individual contribution limits by $5,000 each year for the next five years.
- Cut the payroll tax by at least two percentage points. Payroll tax increases in the last 20 years have canceled out, nearly dollar for dollar, the benefits of the Reagan tax cuts. Middle-class income taxpayers need a break.

Although economic growth can be expected to accelerate with lower taxes, we must always remember that though taxation without representation is not good, taxation with representation isn't so hot either.

Controlling Retirement and Health Care Finally Becomes Personal

The Social Security System is in trouble but it will be fixed. This pay-as-you-go system had 42 workers per retiree in 1940, but by 2040, will only have two. That inevitably means steeply higher taxes. The interest-bearing bonds it holds to represent the accounting surplus of payroll taxes collected minus benefits can only be redeemed by collecting more in taxes.

Further, since benefits are not guaranteed, Congress can reduce them at any time. But here is the good news. President Bush has proposed a system that could provide future retirees with benefits that would return significantly higher rates of return, while still protecting the government's long-term solvency.

In health care, insurance will no longer be predominantly supplied through the workplace; tax policy will shift the current employment-based insurance to a system of tax credits allowing everyone to purchase their own high deductible health insurance and medical savings accounts will be prevalent.

Choosing Your Kids School

The National Assessment of Educational Progress Report was released April 9, 2001. This NAEP study, which the government uses to gauge the state of primary education in the country, shows that two-thirds of the nation's fourth graders lack proficiency in reading. Democrats, naturally, called for more spending on the schools that produce those results. The report also showed that one-third of the fourth graders lack basic reading skills. Democrats, naturally, called for more spending on the schools that produce those results. The report also showed that 63 percent of black fourth graders, 58 percent of Hispanics, 60 percent of children in poverty and 47 percent of children in urban schools scored at "below basic" competency levels, which means they can't read. Democrats, naturally, called for more spending on the schools that produce those results.

Education Secretary Rod Paige remarked, "The first thing you notice from these reading data is that after decades of business-as-usual school reform, too many of our nations children cannot read. After spending $125 billion additional dollars over 25 years, we have virtually nothing to show for it."

What he did not say was 80 of that $125 billion was spent during the Clinton Administration.

Jay Greene, a senior fellow at the Manhattan Institute says, "We've tripled input expenditures over those 25 years and haven't changed output a bit. The education industry suffers from a severe productivity crisis."

Economist Caroline Hoxby of Harvard University released a June 2001 study on school productivity, defined as student performance per dollar spent. Productivity of American schools, she found, fell by 65% between the school years 1970 and 1999. As one example, Washington, D.C.'s spending was in the 99th percentile of all U.S. public schools, but average D.C. student scores were in the 10th to 20th percentile on national tests. These results would get a CEO fired in the private sector. But most public schools are monopolies, not subject to competition.

Despite the obstacles that teachers unions and government school districts place in the way of those who want to enter the educational marketplace, the ongoing lock-hold on our nation's schools will eventually be broken. For-profit education companies are expanding and now hold about ten percent of the $740 billion dollar educational market. The process has just begun. These for-profit educational companies have devised innovative, creative and cost-efficient approaches to meeting the needs of individual students. Edison Schools, National Heritage Academies, the SABIS School Network, Bright Horizons Family Schools, Nobel Learning, Scientific Learning Corporation, Advantage Learning Systems, TRO Learning, and eventually hundreds more will offer a wider range of services and more educational possibilities than ever.

President Bush wants to measure performance and give parents a choice. That's good, but it should happen at the state rather than at the federal level. Anything that gets the federal government deeper into education should be discouraged.

Anything that will curb union control of the teaching profession would be helpful. Anything that would stop mandating what is taught and give more authority to local school districts would be a step in the right direction. President Bush must be very careful about any proposal to give federal aid to private schools. Federal intervention would inevitably follow—overriding state laws and destroying the very reason private schools were started in the first place. The education industry will be revolutionized during the first decades of the twenty-first century. Competition will unleash a dynamism and creativity that will make American schools the best in the world.

Work Choices Everywhere

Many think you have to be a college graduate to succeed in the new economy or be involved in technology. Not true. Education means "to bring out." Fortunately, there are millions of ways to do it in a ten trillion dollar economy. When you don't have an education, you've got to use your brains. Never say, "I don't think." That is exactly what you do best. I know window washers, lawn mowers, baby-sitters and house cleaners who make lots of money, love their jobs and have found their niche because they understand what customer service really means.

As I'm having my shoes shined in the Pittsburgh Airport, I watch this guy stuff five-dollar bills in his pocket every two to three minutes. He applies a gooey substance to my shoes, lights them on fire for a few seconds, and then hits them with a buff rag. Done. Shazam! It all happens so fast. I have mirrors for shoes. It's the best shoe shine I have ever had in my life.

I give him a five-dollar bill—$3 for the shine, $2 for the tip, just like everybody else had done—and say, "I'm an economist and we often ask personal questions. Sir, how much money do you make shining shoes?"

He answers, "This year I should make about $50,000, tax free."

This is not just a shoe-shine. This is a value-added shoe shine.

I get out of an airplane in Atlanta and into a cab for the drive to a downtown hotel. The cab driver gives me a marvelous history lesson of Atlanta. He tells me about people, places, things, sports, and local companies—about everything. It is the best half-hour I have ever spent in a cab. The cab fare is seventeen dollars. I give him a ten-dollar tip. Handing him $27, I say, feeling a bit embarrassed, "You are terrific." "Why, if this cab ride is worth $27, it is worth a $100."

He looks me right in the eye and replies, "Excuse me, sir, but a lot of my customers do tip me $100."

Imagine that. A cab driver getting rich. There are no limits.

Limiting Government: A Never Ending Struggle

The Clinton/Gore Department of Justice anti-trust suit against Microsoft cost Microsoft stockholders between $100 billion and $200 billion and close to $1 trillion on the NASDAQ overall. The cost to the America economy was double that. It represents another sad chapter in the history of anti-trust suits brought against powerful, efficient, competitive companies. (See

Appendix B for further discussion). Government might think that breaking the back of the most important technological company in America would have minimal consequences. It doesn't.

The activist Federal Trade Commission under Clinton and Gore, trying to set up privacy requirements, and the Federal Communications Commission, by imposing a so-called open access regime on broadband providers, not only violates property rights laws by appropriation which unnecessarily disrupts the spread of fast Internet access, but it also sews the seeds of slowdown and disruption of the economy.

As the Internet creates a market structure in which a single broadband connection enables people to speak in real time and access information at the speed of light, the FCC hampers the whole process with outmoded rules. "Last mile" technologies—cable modems, telephones—all being held back by the stifling regulations and "counter incentives" offered through local phone companies. Subsidizing companies that merely resell services developed by local phone companies discourage the building and upgrading of broadband pipelines. Why build them when local phone companies are forced to share them at ridiculously below-cost prices? Why innovate when federal policy makers adopt different regulations for the same competing services? Why should phone companies compete when they are allowed to collect only on charges from subscribers, while cable companies are allowed to capture revenue both from subscribers and from firms that deliver content over their pipelines? It makes no sense. Broadband facilities and services should be set free of stifling regulation and all should be allowed to compete on an equal footing. As telephone switches are replaced by Internet telephony and "soft switches"; as wireless fidelity networks portend a grass-roots network giving new meaning to "power to the people"; wireless access will be the future. The past is not even prologue.

The Best Is Yet To Come

Hopefully President George W. Bush will end the threat of this regulatory recession by appointing market-oriented professionals to head and staff the key federal departments and commissions. Sensible regulators, realizing that broadband is creating an entirely new world, will apply the model used for mobile wireless services in which deregulation has prompted a flood of innovation. It was Bush who said, "Always take the side of innovation over litigation and private initiative over federal regulation." Should he accomplish his hands-off policy of eliminating price regulation and sharing requirements, you will see a proliferation of providers, a big drop in prices, a turbo-charged future, and another reason to be happy.

But Are You Happy?

> You never see the stock called Happiness quoted on the exchange.
> - Henry VanDyke

Sherlock Holmes and Dr. Watson went on a camping trip. After a good meal and a bottle of wine, they lay down for the night and went to sleep.

Some hours later, Holmes awoke and nudged his faithful friend. "Watson, look up at the sky and tell me what you see."

Watson replied, "I see millions and millions of stars."

"What does that tell you?"

Watson pondered for a minute. "Astronomically, it tells me that there are millions of galaxies and potentially billions of planets. Astrologically, I observe that Saturn is in Leo. Horologically, I deduce that the time is approximately a quarter past three. Theologically, I can see that God is all-powerful and that we are small and insignificant. Meteorologically, I suspect that we will have a beautiful day tomorrow. What does it tell you?"

Holmes was silent for a minute, then spoke. "Watson, you idiot. Someone has stolen our tent."

Why is it that even with such economic prosperity so many Americans admit to unhappiness and discontent? Have we forgotten that prosperity is only an instrument to be used, not a deity to be worshipped? Who stole our happiness? The fact that Americans live well cannot ease the pain of not living nobly. Full employment, economic growth and prosperity are of little value if we cannot also live spiritually-enriched and significant lives. Unless we and our children learn to live lives of goodness, mercy and servant leadership, the Great American Experiment, no matter how gilded, will have failed.

People have always been able to lead satisfying lives when they perform the fundamental roles of life: parent, spouse, and neighbor. Why is being a parent satisfying? Because it is about accomplishment and relationship. The greatest happiness of life is found mainly in the regular discharge of some mechanical duty. Often times the greatest reward for doing a task is the opportunity to do more. Parenting always does that. If you changed the diapers, dried the tears, helped with the homework, and lived through all of the things that a child lives through, you can take a great deal of satisfaction in being a parent. Your kind words might be short, but their echoes are truly endless. Unlike sculpting marble, which will perish, or pounding brass, which will efface, or building cathedrals, which will crumble, instilling principles in children brighten with use and light their path for a lifetime.

No great thing is created suddenly. Patience and time are required. Satisfaction comes because we had some responsibility for the outcome. Many times, the harder the task, the sweeter the result. Marriage is hard. Family is hard. A relationship's ultimate test is when you can disagree and still hold hands. But to those who do keep their promises with each other and keep on keeping on, statistics are on your side. Twenty-five percent of husbands kiss their wives goodbye when they leave the house but ninety-five percent of men kiss their houses goodbye when they leave their wives.

Past generations derived most of their fulfillment in life from their struggle to make a living for their families. They worked hard to provide shelter for their kids, to make sure everybody had food to eat that day and that everyone had the proper clothes. Was it often boring and tiresome? Indeed it was. But at the same time it provided a seriousness to life, a sense of victory against a difficult nature and it gave an unquestionable moral depth to their lives. Today, we barely think of those things. Almost all American children have plenty to eat, a nice home to live in, a future that includes college, and when they need something they usually get it. What am I saying? Parents today cannot get the same depth and fulfillment of meeting those basic needs as did their parents. It is now even more imperative to find a moral purpose to life. That idolatry of self as a dead-end street has never been truer.

Twenty years ago, I wrote a book discussing that idea entitled *Crossroads: The Great American Experiment*. I never would have imagined then that America would produce so much wealth-in just two decades. But I also would not have imagined so many people worried about the safety of their kids in school, the pervasiveness of drugs, and the frenzied busyness, and discontentment with life. What's wrong?

Life is more than economics—much more. Money may be the husk of many good things, but not the kernel. It brings food, but not appetite; houses, but not homes; a bed, but not sleep; medicine, but not health; acquaintances, but not friends; servants, but not loyalty; days of enjoyment, but not peace or happiness. So many things in life go beyond the mere material aspects of our existence. If all the gold in the world were melted down into a solid cube, it would fill the rooms of a very large house. But with all those billions and billions of dollars, could you buy a friend or a clear conscience, or an eternal life? Economics can do many things, but it cannot touch the soul nor transform a life.

While prosperity can fulfill many human purposes—food, housing, cars, and education are indeed blessings—we must not let wealth lure us into believing that this is the way to orient our lives. Christian theology or not, the truth is that all the wealth of the world will finally come to nothing. From dust we came and to dust we return. Rich or poor, that is our destination. Humans have come from somewhere and are going somewhere. The God of the universe never built a stairway that leads to nowhere. And since we are spiritual beings, a happy life cannot simply be filled with just good things. It also requires a life that has moral purpose and a concern for eternity.

A transcendent system of sanctions and salvation, such as I find in Christ, is far superior to the Utilitarianism so many practice in the U.S. A transcendent system doesn't drift with the winds of convenience and pleasure, but it holds fast to the fundamental laws ordained by God. We are more than homo-economicus, more than an accident of chance, more than a bundle of nerve endings seeking pleasure and avoiding pain. Every one of us is created in the image of God. We all need a healthy soul.

We must be as concerned with what is on the inside as we are with what is on the outside. Can happiness and "soul caring" be produced without virtue?

The American Founders said no. Unless people are able to put moral chains upon their appetites, unless they can control their intemperate minds, inevitably their passion will forge their fetters. They might be free for a time and temporarily be happy. But over time, they will find it more difficult to enjoy lives of meaning. Our framers strongly believed that virtue was a necessary aspect of a free society. John Adams wrote, "Our Constitution was made only for a moral and religious people. It is wholly inadequate for the government of any other."

Unless we strategically act to nourish and strengthen both our body and soul, we may end up as road-kill on the information highway. Machinery can work 24 hours each day at the speed of light without resting. Humans cannot.

How then should we live? The answer is found in your words when asked, what is most important to you? You have said, probably more than once: faith, family, and work. Without faith, there is no redemption. Faith is not everything, but it should rank right up there with oxygen as to importance. Without family, there is no love. With it, life is rich because family matters. Without work, there is no bread on the table. We cannot repeal the law of supply and demand any more than we can repeal the law of gravity. But at the same time, we must realize that the truths of economics and work, like the truths of science, are not the whole truth.

Dedication to endless acquisition and self-indulgent consumerism at the expense of selfless service, sacrifice, heroism and transcendent soul caring is the sure prescription to an unhappy life. The true question then is not what we have gained, but what we do. Is it possible that contentment now requires less fuel and perhaps even reducing the fire? Don't you have to stop in order to change direction? If success is getting what you want, isn't happiness wanting what you get?

A spiritual life is important. It roots us, anchors us, identifies us, and locates us in this universe. Every person has a God-shaped vacuum and, until it is filled, we never find home. It is a widening of our horizon and a broadening of our vision that reaches out to eternal realities. For me it is, "I live, yet not I live, but Christ lives in me."

There is a desire in all of us to discover the supernatural laws for human happiness, a longing to communicate with the Creator, a willingness to cooperate with a purpose much higher than the transitory human purpose, and last of all to find some security that transcends physical death. As we do that, we find that when the spiritual is right, everything is right, even in difficult circumstances. You realize that the whole exercise of life is not about you, but about God. You begin to see that trials, tribulations and difficulties are frequently God's greatest benedictions. They are often blessings in disguise; angels dressed in black but for a moment. Sometimes the things we think are going to break us are the things that really make us. Human life is frequently in the forge and on the anvil. It is through trials that God shapes us for higher-and better things. And when life gets to hard to stand: kneel.

God is bigger than us and His word is more authoritative than our words. Humbly, we gradually see that life is way bigger than we are. The way to see it is not to think less of ourselves, but to think of ourselves less. It is not to stoop until you are smaller than yourself, but to stand tall against a creator God that will show you what the real smallness of your greatest greatness is. God is supreme. We are not. We worship and serve because we were created to worship and serve. Just as an eagle needs thermals to soar, a sailboat needs wind to sail and a car needs gasoline to run, so do humans need worship and a spiritual life to prosper. Nothing else will do. Nothing makes God more central in worship than when people are utterly persuaded that nothing— not money or prestige or job or family—nothing is going to bring satisfaction to their aching hearts besides filling it with Him. It is a deep, heartfelt satisfaction in your creator God. Without a sense of something bigger than ourselves, the pursuit of possessions becomes a tedious and empty struggle, becoming in the end a joyless quest for joy. The pursuit of success comes up empty. The pursuit of God does not.

Happiness, in the last analysis is not something you arrive at—it is a means of traveling. It is not necessarily doing what you like, but liking what you do. It isn't what you make—it's what you do with what you make. Live to love and you will love to live. And when that happens, when you are thoroughly served up, used up, and loved up, lying exhausted on the battlefield of life, you will know that you have won. Would you ever have guessed that the riches you impart are now the only riches you retain, that giving is the highest level of living?

CHAPTER 12

Tribute to America

America's gift to the world is freedom—the institutions that provide its nexus and the inevitable prosperity that follows. Poverty has always been the natural condition. Wealth is the exception. Breaking the cords of poverty first involves industrious people, but if they are free to choose under a system of capitalism and freedom, the results are truly spectacular.

Sixteen years ago, I wrote a tribute to America and delivered it at the 1986 Statue of Liberty rededication. Both sets of my grandparents came to Ellis Island from Russia at the turn of the century. I'm sure that is the reason why I was invited to speak. This 2001 update is written exactly 100 years after they landed on freedom's soil.

Ladies and gentlemen, my name is the United States of America. I was born on July 4, 1776, conceived in freedom and liberty. That freedom has brought millions to my shores to cast their lot with me. It has also given human incentive its widest scope. Freedom is truly a virus for which there is no antidote.

Now, just 225 years later, I am a diverse, multilingual country that is bound together by a single language, English, the dominant language of the business world, of the Internet world, and the second language for most of the world. Who would have believed that 60 percent of the world's radio broadcasts would be in English? That 70 percent of the world's mail is addressed in English? That 85 percent of all international telephone conversations and 80 percent of all the data in the several hundred million computers in the world is in English? English is one of my most strategic assets.

I am a country where everyone belongs and everyone deserves a chance. America is just another name for opportunity. There are no little people because everyone is created in the image of God. Every person has significance. My incomparable land is blessed by nature with protective oceans and superabundant resources. But resources do not make a nation. People do. When creative and hard-working people are dedicated to the proposition of liberty, anything can happen, and often does. From the Atlantic Ocean in the East to the Pacific Ocean in the West, I look comfortably in every direction to the three key markets of the world—Europe, Asia, and all of the Americas. My local economy consists of a dozen different regional economies, all bound together by a single currency, the dollar. For much of my history I have been the world's largest free trade area, where both goods and entrepreneurs could travel freely without worrying about the tariffs and regulations that governments regularly impose to plague trade and enterprise.

My diverse, innovative and efficient capital markets are the envy of the world. I do not tolerate secrecy. My markets are fully transparent, and my listed companies file timely earnings reports. It all works because the rule of the game is the rule of law, and our generally accepted accounting procedures allow everyone to keep track and to keep score. My property rights protection system is the envy of the world.

I have a deeply rooted entrepreneurial culture and a tax system that allows risk-takers to keep much of what they make. A mere fifty thousand dollars loan to a budding entrepreneur with a great idea might result in the next Microsoft. Even my tiny state of Massachusetts has a bigger venture capital industry than all of Europe put together. To encourage entrepreneurial risk-taking, I have a system of bankruptcy laws that actually encourages people who fail to get up and start over again. One of America's glories is not in failing, but in giving people another chance when they do. Success in America is going from failure to failure without losing enthusiasm. Failures are, after all, the evidence of action, of people doing something, willing to experiment and take risks. The idea is to learn from the mistakes of others because you can't live long enough to make them all yourself. Theodore Roosevelt, my 26th President said this:

> Far better is it to dare mighty things, to win glorious triumphs even though checkered by failure, than to rank with those poor spirits who neither enjoy nor suffer much because they live in the gray twilight that knows neither victory or defeat.

From day one, I've accepted new immigrants from any country in the world and treated them as constitutional equals. I have always believed in differentiation, not uniformity. My open doors have siphoned the best intellects in the world to American companies, universities, and medical centers. Many of my engineers and scientists are foreign-born immigrants. To be Russian you have to be born Russian; to be a German you have to be born German. But to be American, you only have to say I desire to be an American.

Yes, freedom is the mainspring of economic prosperity, and I have lived freedom and limited government longer than anyone else. And yes, freedom does produce incomprehensible wealth. But my history is more than just that. It is also the story of power that went into the world to protect, but not possess; to defend, but not to conquer. For when I see a defeated enemy, I bind its wounds, feed its children, and give it billions of dollars to restore itself to an honorable place among the nations of the world. A nation's character after all, is the sum of its splendid deeds. I have abolished slavery, lifted countless people out of poverty, instituted more humanitarian campaigns against hunger and human suffering than any other, and focused enormous attention on human rights, personal dignity and freedom. If you compare that record with the actual histories of both ancient and contemporary societies, America might not be the best conceivable society, but it might very well be the best society that has ever existed.

Is there any room for complacency? Not at all. One hundred years ago, Great Britain stood at the pinnacle of world power. The sun never set on the British Empire. A few generations later her power and economic leadership were eclipsed. That could easily happen to me. With humility, Americans must realize that complacency toward the defense of freedom and limited government could take us from boom-to-bust as surely as the dusk follows the dawn.

After the Declaration of Independence was signed, Virginia statesman John Page wrote to Thomas Jefferson: "We know the race is not to the swift—nor the battle to the strong. But do you think an Angel rides in the whirlwind and directs the storm?"

The world continues to watch that storm—sometimes admiringly, sometimes grudgingly, and often with both love and envy in their hearts. But whatever they see, they see a work not finished, because my history is His story, filling time and eternity with His purpose.

As the twenty-first century dawns, my hope is to be the best hope for the human race. Once merely a thrilling idea without a speck of a chance, freedom is now a seed sewn upon the wind and sprouting everywhere. And yes, my friend, an angel still rides in the whirlwind and directs each storm.

Postscript July 4, 2002

On page 278 I said "we are bound to be surprised by the reversals, breakthroughs, upsets, volatile swings, and even luck and chance." Who would have predicted a September 11, 2001 terrorist attack on the U.S. mainland? Three thousand American casualties was horrific for the nation and unspeakably tragic for the victims and their families.

These merchants of terror must be made to pay a price so high that they would never again consider such wanton acts of human carnage. Our grief must now be matched by our resolve. This is not a war of revenge, but rather a war of justice and freedom. While freedom is worth fighting for, unfortunately it is not free.

The events of September 11 are a poignant reminder that freedom demands eternal vigilance. For too long we have not been vigilant. We have harbored those who hated us; tolerated those who threatened us; and indulged those who weakened us. As a result, we remain all but defenseless against ballistic missiles that could be launched against our cities. A missile defense system could change that. Thankfully, we have a President who understands these rogue regimes and will provide the robust leadership necessary to upgrade our defenses and protect our homeland. The war against terrorism cannot be won until the war against weapons of mass destruction is lost.

Freedom is still America's best investment.

America's God and Country
Encyclopedia of Quotations
William J. Federer

These astounding quotes are only a few of the thousands in Federer's book. His comprehensive 864 page reference book of quotes includes over 2,100 quotations from nearly 700 sources highlighting America's noble heritage.

John Adams (1735-1826), was the 2nd President of the United States of America and the first president to live in the White House. He had also served as the Vice President for eight years under President George Washington. The Library of Congress and the Department of the Navy were established under his presidency. A graduate of Harvard, John Adams became a member of the Continental Congress and a signer of the Declaration of Independence. In his diary entry dated February 22, 1756, he wrote:

> Suppose a nation in some distant region should take the Bible for their only law book, and every member should regulate his conduct by the precepts there exhibited! Every member would be obliged in conscience, to temperance, frugality, and industry; to justice, kindness, and charity towards his fellow men; and to piety, love, and reverence toward Almighty God . . . What a Utopia, what a Paradise would this region be.

John Quincy Adams (1767-1848), was the 6th President of the United States and son of John Adams, the 2nd President. He was a U.S. Senator; U.S. Minister to France; and U.S. Minister to Britain, where he negotiated the Treaty of Ghent, ending the War of 1812.
On July 4, 1821, he declared:

> The highest glory of the American Revolution was this, it connected in one indissoluble bond the principles of civil government with the principles of Christianity.

Appendix A

The Holy Bible was found to have directly contributed to 34% of all quotes by the founding fathers. This was discovered after reviewing 15,000 items from the founding fathers (including newspaper articles, pamphlets, books, monographs, etc.). The other main sources that the founders quoted include: Montesquieu, Blackstone, Locke, Pufendorf, etc., who themselves took 60% of their quotes directly from the Bible. Direct and indirect quotes combined reveal that 94% of all the quotes of the Founding fathers are derived from the Bible.

William Bradford (1590-1657), the leader of the Pilgrims, was elected as Governor of the Plymouth Colony in 1621, and reelected every year until his death in 1657. In describing the Pilgrims' covenant to establish their church, he wrote:

> They shook off this yoke of anti-Christian bondage, and as the Lord's free people, joined themselves by a covenant of the Lord into a church estate in the fellowship of the gospel, to walk in all His ways, made known unto them, according to their best endeavors, whatsoever it should cost them, the Lord assisting them.

Inscribed on Governor William Bradford's grave at Burial Hill in Plymouth, Massachusetts, are the remarks:

> Under this stone rests the ashes of William Bradford, a zealous Puritan, and sincere Christian Governor of Plymouth Colony from 1621 to 1657, (the year he died) aged 69, except 5 years, which he declined.

Henry Clay (1777-1852), was a powerful U.S. Senator who also served as a Congressman. He was elected Speaker of the House six times, and for nearly 40 years was a leading American statesman. Clay was part of the "Great Triumvirate," with Daniel Webster and John Calhoun, which dominated Congress during the early to mid-1800's. From a speech to the Kentucky Colonization Society, at Frankfort, 1829, Henry Clay proclaimed:

> Eighteen hundred years have rolled away since the Son of God, our blessed Redeemer, offered Himself on Mount Calvary for the salvation of our species; and more than half of mankind still continue to deny His Divine mission and the truth of His sacred Word . . .

Appendix A

Christopher Columbus (1451-1506), after seven years of trying to convince the monarchs of Europe to finance his expedition, won the support of Queen Isabella of Castille and King Ferdinand of Aragon. Columbus set sail on August 3, 1492, and, after the longest voyage ever made out of sight of land, discovered the New World on October 12, 1492. Columbus wrote:

> As they landed on each island, Columbus had his men erect a large wooden cross:

> As a token of Jesus Christ our Lord, and in honor of the Christian faith.

According to Columbus' personal log, his purpose in seeking "undiscovered worlds" was to:

> . . . bring the Gospel of Jesus Christ to the heathens. [And]
> . . . bring the Word of God to unknown coast lands.

> Columbus always loved to apply the Sacred Scriptures to his own life and adventures. That religious elements played a great part in Columbus' thoughts and actions is evident from all his writings. It may be surprising that his concept of sailing west to reach the Indies was less the result of geographical theories than of his faith in certain biblical texts — specifically the Book of Isaiah.

The Library of Congress, from the collected reports of the various patriots, recorded on a famous historical placard the effect of that first prayer upon Congress:

> Washington was kneeling there, and Henry, Randolph, Rutledge, Lee, and Jay, and by their side there stood, bowed in reverence, the Puritan Patriots of New England, who at that moment had reason to believe that an armed soldiery was wasting their humble households.

Continental Congress, September 11, 1777, approved and recommended to the people that 20,000 copies of The Holy Bible be imported from other sources. This was in response to the shortage of Bibles in America caused by the Revolutionary War interrupting trade with England.

> The use of the Bible is so universal and its importance so great that your committee refers the above to the consideration of Congress, and if Congress shall not think it expedient to order the importation of types and paper, the Committee recommends that Congress will order the Committee of

309

Commerce to import 20,000 Bibles from Holland, Scotland, or elsewhere, into the different parts of the States of the Union. Whereupon it was resolved accordingly to direct said Committee of Commerce to import 20,000 copies of the Bible.

On October 18, 1780, issued a Proclamation for a Day of Public Thanksgiving and Prayer. This came after the revealing of and subsequent deliverance from Benedict Arnold's plot to betray General George Washington and his troops to the British:

> It is therefore recommended to the several states . . . a day of public thanksgiving and prayer, that all the people may assemble on that day to celebrate the praises of our Divine Benefactor; to confess our unworthiness of the least of his favors, and to offer our fervent supplications to the God of all grace . . . . to cause the knowledge of Christianity to spread over all the earth.

Constitutional Convention, June 28, 1787, Thursday, was embroiled in a bitter debate over how each state was to be represented in the new government. The hostile feelings created by the smaller states being pitted against the larger states was so bitter that some delegates actually left the Convention. Benjamin Franklin, being the President (Governor) of Pennsylvania, hosted the rest of the 55 delegates attending the Convention. Being the senior member of the convention, at 81 years of age, he commanded the respect of all present, and, as recorded in James Madison's detailed records, he arose to address the Congress in this moment of crisis:

> We have been assured, Sir, in the Sacred Writings, that "except the Lord build the House, they labor in vain that build it." I firmly believe this; and I also believe that without his concurring aid we shall succeed in this political building no better than the Builders of Babel: We shall be divided by our partial local interests. I therefore beg leave to move —that henceforth prayers imploring the assistance of Heaven, and its blessing on our deliberations, be held in this Assembly every morning before we proceed to business.

Congress of the United States of America, May 1854, passed a resolution in the House which declared:

> The great vital and conservative element in our system is the belief of our people in the pure doctrines and divine truths of the gospel of Jesus Christ.

The Declaration of Independence. As the parchment copy of the Declaration of Independence was being signed by the members of the Continental Congress, August 2, 1776, Samuel Adams declared:

> We have this day restored the Sovereign to Whom all men ought to be obedient. He reigns in heaven and from the rising to the setting of the sun, let His kingdom come.

Timothy Dwight, (1752-1817), the President of Yale, was an influential author and educator. He was the grandson of Jonathan Edwards, the famous New England minister and President of Princeton.

> Religion and liberty are the meat and the drink of the body politic. Withdraw one of them and it languishes, consumes, and dies . . . Without religion we may possibly retain the freedom of savages, bears, and wolves, but not the freedom of New England. If our religion were gone, our state of society would perish with it, and nothing would be left.

The Federalist Papers (1787-1788), were a series of articles explaining the need for, and urging the ratification of, the United States Constitution by the individual State governments. Published in New York newspapers, these articles were written by Alexander Hamilton, James Madison and John Jay under the pen name of "Publius." Without the powerful arguments presented in *The Federalist Papers*, the Constitution most likely would not have been ratified.

> Federalist Paper No. 47: When the legislative and executive powers are united in the same person or body, there can be no liberty, because apprehensions may arise lest the same monarch or senate should enact tyrannical laws, to execute them in a tyrannical manner. Were the power of judging joined with the legislative, the life and liberty of the subject would then be the legislator. Were it joined to the executive power, the judge might behave with all the violence of an oppressor.

Simon Greenleaf (1783-1853), the famous Royal Professor of Law at Harvard, succeeded Justice Joseph Story as the Dane Professor of Law. To the efforts of Story and Greenleaf is to be ascribed the rise of the Harvard Law School to its eminent position among the legal schools of the United States.

In correspondence with the American Bible Society, Cambridge, November 6, 1852, Simon Greenleaf wrote:

> Of the Divine character of the Bible, I think no man who deals honestly with his own mind and heart can entertain a reasonable doubt. For myself, I must say, that having for many years made the evidences of Christianity the subject of close study, the result has been a firm and increasing conviction of the authenticity and plenary inspiration of the Bible. It is indeed the Word of God.

Alexander Hamilton (1757-1804), was not only a signer of the Constitution of the United States, but was known as the "Ratifier of the Constitution." It is probable that without his efforts the Constitution may not have been ratified by the states, particularly his own important state of New York. Alexander Hamilton authored 51 of the 85 *Federalist Pap*ers, which were of immense consequence in influencing the ratification of the Constitution, (which needed to be passed in two-thirds of the states in order to go into effect). Shortly after the Constitutional Convention of 1787, Alexander Hamilton stated:

> For my own part, I sincerely esteem it a system which without the finger of God, never would have been suggested and agreed upon by such a diversity of interests.

He expounded:

> I have carefully examined the evidences of the Christian religion, and if I was sitting as a juror upon its authenticity I would unhesitatingly give my verdict in its favor. I can prove its truth as clearly as any proposition ever submitted to the mind of man.

Harvard University (1636), founded in Cambridge, Massachusetts to train a literate clergy.

2. The Rules and Precepts that were observed at Harvard, September 26, 1642, stated:

Appendix A

Let every student be plainly instructed and earnestly pressed to consider well the main end of his life. To know God and Jesus Christ which is eternal life, John chapter 17 verse 3. Christ is the only foundation of all sound knowledge and learning. Only the Lord gives wisdom. Let every one seriously set himself by prayer in secret to seek it of Him, Proverbs chapters 2 and 3.

Prior to the Revolution, ten of the twelve presidents of Harvard were ministers, and according to reliable calculations, over fifty percent of the seventeenth-century Harvard graduates became ministers. It is worthy of note that 106 of the first 108 schools in America were founded on the Christian faith. Harvard college was founded in "Christi Gloriam" and later dedicated "Christo etEcclesiae." The founders of Harvard believed that: All knowledge without Christ was vain.

Patrick Henry (1736-1799), was an American Revolutionary leader and orator, who spoke the now famous phrase, "Give me Liberty or give me death!" He was Commander-in-Chief of the Virginia Militia, a member of the Continental Congress, a member of the Virginia General Assembly and House of Burgesses, and was instrumental in writing the Constitution of Virginia. He was the five-time Governor of the State of Virginia, (the only governor in United States history to be elected and reelected five times). He boldly declared:

It cannot be emphasized too strongly or too often that this great nation was founded, not by religionists, but by Christians; not on religions, but on the Gospel of Jesus Christ. For this very reason peoples of other faiths have been afforded asylum, prosperity, and freedom of worship here.

Andrew Jackson (1767-1845), the 7th President of the United States of America, was also a lawyer, a Congressman, a U.S. Senator and a judge on the Tennessee Supreme Court. Andrew Jackson was credited with proposing the state's name, "Tennessee", while being a member of the state's first convention which adopted its constitution. He wrote a letter to comfort the family of General Coffee who had recently died:

Rely on our dear Savior, He will be father to the fatherless and husband to the widow. Trust in the mercy and goodness of Christ, and always be ready to say with heartfelt resignation, "may the Lord's will be done."

Appendix A

John Jay (1745-1829), was the first Chief Justice of the United States Supreme Court, having been appointed by President George Washington. He was a Founding Father, a member of the First and Second Continental Congresses and served as the President of the Continental Congress. He was very instrumental in causing the Constitution to be ratified, by writing the *Federalist Papers*, along with James Madison and Alexander Hamilton. On October 1, 1816, John Jay admonished:

> Providence has given to our people the choice of their rulers, and it is the duty, as well as the privilege and interest of our Christian nation to select and prefer Christians for their rulers.

On May 13, 1824, while serving as its president, John Jay gave an address to the American Bible Society:

> The Bible will also inform them that our gracious Creator has provided for us a Redeemer, in whom all the nations of the earth shall be blessed; that this Redeemer has made atonement "for the sins of the whole world," and thereby reconciling the Divine justice with the Divine mercy has opened a way for our redemption and salvation; and that these inestimable benefits are of the free gift and grace of God, not of our deserving, nor in our power to deserve.

Thomas Jefferson (1743-1826), author, architect, educator and scientist, was the 3rd President of the United States of America. In 1774, while serving in the Virginia Assembly, he personally introduced a resolution calling for a Day of Fasting and Prayer. Thomas Jefferson penned the words of the Declaration of Independence, on July 4th, 1776:

> We hold these truths to be self-evident, that all men are created equal. That they are endowed by their Creator with certain unalienable rights, that among these are life, liberty and the pursuit of happiness.

In 1781, Thomas Jefferson made this statement in Query XVIII of his Notes on the State of Virginia. Excerpts of these statements are engraved on the Jefferson Memorial in Washington, DC:

> God who gave us life gave us liberty. And can the liberties of a nation be thought secure when we have removed their only firm basis, a conviction in the minds of the people that these liberties are of the Gift of God? That they are not to be

violated but with His wrath? Indeed, I tremble for my country when I reflect that God is just; that His justice cannot sleep forever.

On June 17, 1804, in a letter to Henry Fry, Thomas Jefferson writes:
I consider the doctrines of Jesus as delivered by himself to contain the outlines of the sublimest system of morality that has ever been taught but I hold in the most profound detestation and execration the corruption's of it which have been invented. . . .

On September 6, 1819, Thomas Jefferson wrote:
The Constitution is a mere thing of wax in the hands of the judiciary, which they may twist and shape into any form they please.

On November 4, 1820, Thomas Jefferson wrote to Jared Sparks:
I hold the precepts of Jesus as delivered by Himself, to be the most pure, benevolent and sublime which have ever been preached to man.

Had the doctrines of Jesus been preached always as pure as they came from his lips, the whole civilized world would now have been Christians. I have always said, I always will say, that the studious perusal of the sacred volume will make better citizens, better fathers, and better husbands.

1. The doctrines of Jesus are simple and tend to the happiness of man.
2. There is only one God, and He is all perfect.
3. There is a future state of rewards and punishment.
4. To love God with all the heart and your neighbor as thyself is the sum of all. These are the great points on which to reform the religion of the Jews.

Jefferson declared that religion is:
Deemed in other countries incompatible with good government and yet proved by our experience to be its best support.

The Liberty Bell (August 1752), was cast in England by an order of the Pennsylvania Assembly to commemorate the fiftieth anniversary of the colony's existence. The inscription cast onto the Liberty Bell in August 1752 is an excerpt from Leviticus 25:10.

> And you shall make hallow the fiftieth year, and proclaim liberty throughout all the land unto all the inhabitants thereof; it shall be a jubilee.
>
> Proclaim liberty through all the land and to all the inhabitants thereof. (Leviticus XXXV.10)

The Liberty Bell got its name from being rung July 8, 1776, at the first public reading of the Declaration of Independence. It cracked as it rang at the funeral for Chief Justice Marshall in 1835.

Library of Congress (1800), was set up primarily to assist Congressmen in preparing laws, although it is open to all scholars. Burned by the British during the War of 1812, it was subsequently rebuilt. President Eliot of Harvard selected the following verse to be inscribed on the walls:

> He hath showed you, O man, what is good; and what does the Lord require of you, but to do justly and love mercy and walk humbly with your God. (Micah 6:8)

The lawmaker's library has engraved the quote from the Psalmist:

> The heavens declare the glory of God, and the firmament shows His handiwork. (Psalm 19:1)

John Locke (1621-1704), was an English philosopher whose writings had a profound influence on our Founding fathers, and, in turn, on the writing of the Constitution. Of nearly 15,000 items of the Founding fathers which were reviewed, including books, newspaper articles, pamphlets, monographs, etc., John Locke was the third most frequently quoted author. In his Two Treatises of Government, 1690, he cited 80 references to the Bible in the first treatise and 22 references to the Bible in the second. John Locke elaborated on fundamental concepts, such as: unalienable rights, separation of powers, parental authority, private property, the right to resist unlawful authority, and government by consent (whereby governments "derive their just powers from the consent of the governed"). He built the understanding of the "social compact" (a constitution between the people and the government). He wrote in The Second Treatise on Civil Government, 1690:

Appendix A

Human Laws are measures in respect of Men whose Actions they must direct, albeit such measures they are as have also their higher Rules to be measured by, which Rules are two, the Law of God, and the Law of Nature; so that Laws Human must be made according to the general Laws of Nature, and without contradiction to any positive Law of Scripture, otherwise they are ill made.

John Locke wrote, in 1695, a seldom mentioned book entitled *A Vindication of the Reasonableness of Christianity.* In it he wrote:

He that shall collect all the moral rules of the philosophers and compare them with those contained in the New Testament will find them to come short of the morality delivered by our Savior and taught by His disciples: a college made up of ignorant but inspired fishermen . . .

Such a law of morality Jesus Christ has given in the New Testament, but by the latter of these ways, by revelation, we have from Him a full and sufficient rule for our direction, and conformable to that of reason. But the word and obligation of its precepts have their force, and are past doubt to us, by the evidence of His mission.

He was sent by God: His miracles show it; and the authority of God in His precepts cannot be questioned. His morality has a sure standard, that revelation vouches, and reason can no gainsay nor question; but both together witness to come from God, the great Lawgiver.

And such a one as this, out of the New Testament, I think, they would never find, nor can anyone say is anywhere else to be found. . . .

To one who is persuaded that Jesus Christ was sent by God to be a King and a Saviour to those who believe in Him, all His commands become principles; there needs no other proof for the truth of what He says, but that He said it; and then there needs no more but to read the inspired books to be instructed.

James Madison (1751-1836), known as the "Chief Architect of the Constitution," was the 4th President of the United States, 1809-17. He was an instrumental member of the Constitutional Convention, speaking 161 times (more than any other founder except Governor Morris). James Madison's records of the debates in the Constitutional Convention are the most accurate

317

and detailed that exist. He authored 29 of the 95 *Federalist Papers,* which argued successfully in favor of the ratification of the Constitution. Home-schooled as a child, Madison attended Princeton University. On June 20, 1785, he wrote in regard to the relationship between religion and civil government. Religion [is] the basis and Foundation of Government.

James Madison, on the future of America, wrote:

> We have staked the whole future of American civilization, not upon the power of government, far from it. We have staked the future of all of our political institutions upon the capacity of mankind for self-government; upon the capacity of each and all of us to govern ourselves, to control ourselves, to sustain ourselves according to the Ten Commandments of God.

James Madison, known to regularly lead his household in the observance of family devotions, was an adamant defender of religious liberty. On November 20, 1825, he wrote in a letter to Frederick Beasley:

> The belief in a God All Powerful wise and good, is so essential to the moral order of the World and to the happiness of man, that arguments which enforce it cannot be drawn from too many sources nor adapted with too much solicitude to the different characters and capacities to be impressed with it.

James Madison, who outlived all of the other 54 founders of the American Republic, wrote on November 9, 1772, to his close college friend, William Bradford:

> A watchful eye must be kept on ourselves lest while we are building ideal monuments of renown and Bliss here we neglect to have our names enrolled in the Annals of Heaven.

George Mason (1725-1792), was a famous American Revolutionary statesman and delegate from Virginia to the Constitutional Convention. He was a member of the Virginia House of Burgesses, a lawyer, judge, political philosopher and planter. The richest man in Virginia, he owned 15,000 acres in Virginia and 80,000 acres in the Ohio area. George Mason was the author of the Virginia Constitution and the Virginia Bill of Rights. He was a delegate to the Constitutional Convention of the United States, but refused to sign the Constitution as it did not sufficiently limit the government's power from infringing on the rights of citizens. He is called the "Father of the Bill of Rights," as he insisted that Congress add the Bill of Rights (the first ten amendments) to the Constitution. George Mason practically wrote the

first ten amendments to the United States Constitution, limiting the power of the government. He stated before the General Court of Virginia:
>The laws of nature are the laws of God, whose authority
>can be superseded by no power on earth.

In his *Last Will and Testament*, George Mason wrote:
>My soul, I resign into the hands of my Almighty Creator, whose tender mercies are over all His works, who hates nothing that He hath made and to the Justice and Wisdom of whose dispensation I willingly and cheerfully submit, humbly hoping from His unbounded mercy and benevolence, through the merits of my blessed Savior, a remission of my sins.

Cotton Mather (1663-1728), an American colonial clergyman, received his degree from Harvard at the age of 18 and joined his father, Increase Mather, in the pastorate of Second Church in Boston. Author of 450 books and a Fellow of the Royal Society, Cotton Mather was regarded as the most brilliant man in New England in his time. Among his many accomplishments is the introduction of the smallpox inoculation in 1721, during an epidemic. In 1702, Cotton wrote *Magnalia Christi Americana*, (The Great Achievement of Christ in America), the most detailed history written of the first 50 years of New England. In it he wrote:
>The sum of the matter is that from the beginning of the Reformation in the English nation, there had always been a generation of godly men, desirous to pursue the reformation of religion, according to the Word of God . . . [The Puritans were] driven to seek a place for the exercise of the Protestant religion, according to the light of conscience, in the deserts of America.

George Washington (1732-1799), the 1st President of the United States, was the Commander-in-Chief of the Continental Army during the Revolutionary War. He was also a surveyor, a planter, soldier, and a statesman. In his Inaugural Address to Both Houses of Congress, April 30, 1789, George Washington proclaimed:
>Such being the impressions under which I have, in obedience to the public summons, repaired to the present station, it would be peculiarly improper to omit, in this first official act, my fervent supplications to that Almighty Being

who rules over the universe, who presides in the councils of nations and whose providential aids can supply every human defect, that His benediction may consecrate to the liberties and happiness of the people of the United States a Government instituted by themselves for these essential purposes; and may enable every instrument employed in its administration to execute with success, the functions allotted to his charge.

On March 11, 1792, from Philadelphia, President George Washington wrote a letter to John Armstrong:

I am sure that never was a people, who had more reason to acknowledge a Divine interposition in their affairs, than those of the United States; and I should be pained to believe that they have forgotten that agency, which was so often manifested during our Revolution, or that they failed to consider the omnipotence of that God who is alone able to protect them.

George Washington stated:

It is impossible to rightly govern the world without God and the Bible.

John Marshall, Chief Justice of the Supreme Court, who had previously fought with Washington in the Revolutionary War and served with him at Valley Forge, said of Washington:

Without making ostentatious professions of religion, he was a sincere believer in the Christian faith, and a truly devout man.

Daniel Webster (1782-1852), was a famous American politician and diplomat. He is considered one of the greatest orators in American history. He served as a U.S. Congressman, a US. Senator and as the Secretary of State for three different Presidents: William Henry Harrison, John Tyler and Millard Fillmore. His political career spanned almost four decades:

If there is anything in my thoughts or style to commend, the credit is due to my parents for instilling in me an early love of the Scriptures. If we abide by the principles taught in the Bible, our country will go on prospering and to prosper; but if we and our posterity neglect its instructions and authority, no man can tell how sudden a catastrophe may overwhelm us and bury all our glory in profound obscurity.

Appendix A

In a speech at the Bunker Hill Monument, Charleston, Massachusetts, on June 17, 1843, Daniel Webster spoke of the founding father's regard for the Bible:

> The Bible came with them. And it is not to be doubted, that free and universal reading of the Bible, in that age, men were much indebted for right views of civil liberty. The Bible is a book of faith, and a book of doctrine, and a book of morals, and a book of religion, of special revelation from God; but it is also a book which teaches man his own individual responsibility, his own dignity, and his equality with his fellow-man.

In a discussion as he sat in a drawing room, Daniel Webster laid his hand on a copy of the Holy Scriptures and proclaimed:

> This is the Book. I have read the Bible through many times, and now make it a practice to read it through once every year. It is a book of all others for lawyers, as well as divines; and I pity the man who cannot find in it a rich supply of thought and of rules for conduct. It fits man for life — it prepares him for death.

In stating his convictions, Daniel Webster declared:

> The Gospel is either true history, or it is a consummate fraud; it is either a reality or an imposition. Christ was what He professed to be, or He was an impostor. There is no other alternative. His spotless life in His earnest enforcement of the truth — His suffering in its defense, forbid us to suppose that He was suffering an illusion of a heated brain. Every act of His pure and holy life shows that He was the author of truth, the advocate of truth, the earnest defender of truth, and the uncompromising sufferer for truth.

Yale College (1701), was founded as the Collegiate School at Saybrook, Connecticut, by ten Congregational ministers. It was moved to New Haven, Connecticut, and renamed for Elihu Yale (1649-1721), an American-born English merchant and governor of the East India Company. The requirements for the students included:

321

Appendix A

All scholars shall live religious, godly, and blameless lives according to the rules of God's Word, diligently reading the Holy Scriptures, the fountain of light and truth; and constantly attend upon all the duties of religion, both in public and secret.

The primary goal, as outlined by the founders, stated:
Every student shall consider the main end of his study to wit to know God in Jesus Christ and answerably to lead a Godly, sober life.

Appendix B

The Question of Monopoly

Barry Asmus and Don Billings, *Crossroads: The Great American Experiment*, (University Press, 1984), p. 208-215.

Arising in part from the confusion over the role of profits in the free market system and the large size of many American corporations, it is frequently asserted that American industry is characterized by monopoly. The Marxist economists Paul Baran and Paul Sweezy have written of "monopoly capitalism" as if they have identified the essential character of our economic environment. But their view is both factually wrong and influenced by an inappropriate interpretation of the competitive process. In the market economy, whenever competitors are not restricted from offering more attractive opportunities to other buyers or sellers, competition is potentially present. From this perspective, monopoly power can arise only if entry barriers are erected which prevent market transactions between consumers and producers. As the entrepreneurial process is inherently competitive, limits or restrictions to market exchange must be imposed externally. In fact, these outside impediments to the competitive process invariably originate in government. Government, employing its monopoly on the use of force, is the source of monopoly power.

The market process is always competitive unless government barriers to entry are enacted. It follows that the number of sellers in a particular industry provides little reliable evidence on the degree of rivalry in a market. Size, or what economists call industrial concentration, is a poor indicator of monopoly power. Harold Demsetz, Yale Brozen, Dominisk Armentano, J. Fred Weston, and John S. McGee are just a few of the contemporary economists whose scholarship documents this proposition.

There are essentially two ways to restrict entry and curtail the competitive process. First, monopoly positions can be held if the control and ownership of an important resource is necessary to a particular activity. This might involve the exclusive ownership of a mineral resource and/or the possession of a patent or secrete technology unavailable to potential competitors. Luciano Pavorotti, the great tenor, in this sense has monopoly power as a result of "owning" those remarkable vocal cords. However, resource monopoly tends to dissipate through time when new production processes, substitutes, and technologies are discovered.

Second and by far the most important source of protection from competition involves the barriers to market entry enforced by the power of government. Examples are the granting of an exclusive franchise for intercity truck routes, garbage collection services, cable television, the licensing of professions and taxicabs, and other government interventions used to prevent competition. Even our so-called antitrust laws have impeded the competitive market process and encouraged monopoly. Since government is the source of monopoly in the American economy, it follows that the most effective way to deal with the "monopoly problem" would be to eliminate government imposed barriers to participation in the market process.

The Antitrust Laws and Competition

Perhaps the most unfortunate, but predictable, implication of government monopoly laws is the extent to which they protect competitors rather than the competitive process. The competitive market is inherently risky. From the community's point of view it is desirable that there be both winners and losers, both profits and losses. Competitive capitalism is a great "flushing system" through which scarce resources are inevitably withdrawn from lower valued uses and mobilized for higher ones. Therein lies one of its great values. A necessary consequence of this rivalrous process is the disappointment and financial loss of those who fail to correctly anticipate consumer preferences or underestimate production costs. Thomas Sowell, in his book *Knowledge And Decisions* has summarized the essential character of a truly open competitive process:

> The advantages of market institutions over government institutions are not so much in the particular characteristics as institutions but in the fact that people can usually make a better choice out of numerous options than by following a single prescribed process. The diversity of personal tastes insures that no given institution will become the answer to a human problem in the market . . . Responsiveness to individual diversity means that market processes necessarily produce 'chaotic' results from the point of view of any single given scale of values. . . . People who are convinced that their values are best - - not only for themselves but for others - - must necessarily be offended by many things that happen in a market economy . . . The diversity of tastes satisfied by a market may be its greatest economic achievement, but it is also its greatest political vulnerability.

324

Appendix B

As already noted, federal antitrust legislation has more often than not been a government enforced device to restrict competition and protect competitors from more efficient rivals. The argument and evidence for this point of view has been forcefully made by the economist Dominick Armentano in his book *Antitrust and Monopoly*. This startling and radical indictment of American antitrust is described by Armentano:

> The general public has been deluded into believing that monopoly is a free-market problem, and that the government, through antitrust enforcement, is on the side of the 'angels.' The facts are entirely the opposite. Antitrust, therefore, whatever its intent, has served as convenient cover for an insidious process of monopolization in the marketplace. Such is the deeper and more subtle meaning of antitrust policy.

A good example of legislation which protects particular competitors from the rigors of the competitive process is Section II of the Clayton Act (1914) as amended by the Robinson-Patman Act (1936). In this instance an overwhelming majority of economists generally agree on the undesirable consequences of the so-called price discrimination laws. Passed to protect small, independent businesses from "unfair" competition of the large regional and national chains evolving during the early part of this century, this legislation in fact suppressed price competition. In the name of "unreasonable" economic power, and of course always in the "public interest," special interest groups used government to obtain protection from the rigors of the market. Naturally, political entrepreneurs were prepared to sell these favors for campaign money and votes. Robinson-Patman is quite explicit in its intentions. Certain parts of Section II suggest that price cuts, even when justified by cost differences, are not defensible and, therefore, price competition is illegal per se. As Armentano points out: "At least the price discrimination law is refreshingly honest concerning its intent to limit price competition and restrain the rivalrous process of an open market."

Among the many court cases on this issue was the much publicized complaint brought by the Federal Trade Commission in the early 1960's against the Borden Company. Accused of selling its own brand of evaporated milk at a higher price than its private label milk, a complaint was brought against Borden. The law suite charged that Borden's private label business had " . . . placed severe competitive pressures on the entire unadvertised brand of private label milk structure and that has . . . largely been felt in the way of lowered market price." Incredibly, we have turned the whole notion of free market competition upside down! Borden was condemned for offering a product to the public at a lower price which in turn stimulated competition among rivals. As one witness before the FTC complained: "The competition has forced our prices down from the level we had previous to that . . . and it is made highly competitive because of these factors."

The good news is that a hearing examiner for the FTC was unwilling to accept the idea that the law's intention was to protect competitors. Armentano quotes the examiner's recommendation which provides an eloquent statement of the benefits to be expected from the competitive process:

> These competitive advantages which counsel supporting the complaint would have us condemn as unlawful are the accumulated benefits of that private initiative, industry, and business acumen which our system of free enterprise is designed to foster and reward.

The bad news, however, was that the Federal Trade Commission reversed the hearing examiner's decision and found Borden guilty of illegal price discrimination. Finally, and unfortunately for economic efficiency and a free society, the U.S. Supreme Court in 1966 upheld the FTC ruling. In a powerful dissent, Justice Stewart of the Court tried in vain to defend the competitive market process:

> In the guise of protecting producers and purchasers from discriminatory price competition, the Court ignores legitimate market preferences and endows the Federal Trade Commission with authority to disrupt price relationships between products whose identity has been measured in the laboratory but rejected in the marketplace. I do not believe that such power was conferred upon the Commission by Congress.

The Borden case, represents the "climax of absurdity" in a long list of price discrimination suits. Space does not permit an enunciation of the anti-competitive implications of other cases like Morton Salt, Minneapolis-Honeywell, Sun Oil, Standard Oil of Indiana, and many others. Suffice it to say that a number of prestigious committees in recent years have condemned the suppression of the competitive process through the Robinson-Patman Act. To summarize, from Armentano's excellent analysis of this issue in Antitrust and Monopoly: "The economic nightmare that is Robinson-Patman is working

326

exactly as it was intended to work back in 1936 when the important amendments were drafted. The law, through the threat of enforcement or actual enforcement, can make serious price competition almost impossible, and that may have been exactly the purpose of the statute."

There is little debate among informed observers concerning the socially undesirable consequences of price discrimination laws. Unfortunately, there is much less unanimity of opinion regarding the consequence of the other major monopoly laws: specifically the Sherman Act (1890), the Clayton Act's other major provisions, and the Federal Trade Commission Act (1914). Many economists continue to believe that the Sherman Act and the others have, on balance, been socially beneficial. However, following the important studies by Armentano, Richard Posner, Donald Dewey, Harold Demsetz, Wesley Liebeler, Yale Brozen, J. Fred Weston, John S. McGee, and others, important reservations are appropriate regarding the likelihood that the antitrust laws have increased economic efficiency and served the American consumer.

An excellent illustration of the relevance of this alternative viewpoint is found in the classic case of "witch-hunting for Robber Barons," the Standard Oil of New Jersey Supreme Court case of 1911. Supported by the highly biased and incomplete work of writers like Ira Tarbell in *The History of the Standard Oil Company*, it was argued that this was a classic example of "monopoly" power. This conventional view was roughly as follows: through predatory pricing and restrictions of output, monopoly profits were achieved by the Standard Oil Company. The Company was accused of monopolizing the petroleum industry and therefore deserving of government dissolution. According to a noted historian: "He [Rockefeller] iron-handedly ruined competitors by cutting prices until his victim went bankrupt or sold out, whereupon higher prices would be likely to return." In another text book two historians maintain that ". . .Rockefeller was a ruthless operator who did not hesitate to crush his competitors by harsh and unfair methods." However, this conventional point of view is inconsistent with the facts.

More than a quarter of a century ago economist John S. McGee, after reviewing more than 10,000 pages of the Standard Oil trial record, demonstrated on both theoretical and empirical grounds " . . . that Standard Oil did not systematically, if ever, use local price cutting in retailing, or anywhere else, to reduce competition. To do so would have been foolish; and, whatever else has been said about them, the old Standard organization was seldom criticized for making less money when it could readily have made more."

The rapid increase in Rockefeller's share of total refining capacity in the United States (from 4 percent in 1870 to more than 80 percent in 1880) resulted from a combination of influences. Economic efficiency, entrepreneurial management, the generally depressed conditions during the 1870's, and the excess capacity in refining which had appeared following the Civil War were the most important factors. Rockefeller's acquisitions, an exchange of money for assets agreed to by all parties, were evidently favorable to the sellers, especially when the generally low market values of the depressed times are considered. Some refineries were anxious to be purchased, and frequently Standard Oil thought the asking price "outrageous."

Furthermore, the techniques of production were changing during this period, and the economically efficient scale of refinery output was increasing rapidly. Larger capital requirements meant that bigger firms had advantages not available to small producers. Most important of all, however, the Rockefeller organization exhibited the classic attributes of entrepreneurial alertness which are the fundamental source of new ideas, products, production techniques and over the long haul, rising real standards of living for the population. Armentano's summary description of those momentous events of the 1870's captures the exciting flavor of the competitive process at work in this important industry:

> Efficient operations in the 1870's meant tank cars, pipelines, adequate crude sources, cheap barrels, huge storage facilities, and export capabilities, all of which the Standard Oil Company had invested in heavily, and most of which the smaller competitors had not. The Standard Oil Company has often been criticized for the fact that its competitors could not enjoy the efficiencies of a tank car fleet, access to cheap pipelines, and large storage facilities. But, surely, the fact that competitors would not or could not be as efficient as Standard in these areas was not Standard's responsibility. Was it unfair to buy or build pipelines and then employ them to obtain lower rates for railroad freight? Was it unfair to invest millions in storage facilities to take advantage of slight variances in the demand and supply of crude or refined petroleum? And was it unfair for Rockefeller to surround himself with singular men of exceptional 'brainpower, astuteness, and foresightedness'? While competitors that could not or would not do these things might have regarded these activities as unfair, the ultimate justification of these

policies was proven again and again in the market place: they
lowered the costs of production and the price of the product
and raised the profits of the Standard Oil Company.

Economists are in general agreement with the textbook argument against
monopoly: barriers to market entry permit the restriction of production levels,
facilitate a higher 'monopoly price," and   therefore permit higher profits
and an inefficient allocation of resources. Presumably the Supreme Court, in
ruling that Standard Oil was in violation of the Sherman Act, interpreted this
to be the case. Again, however, the facts run contrary to the Court's decision.
Between 1870 and 1885, the period during which the Rockefeller organization
reached the zenith of its "power," refined kerosene prices *fell* from 26 cents
per gallon to just 8 cents. Average costs per gallon were reduced by a factor
of six.   From 1880 to 1897, when Standard Oil supposedly possessed this
monopoly power, or more than 90 percent of refinery capacity in the United
states, the price of refined oil per gallon in barrels *declined* from 9.33 cents to
5.91 cents.   At the same time the quality of petroleum products was being
significantly improved.   Furthermore, the volume of production increased
rapidly throughout the period, a performance which directly contradicts the
traditional case against monopoly.

In fact, the history of Standard Oil represents an important example of the
power and socially beneficial implications of the competitive process when
barriers to market participation are absent. Long before the breakup of the
Standard combination, according to one student of this period, " . . . the
process of whittling Standard Oil down to reasonable size within the industry
was already far advanced." While Standard's volume of refined production
increased from 39 million barrels in 1892 to 99 million barrels in 1911 (hardly
a monopolist output!), its share of the petroleum product's market had
declined to 64 percent in 1911 from almost 80 percent in 1890. With the
expansion of the industry and newly discovered crude oil supplies in the West
and Southwest, new companies were formed including the Pure Oil Company,
Texaco, Union Oil, and Gulf Oil Company. On the eve of the Supreme
Court's verdict against Standard Oil, there were at least 147   independent
refineries   in the United States.   In conclusion, and once again quoting
Armentano in his book *Antitrust and Monopoly*: "To seriously maintain that
Standard was increasingly monopolizing the petroleum industry at the turn of
the century, or that the antitrust suit against Standard . . . was a legitimate
response to almost complete monopolistic control, is patently absurd."

Appendix B

It is interesting that in recent decades the coercive power of government has been used to erect barriers to competition in the petroleum industry and thereby protect certain sectors from the rigors of competition. Through import quotas, restrictions on well-head production, and more recently in the government intervention which came out of the "energy crisis," the federal government has in effect cartelized the petroleum industry in a manner which had been found to be impossible for Rockefeller and his powerful combination. Once again the hard facts of reality must be recognized: government has invariably been the source of long-lasting monopoly power. The competitive process can only be suppressed by a force external to the market.

These conclusions regarding the Standard Oil example are generally applicable to the other cases brought under the Sherman Act and the Clayton Act. Almost without exception the record shows that government intervention is brought to bear against businesses which are *increasing output, innovating, reducing* costs and *passing these lower costs along in large part to the ultimate consumer.* For example, part of the brief against the Aluminum Company of American (Alcoa) in the antitrust suit before the special federal court in 1945 was that the company continued to research, innovate, lower their costs, and pass these savings on to the buyer in the form of lower prices, thereby precluding profitable entry by potential competitors. Alcoa had no competitors in the production of primary aluminum ingots because potential entrants simply could not match the company's economic efficiency. Appeals Court Justice Learned Hand seemed totally confused about the nature of competition and its benefits when he concluded that Alcoa "forestalled" competition by encouraging the consumption of aluminum and then "doubled and redoubled" its refining capacity to meet that demand. Striving for more business and increased economic efficiency, their actions were interpreted as restraints of trade. Antitrust had literally been turned on its head, penalizing what it allegedly was designed to promote.

The Sherman Act provides that ". . . every contract, combination, or conspiracy, in restraint of trade is hereby declared to be illegal," that *restraint* of production and trade is a violation of the law. Like Standard Oil, Alcoa, U.S. Steel, Brown Shoe Company, and many others, the evidence of actual behavior contradicts the indictments. Du Pont is a case in point. In the 1970's the Federal Trade Commission charged that du Pont's new low-cost method of producing titanium dioxide pigments had enabled it to gain forty percent of the domestic market. Not only had they acquired a larger share of the market through increased efficiency, but their new, efficient plant in Mississippi also increased their capacity to serve even more customers. University of Chicago

330

economist Yale Brozen identified the fundamental point: "Can you imagine that any enterprise would engage in such a nefarious activity? It should, according to the FTC, behave like a monopolist. It should restrict its output, instead of expanding, and charge higher prices." Examples of this confusion between protecting competitors from the market process and the desirable goal of encouraging entrepreneurial rivalry could fill volumes.

Armentano has summarized the role "anti-monopoly" statutes have played in actually suppressing the benefits derivable from the market process:

> The most important conclusion is that the entire antitrust system allegedly created to protect competition and increase consumer welfare has worked, instead, to lessen business competition and lessen the efficiency and productivity associated with the free-market process. Like many other governmental interventions, antitrust has produced results that are far different from those that were allegedly intended . . . In each and every case the indicted corporations were engaging in an intensely competitive process, yet in each and every case, such behavior was condemned by the FTC or by the Justice Department, as a 'restraint of trade' and as an alleged violation of the antitrust laws . . . in the vast majority of . . . private cases, it is perfectly clear that the legal concern is not monopoly or resource misallocation at all, but an obvious and blatant attempt by the plaintiff to retain and restrict the competitive rivalry emanating from the more efficient defendant company.

Although Microsoft was being sued by the Clinton "Justice" Department, the real reason for the lawsuit was the result of an effort by competitors to make government do what they could not do themselves: compete successfully against Microsoft. George W. Bush should drop the case and appoint new heads of the Anti-trust Division and Federal Trade Commission.

The Best Is Yet To Come

Notes

Chapter 1

The Triumph of Liberty

Footnotes

1. Barry Goldwater, Goldwater, (Doubleday 1988)
2. Ed Hewett, Reforming the Soviet Economy, (Brookings Institution, 1988)
3. Thomas Fleming, The New Dealers War, (Basic 2001)
4. Kenneth S. Davis, FDR: The War President, (Random House, 2001)

Chapter 2

Religion, Limited Government and the American Republic

Footnotes

1. M. Stanton Evans, The Theme is Freedom, (Prentice Hall, 1999), p. 117
2. Ibid. p. 133
3. Fustel de Coulanges, The Ancient City, (Doubleday, 1956), p. 181
4. F. M. Cornford, ed., The Republic of Plato, (Oxford, 1957), p. 232
5. Ibid. p. 234
6. Richard McKeon, ed., The Basic Works of Aristotle, (Random House, 1941), p. 132-137
7. M. Stanton Evans, The Theme is Freedom, (Prentice Hall, 1999), p. 144
8. New American Standard Bible, (Creation House, 1971), p. 402
9. M. Stanton Evans, The Theme is Freedom, (Prentice Hall, 1999), p. 136-141
10. Judaism and Modern Man, (Meridian, 1953), p. 50
11. Christopher Dawson, The Historic Reality of Christian Culture, (Harper, 1965), p. 35
12. Charles Colson, How Now Shall We Live?, (Tyndale House Publishers, Inc., 1999) p. 401
13. Paul Johnson, "Laying Down the Law", Wall Street Journal, March 10, 1999, p. A22
14. Charles Colson, How Now Shall We Live?, (Tyndale House Publishers, Inc., 1999) p. 402
15. Perry Miller and Thomas Johnson, eds., The Puritans (Harper, 1963), p. 212-213

16. M. Stanton Evans, The Theme is Freedom, (Prentice Hall, 1999), p. 146
17. Bernard Bailyn, Ideological Origins of the American Revolution, (Harvard, 1973), p. 57-60
18. William J. Federer, America's God and Country, (Fame Publishing, 1994) p. 317
19. M. Stanton Evans, The Theme is Freedom, (Prentice Hall, 1999), p. 262-263
20. The Political Writings of Thomas Jefferson, (Liberal Arts press, 1956), p. 161
21. Gary DeMar, American Christian History (American Vision, Inc., 1995), p. 152-159
22. M. Stanton Evans, The Theme is Freedom, (Prentice Hall, 1999), p. 300
23. William J. Federer, America's God and Country, (Fame Publishing, 1994) p. 409-413
24. Alex de Tocqueville, Democracy in America, (Vintage, 1955), Vol. I. p. 316

Chapter 2

Religion, Limited Government and the American Republic

It was certainly my good fortune to read M. Stanton Evans book, *The Theme is Freedom*, in 1995. As director of the National Jounalism Center in Washington, D.C. and former editor of The Indianapolis News, Evans convincingly makes the case that Western liberty and America's free institutions are products of our religious faith. "Our liberties," he says, "have always been dependent on the religious traditions of the West." Chapter 2 of this book is but a taste of the more filling meal found in *The Theme is Freedom*.

If one wanted to compress the best advice about studying politics into a single phrase, it would be: read Edmund Burke. Modern Library volume, *Selected Writings of Edmund Burke* (1960), edited by Walter Bate, and Burke's *Selected Writings and Speeches* (Doubleday, 1963), edited by Peter Stanlis. Also, Professor Stanlis' *Edmund Burke and the Natural Law* (Ann Arbor, 1965), is highly recommended.

Alexis de Tocqueville, whose insights into our political system, and Western freedom generally, remain as cogent today as when they were written in the 1830s. *Democracy in America* (two vols., 1956) is available in the Vintage Books edition.

Among expositors of the chapters central theme concerning the unity of our freedom and the Christian religion, the greatest by far, as most readers doubtless know, is Lord Acton, *Essays on Freedom and Power* (Gertrude Himmelfarb, ed., Meridian, 1955) is an excellent compendium of his *Lectures on Modern History* (Meridian, 1951). For those who want to delve further in Acton's fabled erudition, Liberty Fund of Indianapolis has brought out a handsome three-volume set, edited by Rufus Fears (*Selected Writings of Lord Acton*, 1986). He who has reads Burke, Tocqueville, and Acton will know most of what is worth knowing on these topics.

For one of the great books on the Christian faith, I would recommend C.S. Lewis, *Mere Christianity*, (Touchstone, 1980). Lewis was a professor of medieval and Renaissance literature at Oxford and Cambridge Universities who wrote more than thirty books in his lifetime, including *The Screwtape Letters*, the *Chronicles of Narnia*, and *The Space Triology*.

Eric Voegelin, a four-volume *Order and History* (Louisiana, 1957-74), and a monument of scholarship and analysis, traced the idea of transcendence, its origins and applications, from ancient societies to Israel to the modern era by providing unique comparative study in philosophy and religion. Another great source is Frank S. Meyer's, *In Defense of Freedom* (Regnery, 1962) and *The Conservative Mainstream* (Arlington House, 1969). Russell Kirk, *The Conservative Mind* (Regnery, 1953) is a classic. Already mentioned, of course, and a main subject to Chapter 3 is F. A. Hayek, Nobel Laureate and tireless exponent of free markets, *The Road to Serfdom* (Chicago, 1944), *The Constitution of Liberty* (Chicago, 1960), and *Individualism and Economic Order* (Routledge & Kegan Paul, 1949).

Others who specifically trace our freedoms to their religious roots, should also be mentioned: Michael Novak, *The Spirit of Democratic Capitalism* (Simon and Schuster, 1982), Edmund Opitz, *Religion and Capitalism: Allies, Not Enemies* (Arlington House, 1970), John Courtney Murray, *We Hold These Truths* (Image Books, 1964), and George Gilder, *Wealth and Poverty* (Basic Books, 1981).

On the covenantial precepts of the early settlers, the reader is especially referred to Perry Miller's *Orthodoxy in Massachusetts* (Beacon, 1959), Samuel Eliot Morison's *Builders of the Bay Colony* (Houghton Miffin, 1964), Edmund Morgan's *The Puritan Dilemma* (Little Brown, 1958) and Daniel Wait Howe's *The Puritan Republic* (Bowen-Merrill, 1899), as well as David Lovejoy's *The Glorious Revolution in America* (Harper, 1974).

America's Founding Fathers represent an accumulation of talent perhaps never again to be duplicated. *The Life and Selected Writings of Thomas Jefferson* (Modern Library, 1944), *The Political Writings of John Adams* (Liberal Arts Press, 1956), and *The Complete Madison* (Harper, 1953) are all invaluable sources to those men and those times.

Appendix A shares a few hundred quotes from a a selection of founders, justices, and government leaders concerning Christianity.

Chapter 3

Ideas Have Consequences

Of mankind's greatest achievements over the last twenty centuries, one towers over all the rest. It was the long, painstaking task of the triumph of liberty by limiting government. Wresting liberty from tyranny's iron fist still has a long way to go. Some countries have not yet started. Millions of men and women have worked and struggled and even given their lifeblood to fight for the greatest cause that humankind has ever known. There are millions of heroes.

In addition, tens of thousands of economists have described the workings of the market, a spontaneous order of natural self-interest working without a plan or government. F.A. Hayek and Milton Friedman are but two of the important contributors. Limited government and private property leads to freedom and freedom produces the most efficient of competitive market outcomes. Stable money, low taxes, and free trade are policies that can be chosen which only enhance the workings of a free market system. All are important. All were briefly discussed in this chapter.

An important source of information for this chapter was, *What Everyone Should Know About Economics and Prosperity* by James Gwartney and Richard Stroup, published by The Goldwater Institute. Dr. Stroup was my Ph.D. thesis advisor and has been a source of wisdom for me for over 30 years. In addition, Leonard Read (now deceased) and the Foundation for Economic Education have been most helpful. As executive director of the Center for Market Alternatives in Boise, Idaho, I brought Leonard and his group of scholars to Idaho on at least six different occasions for a weekend FEE Seminar. Articulate and outspoken scholars of the free market, limited government point of view, the Foundation for Economic Education is still one of the outstanding defenders of freedom.

Chapter 4

U-Turn on the Road to Serfdom

The initial impetus for this chapter came from Daniel Yergin's wonderful book *Commanding Heights*. While the brief development of Augusto Pinochet, Margaret Thatcher, Ronald Reagan, and Deng Xiaoping borrowed a few ideas from his book, the main part of the chapter came from my book *CrossRoads: The Great American Experiment*, published in 1984 by University Press, and subsequent writing.

The discussion of Ronald Reagan was aided by a book by his Attorney General Edwin Meese III entitled *With Reagan*, published in 1992. Meese worked with Reagan during his governorship of California as well as Reagan's two terms in the White House. The modern day Rip van Winkle idea of comparing 1980 with 1990 and awakening to an entirely different country was enlightening. Thank you Ed. And by the way, my son has heard me talk so fondly of Ronald Reagan for so long that he named his son Raegan—a bit different spelling, but the thought was there. Grandpa Barry is enjoying his two grandsons, Andrew and Raegan.

Chapter 5

Freedom and the Developing Countries

Footnotes

1. Gerald O. Driscoll, Kim Holmes, and Melanie Kirpatrick, *2001 Index of Economic Freedom*, The Heritage Foundation and the Wall Street Journal.
2. Thomas L. Friedman, *The Lexus and the Olive Tree* (Farrar Straus Giroux, 1999) p. 307.
3. Hernando DeSoto, *The Mystery of Capital*, (Basic Books, 2000), p. 13.
4. Ibid. p. 23.
5. Ibid. p. 7.
6. Driscoll, et al., p. 327

Chapter 6

Anatomy of Government Failure

A brief but excellent summary of the issues in this chapter concerning the question of government's limitations as a delivery system is William C. Mitchell, *The Anatomy of Public Failure: A Public Choice Perspective*, (International Institute for Economic Rearch: Los Angeles).

Another important summary of the theory of public choice is Henry LePage, *Tomorrow, Capitalism*. A few of the more accessible sources would include the relevant chapters in Milton and Rose Friedman, *Free to Choose*, (Harcourt, Brace Jovanovich: New York), William E. Simon, *A Time for Truth* (McGraw Hill); Bernard H. Siejen, *Economic Liberties and the Constitution*, (University of Chicago Press), and Richard B. McKenzie and Gordon Tullock, *Modern Political Economy: An Introduction to Economics*, (McGraw Hill: New York).

The following are generally more demanding reading but they are classics. The pioneering study of the ideas contained in the public choice model was Anthony Downs, *An Economic Theory of Democracy*, (Harper and Row Publishers: New York, 1957). Other key contributions to our understanding of the anatomy of government failure include James Buchanan and Gordon Tullock, *The Calculus of Consent: Logical Foundations of Constitutional Democracy*, (University of Michigan Press: Ann Arbor), 1962; William Niskannan, *Bureaucracy and Representative Government*, (Aldine Atherton: Chicago), 1981.

Two fairly short and very readable discussions of the defects in our democratic institutions can be found in Robert A. Nisbet, *The New Despotism*, (Institute for Humane Studies: Menlo Park, Calif. 1976), and Richard E. Wagner and Robert D. Tollison, *Balanced Budgets, Fiscal Responsibility, and the Constitution*. Henri Lepage in Tomorrow, Capitalism, Chapter 7 — "*Reinventing the Market*" also offers a good summary of the means by which government might be made more responsive to individual wants.

From a somewhat different approach than the public choice people, the "Austrian School" has also made important contributions to our understanding of the limitations of government as a delivery system. See for example the classic Ludwig von Mises *Bureaucracy*, (Hale University Press: New Haven 1946), and Socialism, (Liberty Fund, Inc.: Indianapolis 1981), and in the work of Friedrich A. Hayek, *The Road to Serfdom* and *Part III of The Constitution of Liberty*. A powerful account of the implications of government intervention in the free market is the important book by Murray N. Rothbard, *Power and Market: Government and the Economy.* An excellent short summary of the factors contributing to the growth in government is Allen H. Meltzer, *Why Government Grows*, (International Institute for Economic Research: Los Angeles August 1976).

Chapter 7

The Microsoft Debacle

Footnotes

1. With respect to the question of monopoly and the antitrust laws the basic contribution is Dominick T. Armentano, *Antitrust and Monopoly: Anatomy of a Policy Failure*, (John Wiley & Sons: New York, 1982). An important collection of papers on this issue is H.J. Goldschmid, H.M. Mann, and J. F. Weston, eds., *Industrial Concentration: The New Learning*, (Little, Brown and Company: Boston, 1974). Among other important and readable sources on the question of monopoly power and industrial concentration, the following are recommended: Yale Brozen, *Is Governemnt the Source of Monopoly? And Other Essays* (CATO Institute: Washington, DC 1980); Harold Demsetz, *The Market Concentration Doctrine*, (American Enterprise Institute: Washington, DC August 1973); and Harold Demsetz, *The Trust Behind Antitrust*, (International Institute for Economic Research: Los Angeles, March, 1978).

2. The power and relevance of Friedrich A. Hayek's views on "social justice" are found in *The Constitution of Liberty: Law, Legislation and Liberty: The Mirage of Social Justice*, (University of Chicago Press, Vol. II, 1976); and *"The Atavism of Social Justice,"* in *Social Justice, Socialism and Democracy*, (Center for Independent Studies: Sydney, Australia, Occasional Papers 2, 1979).

3. The revisionist view of the importance of monopoly in the post-Civil War period can be found in Gabriel Kolko, *The Triumph of Conservatism: A Reinterpretation of America's History*, 1900-1916, (Free Press 1977).

And, Dominic T. Armentano, *Antitrust and Monopoly: Anatomy of a Policy Failure*, (John Wiley & Sons: New York, 1982). The classic illustration of the robber barons interpretation of this period is de-bunked in Lawrence W. Reed, *"Witch Hunting for Robber Barons: The Standard Oil Story"*, The Freeman (Foundation for Economic Education: Irvington-on-Hudson, New York, March 1980).

Chapter 8

Jobs That Work

This chapter is a compilation of thirty years of reading *The Wall Street Journal, Forbes, Business Week, The Economist, Harvard Business Review*, several daily newspapers, and the hundreds of books I've read on the subject.

My public presentations have used these daily and weekly publications for over 30 years. When it comes to who said what, I am not sure, only to say Chapter 6 is loaded with the great ideas that appeared numerous times in those newspapers, journals, and magazines. *Salt and Pepper* in the Wall Street Journal, the last page of Forbes magazine, the cartoons in Harvard Business Review, and the distinctive humor of the British Economist have given me enough one-liners to last a lifetime.

Ten years ago I read a small pamphlet by Price Pritchett entitled *New Work Habits for a Radically Changing World*. Since then, I have used many of his wonderful ideas in my presentations. Thank you Price. Your insights are truer today than when you wrote them.

Authors Tom Peters, Thomas Malone, Robert Laubacher and William Bridges should be also noted for their ongoing books on management, leadership and job shifts of the future. Parts of this chapter have been influenced by their work.

Thanks also to Coach John Wooden. Anybody that can win 10 national championships in 12 years has to be the most truly remarkable of men. John, you are.

Chapter 9

Globalism and the Internet

Footnotes

1) Barry Asmus, When Riding a Dead Horse, For Heaven's Sake . . . Dismount, p. 68.
2) Bill Gates, Business at the Speed of Thought (Warner Books, 1999).
3) David Burnell, Making the Cisco Connection, (John Wiley and Sons, 2000).

I want to thank Thomas Friedman for his book, *The Lexus and the Olive Tree*. Twenty years ago, he was a great liberal spokesman. Today, he is still a great writer, thinker, but now liberal is used in the eighteenth century sense. His book is one of the best reads of the decade on understanding globalization.

Mark Helprin, a novelist and contributing editor to *The Wall Street Journal*, and author of *Refiner's Fire*, *Ellis Island and Other Stories*, was a source of many of the ideas in this section.

Chapter 10

American Policy and Free Market Reforms

Footnotes

1. Peter M. Flanigan, Chairman of Children First America, the Development of Private Voucher Programs. NCPA: An Education Agenda, p. 28.
2. Ibid. p. 30
3. Wall Street Journal, Review and Outlook, p. A-22, Wednesday, December 20, 2000
4. Barry Asmus, When Riding a Dead Horse, for Heaven's Sake . . . Dismount, (AmeriPress, 1995) p. 87
5. Steve Forbes, A New Birth of Freedom, (Regnery Publishing, 1999), p.106
6. Ibid. p. 107
7. John Goodman, Patient Power, (Cato Institute, 1992), p. vii

8. Barry Asmus, When Riding a Dead Horse, For Heaven's Sake . . . Dismount, (AmeriPress, 1995) p. 145
9. Barry Asmus, ClintonCare: Putting Government in Charge of Your Health, (AmeriPress, 1995).p. 66
10. Bill Gates, Business at the Speed of Thought, (Warner Books, 1999), p. 333-335
11. Milton Friedman, Free to Choose, (Harcourt Brace Janovich, 1981), p. 113.

Thanks to the National Center for Policy Analysis and the talented staff, Sr. Fellows and great economists who associate with the center. I learn the ideas from you and am then privileged to share them with the world.

Notes

Education

On the history and success of private education in the United States before the Civil War see Samuel L. Blumenfeld, *"Why Schools Went Public,"* Reason, March 1979 and his book *Is Public Education Necessary*, (Devin-Adair Co., Inc.: Old Greenwich, Connecticut), 1981. An important work on the evolution of the relationship between government and education and an evaluation of proposals for privatization is Robert B. Everhart, ed., *The Public School Monopoly: A Critical Analysis of Education and the State in American Society*, (Pacific Institute for Public Policy Research : San Francisco), 1982. Another important collection of articles can be found in James S. Coleman, et. al., *Parents, Teachers, and Children: Prospects for Choice in American Education*, (Institute for Contemporary Studies: San Francisco). Two short pieces by Thomas Sowell provide some interesting facts on the viability of private schools: *"Educators' Treat Parents Like Children,"* and "Educational Draftees," in his *Pink and Brown People and Other Controversial Essays*, (Hoover Institute Press: Palo Alto, Calif., 1981).

Milton Friedman, Capitalism and Freedom (Chicago: University of Chicago Press, 1962), 85-107; Robert B. Everhart, ed., *The Public School Monopoly* (San Francisco: Pacific Institute for Public Policy Research, 1981); and Paul E. Peterson, "Monopoly and Competition in American Education," in William H. Clune and John F. Witte, eds., *Choice and Control in American Education* (New York: Falmer Press, 1990), 47-78. A blistering critique of our failing public schools and our fuzzy thinking about how to fix them,

Myron Lieberman's book, *Public Education: An Autopsy*, explains why public education is in irreversible and terminal decline and tells us what we must do to get American schooling back on track. Few other books on educational policy or reform cover such a broad range of issues or draws upon such extensive empirical data across such diverse academic disciplines. His is a refreshingly clear analysis of our educational crisis and a rallying cry for market-system approaches to school reform. Lieberman contends that the major deficiencies of public education are inherent in the fact that government provides the service: the government's role as producer of education conflicts with its role as protector of consumer interests, and the conflicts are overwhelmingly resolved in favor of its producer role. He presents a comprehensive analysis of the alternatives, concluding that the existing system must be replaced by a three-sector industry encompassing public, non-profit, and for-profit schools, with for-profit schools playing an important role.

Different children need to be educated differently and we need a vast array of competitive choices. His analysis covers the enormous underestimation of the real cost of public education, the overestimation of its benefits, the breakdown of its information system, the destructive role of higher education, the media emphasis on secondary issues such as multiculturalism, the futility of educational research and development, the role of teacher unions in protecting the status quo, and the antimarket bias that pervades every aspect of public education. Lieberman also analyzes the implications of a market system for equality of educational opportunity: in his view, the critics of a market system of education have ignored the evidence that free enterprise has done more than government to equalize the human condition. His Privatization and Educational Choice, (St. Martin's Press, 1989) is another of Lieberman's many books making a clear and convincing argument for parental choice and privatization. Myron Lieberman, an educational consultant and writer, has served most recently as Visiting Scholar, Social Philosophy and Policy Center, Bowling Green State University. He is presently a consultant to federal, state and local education agencies and is a nationally recognized analyst of educational issues.

Notes

Health Care

Blank, Robert H. *Rationing Medicine*, (Columbia University Press, 1988).
Goodman, John, *Patient Power: Solving America's Health Care Crisis*, (Cato, 1992), *Regulation of Medicare Care: Is the Price Too High?* (1980).
Herzlinger, Regina, Creating New Health Care Ventures, 1991. Task Force Report, *An Agenda for Solving America's Health Care Crisis*, NCPA Policy Report No. 151, Dallas, 1990.

Social Security

Four central changes in our economic and social life since the thirties have altered the costs and benefits of Social Security, yet have had almost no effect on the design of the program. These are the great expansion in employer-provided pensions and other sources of retirement income; the steady increase in life expectancy (since 1930, life expectancy at birth has increased from 58 to 71.6 years among males, and from 61.3 to 78.6 years among females); the steady improvement in the financial well-being of the elderly relative to other age groups; and changes in federal policy itself, which have resulted in an array of programs providing assistance to the elderly poor and medical care coverage for virtually all of the nation's elderly. U.S. retirement income policy can continue to ignore these developments only at great cost.

Further reading on Social Security:

Barro, Robert J. *The Impact of Social Security on Private Saving: Evidence from the U.S. Time Series* (1978).
Board of Trustees of the Federal Old-Age and Survivors Insurance, Disability and Hospital Insurance Trust Funds. *1992 Annual Report* (1992).
Boskin, Michael J. *Too Many Promises: The Uncertain Future of Social Security* (1986).
Campbell, Colin D. *Social Security's Financial Crisis*, (International Institute for Economic Research: Los Angeles (October, 1983).
Feldstein, Martin, *"Social Security, Induced Retirement, and Aggregate Capital Accumulation"* Journal of Political Economy 82, No. 5 (1984): 905-27.
Ferrera, Peter J. *Social Security: Averting the Crisis*, (CATO Institute, Washington , DC 1982).

Notes

Hurd, Michael D., and Michael J. Boskin. "The Effect of Social Security on Retirement in the Early 1980s." *Quarterly Journal of Economics 99* (November 1984): 767-90.

Kollman, Geoffrey, "Social Security: The Relationship of Taxes and Benefits." Congressional Research Service Report no. 92-956 EPW. December 16, 1992.

Quinn, Joseph F., Richard V. Burkhauser, and Daniel A. Myers. *Passing the Torch: The Influence of Economic Incentives on Work and Retirement.* 1990.

Weaver, Carolyn L. *The Crisis in Social Security: Economic and Political Origins.* 1982.

The Best is Yet to Come

Selected Bibliography

Asmus, Barry, *When Riding a Dead Horse for Heaven's Sake . . . Dismount*, (AmeriPress, 1995). *ClintonCare: Putting Government in Charge of Your Health*, (AmeriPress, 1995). Co-author with Don Billings *Crossroads: The Great American Experiment*, (University Press, 1983).

Bailyn, Bernard, *Ideological Origins of the American Revolution*, (Harvard, 1973)

Bartley, W.W., III, ed. *The Collected Works of Friedrich August Hayek, Vol. 1*, (Routledge, 1988)

Baum, Richard, *Buying Mao: Chinese Politics in the Age of Deng Xiaoping*, (Princeton University Press, 1966)

Bell, Daniel, *The Cultural Contradictions of Capitalism*, (Basic Cooks, 1976)

Berman, Harold , *Law and Revolution*, (Harvard, 1983)

Bridges, William, *Job Shift*, (Perseus Books, 1994)

Bryan, Lowell and Diana Farrell, *Market Unbound: Unleashing Global Capitalism*, (John Wiley & Sons, 1996)

Buchanan, James, *The Calculus of Consent: Logical Foundations of Constitutional Democracy*, (University of Michigan Press: Ann Arbor, 1962)

Colson, Charles, *How Now Shall We Live*, (Tyndale House Publishers, Inc., 1999)

Cornford, F. M., *The Republic of Plato*, (Oxford, 1957)

Coulanges, Fustel de, *The Ancient City*, (Doubleday, 1956)

Davis, Kenneth S., *FDR: The War President*, (Random House 2001)

Dawson, Christopher, *The Historic Reality of Christian Culture*, (Harper, 1965)

DeMar, Gary, *American Christian History*, (American Vision, Inc., 1995)

DeSoto, Hernando, *The Mystery of Capital*, (Basic Books, 2000).

D'Souza, Dinesh, *The Virtue of Prosperity: Finding Values in an Age of Techno-Affluence,* (Simon & Schuster, 2000)

Downs, Anthony, *An Economic Theory of Democracy*, (Harper and Row Publishers: New York, 1957)

Drucker, Peter, *Managing in a Time of Great Change*, (Truman Talley, 1996)

Ebenstein, Alan, *Friedrich Hayek* (St. Martins 2001)

Evans, M. Stanton, *The Theme is Freedom*, (Prentice Hall, 1999)

Federer, William J., *America's God and Country*, (Fame Publishing, 1994)

Forbes, Steve, *A New Birth of Freedom,* (Regnery Publishing, 1999)

Fleming, Thomas, *The New Dealers War*, (Basic 2001)

Friedman, Milton, *Free to Choose*, (Harcourt Brace Janovich, New York, 1981). Co-author Rose Friedman, *Two Lucky People*, (University of Chicago Press, 1998)

347

Selected Bibliography

Friedman, Thomas L., *The Lexus and the Olive Tree*, (Farrar Straus Giroux, 1999)

Fukuyama, Francis, *The End of History and the Last Man*, (Free Press, 1992)

Gates, Bill, *Business at the Speed of Thought*, (Warner Books, 1999)

Gilder, George, *Wealth and Poverty*, (Basic Books, 1981)

Goldwater, Barry, *Goldwater*, (Doubleday, 1988)

Goodman, John, *Patient Power*, (Cato Institute, 1992)

Hayek, Friedrich A., *The Road to Serfdom*, (Chicago, 1944)

Helprin, Mark, *Ellis Island and Other Stories*, (Harcourt Brace, 1991)

Hewett, Ed, *Reforming the Soviet Economy*, (Brookings Institution 1988)

Howard, Michael and William Louis, eds., *The Oxford History of the Twentieth Century*, (Oxford University Press, 1998)

Jardin, Andrè, *Tocqueville, a Biography*, (Farrar, Straus, and Giroud, 1988)

Johnson, B. Bruce, *"Planning Without Prices: A Discussion of Land Use Regulation Without Compensation"*

Johnson, Thomas, *The Puritans*, (Harper, 1963)

Judaism and Modern Man, (Meridian, 1953)

Kahn, Alfred, *Economics of Regulation: Principles and Institutions*, (Wiley, 1970)

Kindleberger, Charles, *The World in Depression, 1929-1939*, (University of California Press, 1986)

Klaus, Vàclav, *Renaissance: the Rebirth of Liberty in the Heart of Europe*, (Cato Instiute, 1997)

Kotkin, Joel, *Tribes: How Race, Religion and Identity Determine Success in the New Global Economy*, (Random House, 1992)

Mayer, David N., The Constitutional Thought of Thomas Jefferson, (University Press of Virginia, 1994)

McKenzie, Richard B., *Modern Political Economy: An Introduction to Economics*, (McGraw Hill: New York, 1992)

McKeon, Richard, *The Basic Works of Aristotle*, (Random House, 1941)

Meese, Edwin III, *With Reagan*, (Regnery Gateway, 1992)

Meyer, Frank S., *In Defense of Freedom*, (Regnery, 1962)

Micklethwait, John and Adrian Wooldridge, *A Future Perfect*, (Crown Business, 2000)

Miller, Perry, *The Puritans*, (Harper, 1963)

Mises, Ludwig von, *Bureaucracy*, (Hale University Press: New Haven, 1946). *Socialism*, (Liberty Fund, Inc.: Indianapolis 1936)

Morley, Felix, *The Christian History of the Constitution and Self Government with Union*, (American Christian Constitution Press, 1962)

Selected Bibliography

New American Standard Bible, (Creation House, 1971)

Nisbet, Robert A., *The New Despotism*, (Institute for Humane Studies: Menlo Park, Calif., 1976)

Niskanen, William A., *Reaganomics: An Insiders Account of the Policies of the People,* (Oxford University Press, 1988)

Niskarran, William, *Bureaucracy and Representative Government*, (Aldine Atherton: Chicago, 1981)

Novak, Michael, *The Spirit of Democratic Capitalism*, (Simon & Schuster, 1982)

Ohmae, Kenichi, *The Borderless World*, (Harper Business, 1990)

Opitz, Edmund, *Religion and Capitalism: Allies, Not Enemies*, (Arlington House, 1970)

O'Rourke, P.J., *Eat the Rich*, (Atlantic Monthly Press, 1998), *Parliament of Whores,* (Atlantic Monthly Press, 1991)

Palm, Daniel C, *On Faith and Free Government*, (Roman and Littlefield, 1997)

Peters, Tom, *The Brand You: 50 Ways to Transform Yourself From an "Employee" Into a Brand that Shouts Distinction, Commitment, and Passion*, (Alfred A. Knopf, 1999)

Powell, Jim, The Triumph of Liberty, (The Free Press, 2000)

Ramsay, I.T., ed *John Locke, The Reasonableness of Christianity With a Discourse of Miracles*, (Stanford University Press, 1989)

Read, Leonard, *Anything That's Peaceful*, (Foundation for Economic Education, 1993)

Rohwer, Jim, *Asia Rising: Why America Will Prosper as Asia's Economies Boom*, (Simon & Schuster, 1995)

Rothbard, Murray N., *Power and Market: Government and the* Economy, (Sheed Andrews and McNeal, Inc. 1970)

Samuels, Warren J., Ed., *The Chicago School of Political Economy*, (Transaction Publishers, 1993)

Schumpeter, Joseph A., *Capitalism, Socialism, and Democracy*, (Routledge, 1994)

Shanahan, John M., *The Most Brilliant Thoughts of All Time*, (Harper Collins, 1999)

Siegen, Bernard H., *Planning Without Prices*, (DC Heath: Lexington, Mass., 1977). *Economic Liberties and the Constitution,* (University of Chicago Press)

Skidalsky, Robert, *John Maynard Keynes: The Economist as Savior*, (Macmillan, 1992)

Simon, William E., *A Time for Truth*, (McGraw Hill, 1980)

349

Selected Bibliography

Sowell, Thomas, *Knowledge and Decisions*, (Basic Books, 1980)

Stroup, Richard, *What Everyone Should Know About Economics and Prosperity*, (The Goldwater Institute, 1993)

Templeton, Sir John Marks, *Story of a Claim: A Fable of Disenchantment and Enlightenment*, (Templeton Foundation Press, 2001)

Thatcher, Margaret, *The Downing Street Years*, (Harper Collins, 1993)

Tocqueville, Alex de, *Democracy in America*, (Vintage, 1955)

The Political Writings of Thomas Jefferson, (Liberal Arts press, 1956)

Toffler, Alvin, *The Third Wave*, (Morrow, 1980), *Powershift* (Bantam, 1990)

Tullock, Gordon, *Modern Political Economy: An Introduction to Economics*, (McGraw Hill: New York) *The Calculus of Consent: Logical Foundations of Constitutional Democracy*, (University of Michigan Press: Ann Arbor, 1962)

Valdez, Juan Gabriel, *Pinochet's Economists: The Chicago School in Chile*, (Cambridge University Press, 1995)

Weaver, Richard, *Ideas Have Consequences*, (Chicago, 1948)

Weber, Max, *The Protestant Ethic and the Spirit of Capitalism*, (Unwin Hyman, 1989)

West, Thomas G., *Vindicating the Founders*, (Roman and Littlefield, 1997)

Wooden, John, *Wooden*, (Contemporary Books, 1997)

Wriston, Walter, *The Twilight of Sovereignty*, (Scribner, 1992)

Yergin, Daniel, *Commanding Heights*, (Simon & Schuster, 1998)

Young, Hugo, *The Iron Lady: A Biography of Margaret Thatcher*, (New York: Farrar, Straus, and Giroux, 1989)

Acknowledgments

I want to thank the following people (or staff) for their interviews, ideas, insights, and many helpful suggestions along the way.

Ed and Esther Asmus: parents, life-givers, life-lovers, and wisdom dispensers; **Fred Beasely:** builder of houses and men, Pastor of Outreach, Scottsdale Bible Church, best friend; **James Buchanan:** famous public choice economist from George Mason University; **William F. Buckley:** author of over forty books, founder of the influential magazine *National Review*, and host of the 30 year running television show, *Firing Line*; **William Bridges:** a consultant, lecturer, and author of the classic book, *Transitions*, and one of the top five executive development consultants in the U.S.; **Bob Buford:** President of a successful cable television company and the founder of Leadership Network; **Charles Colson:** a popular and widely known author, speaker, radio commentator, and winner of the prestigious Templeton Prize for Progress in Religion; **Dorman Cordell:** Editor of Executive Alert, National Center for Policy Analysis; **Edward Crane:** President of the Cato Institute, one of Washington's most important think tanks; **Hernando deSoto:** President of the Institute for Liberty and Democracy, headquartered in Lima, Peru and named by the Economist as the second most important think tank in the world; **Richard Ebeling:** Professor of Economics, Hillsdale College, and top rate scholar of the Austrian School; **M. Stanton Evans:** Director of the National Journalism Center in Washington DC and prestigious American columnist; **Milton Friedman:** Nobel Laureate in Economics, now with the Hoover Institution and arguably the world's most influential economist; **Steve Forbes:** International business leader, President and CEO of *Forbes, Inc.*, as well as Editor-in-Chief of *Forbes*, and Republican Presidential candidate; **William Federer:** author of *America's God and Country*, with over 2,100 quotations has given us an invaluable encyclopedia of America's noble heritage; **Thomas Friedman:** won two Pulitzer Prizes for his reporting for *The New York Times* as bureau chief in Beirut and Jerusalem, and author of the acclaimed *The Lexus and the Olive Tree*; **John Goodman:** President of the National Center for Policy Analysis, an original manufacturer of ideas, author, professor, debater, and a very good friend; **George Gilder:** best selling author and technological guru, always seeing what others cannot; **David Henderson:** editor of the *Fortune Encyclopedia of Economics*, Professor of Naval Postgraduate School in Monterey, California and a former Senior Economist for President Reagan's Council of Economic Advisors; **Rena Henderson:** book editor extraordinaire, full of perspective and wisdom, deserves much credit for the flow of this book; **P. J. Hill:** Professor of Economics, Wheaton

351

Acknowledgments

College, author, Ph.D. from the University of Chicago, the man who most influenced my views economically and spiritually; **Michael Lyon**: Professor of Finance, a colleague for thirteen years and friend for thirty; **Raymond Manning**: Program Director, B2B Marketplaces of Oracle, Inc., a great friend, and my son's father-in-law; **Marvin McCarthy**: engineer, technological guru, consultant and book editor; **Michael Novak**: noted historian, theologian, and policy analyst with the American Enterprise Institute, and one of America's best spokesman for both Christianity and capitalism; **Ed Opitz**: Christian theologian with The Foundation for Economic Education, has been clarifying spiritual and economic ideas for me for over forty years; **Mary O'Grady**: editor of The America's column in *The Wall Street Journal*, great mind and even better personal friend; **Jim Powell**: Senior Fellow at the Cato Institute and editor of Laїssez-Faire Books, important author and prolific spokesman for liberty; **Tom Peters**: America's most recognized business guru, author of the famous *In Search of Excellence* and founder of the Tom Peters Group; **Llewellyn Rockwell**: founder and President of the Ludwig von Mises Institute and insightful Austrian scholar; **Tom Schrader**: businessman, Senior Pastor of East Valley Bible Church, and one of my best mentors; **Dr. Robert A. Sirico**, President of the Acton Institute for the study of Religion and Liberty, a tireless proponent of the theological basis for limited government and liberty; **Richard Stroup**: author of the best selling textbook *Economics: Private and Public Choice*, my Ph.D. thesis advisor and an academic who has influenced my thinking for 35 years; **Thomas Sowell**: Senior Fellow at the Hoover Institution, Stanford University, famous author, and influential thinker on social issues and intellectual controversies; **Tom Swanson**: author of *Words From the Street: Overheard From Commonfolk*, high school math and social science teacher, my personal friend and pithy statement dispenser for almost three decades; **Gayle Tofani**: wonderful sister for 45 years, secretary and office manager for almost 15 years, and, next to my wife, my best female friend; **Alvin Toffler**: his books *Future Shock, The Third Wave*, and *PowerShift* were enormously successful and very influential; **Walter Williams**: well known economist, social critic, and author of many books including *The State Against Blacks*; and **Daniel Yergin**: author of the Pulitzer Prize book, *The Prize: The Epic Quest for Oil, Money and Power* and *Commanding Heights,* also President of Cambridge Energy Research.

The staff of The National Center for Policy Analysis, as always, were especially helpful. Appreciation. Kudos. Thanks. Any mistakes or ideas not properly credited, of course, are mine. Many authors often stand on the shoulders of intellects more powerful than themselves. The names listed above are definitely in that category for me. And now, the best for last.

352

Acknowledgments

Amanda Phelps Asmus: elegant lady, mother, life partner and my very best friend. We met at age 18, fell in love at 19, married as twenty year olds and spent the next 40 years growing together. Your commitment to our children and our parents; your enthusiasm for sports; your instinctual reaction to always think the best of everyone; and your oh so helpful interest in economics and world events make you a woman designed in heaven for me. You taught me that the adventure of faith and our spiritual walk were far more important than any possible happenings in the marketplace. Thank you for giving up hundreds of hours of what should have been "our time" for this book. Once again, sweetheart, you were my encouragement and support.

I love you very much.

INDEX

(main discussion-bold-faced numbers)

A

INDEX
(main discussion-bold-faced numbers)

B

C

INDEX
(main discussion-bold-faced numbers)

INDEX
(main discussion-bold-faced numbers)

G

GDP   72, 96, 114, 137
GM   82, 219, 227
GM Brazil   227
Gates, Bill (Microsoft)   165-181
General Electric   187, 205, 223
General Motors   249
General Theory of Employment, Interest and Money   21
Genesis 1:1   39
George, Henry   91
Gerstner, Lou   223
global capitalism   123, 164
global economy   29, 89, 90, 209
globalism   **207-210**, 212, 232
globalization   117, 121, 277
gold standard   20
Goldman Sachs   219
Goldwater, Barry   14-15
Gooding, Cuba, Jr.   175
Gorbachev, Mikhail   17
Gore, Albert   162, 254, 271
Gray, Lee   15
Great Britain   19, 21, **99-103**, 109, 120, 160, 252
Great Depression   15, **19-23**, 24, 275
Great Leap Forward   111, 113
Greenleaf, Simon   312
Greco-Roman   35
Greenspan, Alan   3, 255
Grove, Andy   228
Gutenberg   110

H

Haiti   128
Hamilton, Alexander   55, 311, 312, 314
happy? Are you   294-300
Harris, Ralph   100
Harvard University   24, 312
Hayek, Friedrich A.   v, 4, 22, **65-69**, 72-76, 95, 99-101, 107, 113, 279, 283

359

INDEX

(main discussion-bold-faced numbers)

INDEX
(main discussion-bold-faced numbers)

INDEX
(main discussion-bold-faced numbers)

INDEX
(main discussion-bold-faced numbers)

S

INDEX
(main discussion-bold-faced numbers)

V

Veterans   24
Virginia, West   9, 304
voluntary exchange   6, 62, 71, 74, 79, 85, 92, 123, 178, 197, 210, 281, 285
vouchers   69, 71, 159, **245-248**, 272, 290

W

Wal-Mart   221
Wall Street Journal   4, 119, 125, 162
Washington, George   50, 55, 158, 307, 310, 314, 319, 320
Washington Post   247
wealth   4, 10, 23, 27, 52, 54, 74, 83, 89, 110, 119, 120, 123, 125, 127, 132,
        134, 136, 178, 183, 197, 198, 214, 233, 296, 297, 301, 304
Webster, Daniel   40
Welch, Jack   187, 205, 223
welfare state   2, 19, 29, 99, 142, 287
Whigs   53
Wilson, Woodrow   31
Windows   165, 167, 168, 170, 172-177, 179, 191
Windsor Town Hall   27, 28
Winkle, Rip Van   103
wireless Internet   215, 230
Wooden, John   204
World Series   10
work choices   185-206
World War II   5, 18, **23-25**, 27, 66, 253
World Wide Web   117, 214, 218, 280
Wren, Sir Christopher   27

X

Xiaoping, Deng   109, **112-114**

Y, Z

Yergin, Daniel   68, 337
Young Presidents Organization   131

About the Author

Dr. Barry Asmus speaks, testifies, writes and consults on political and business issues facing America. He was named by *USA Today* as one of the five most requested speakers in the United States. Barry was twice voted the Outstanding Professor of the Year, as well as honored with the Freedom Foundation Award at Valley Forge for Private Enterprise Education.

As the Senior Economist with the National Center for Policy Analysis, Dr. Asmus does not just speak on policies - - he is also involved with implementation. He has testified before the House Ways and Means Committee on switching from an income tax to a consumption tax; was a featured speaker in a privatizing Social Security Conference for Western European leaders held in France, and has just returned from an engagement speaking as part of the faculty for the Young President's Organization in Cape Town, South Africa. His Fall 2001 appearance at the Forbes' Château de Balleroy in France with former Czech Prime Minister Vaclav Klaus, members of the British Parliament, and other western European leaders focused on the importance of public policy decisions in Europe and how they might meld with the global economy.

Dr. Asmus likes to explain the economic concepts needed to navigate the evolving network economy to worldwide firms like Compaq, Hewlett Packard, IBM and a host of other audiences. Based on durable free market economic principles, his presentations apply the current issues of the information economy to help decision-makers formulate informed and effective choices in a global, e-commerce world.

"I try never to forget," he says, "that the presentation I am about to give prospers in direct proportion to the way my audience responds. Will they enjoy it? Will they learn? Is there something special about this talk? Exceptionalism is not a one-time event. It is a process which starts with knowing your audience and then delivering with content, enthusiasm, and humor."

Hopefully some of the natural advantages and nuances of the spoken word addressed to a live audience were transferred in this book to you, the thoughtful reader. No exclamation marks, no bold faced type, no underlines—just the carefully selected words of a mostly quiet voice to cause a frequent smile, a learning experience, and a new appreciation of freedom. There are few things more wonderful than a comfortable chair, a good book and being with a special friend. Thanks for spending a few of your valuable moments with me.

Other books by Barry include: *When Riding a Dead Horse, For Heaven's Sake . . . Dismount*; *It's Tea Time Again: The Original American Dream*; *ClintonCare: Putting Government in Charge of Your Health; and CrossRoads: The Great American Experiment*. His most acclaimed book is a children's book that has been consistently ordered for every student in an entire school. It is a space fiction story containing many of the economic concepts found in this book. *Apollo: An Outer Space Economic Adventure* is about freedom, limited government, market solutions and dozens of other concepts explaining how capitalism, markets and entrepreneurship actually work. It's a book that your kids will long remember. Call the toll-free number listed on the title page of this book, or go to website www.barryasmus.com to order this potentially life-impacting book for the child or grandchild that matters the most: yours.